YOUR SUN SIGNS

by

Russell Grant

Published by
the Paperback Divi...
W.H. ALLEN & C...

This book is dedicated to the following people
who have all played a part in furthering my career:

Her Majesty Queen Elizabeth the Queen Mother

Jacque Evans
Anthony Peagam
Ron Neil and Lino Ferrari

A Virgin Book
published by
the paperback division of
W. H. Allen & Co. Plc,
44 Hill Street, London W1X 8LB

Reprinted 1985, 1987

Printed in Great Britain by
Anchor Brendon Ltd, Tiptree, Essex

ISBN 0 86369 055 6

Designed by Type Generation
Illustrated by Sue Walliker
Cover design by Ken Ansell
Cover photographs by Davies/Starr

Contents

Foreword

The zodiac is like the most delicious cake in the world, made from a host of celestial ingredients – all the planets in our solar system – and covered with heavenly marzipan and icing. To understand astrology, we must realise that every planet plays a particular role in our lives. Mars adds spice, Jupiter allows us to grow and expand, Saturn gives us our backbone, Venus lets us appreciate all the sweet things of life, Uranus makes each of us an individual, Pluto lets us cut ourselves off from our pasts and transform our lives, Neptune gives us our dreams, Mercury lets us communicate with others, the Sun gives us our creative urge, and the Moon our emotional drive. Each of us is unique, because we're all made up from a different astrological recipe, with added dashes of some planets, and a light dusting of others. Analyse the recipe and you have the key to someone's character.

Your Sun Signs is very general – as are my stars in *TV Times* magazine, and my myriad of newspaper columns throughout the country – but it will set you on the right track to understanding someone through their Sun sign. You'll be able to fathom out not just yourself, but your partner, workmates, family and friends – and even the person who sits next to you on the bus! What's more, very often we underestimate our potential and talents, and this book will help you to discover parts of your personality that you didn't know existed. Remember, this is only the start of your journey into astrology. Once you've finished this trip into the celestial universe you'll want to travel more with me on my voyage through the realms of astrology, and make your world a brighter, better place in which to live.

Russell Grant

Aries

21 March – 20 April

What Makes Aries Tick

Me, me, me, me! No, it's not an opera singer practising the scales, but the Arian catch-phrase. This is the first sign of the zodiac, and Arians like everyone to remember that. (First come, first served, is the Martian motto.) And because this is such a fun-loving, frisky sign, Arians can get away with it.

The positive side of Aries is like a scene from *The African Queen,* in which our intrepid explorers boldly go where only crocodiles have gone before. Arians are active, alive, awake (usually), assertive and adventurous, hacking their way through the undergrowth of life like Marlon Brando in a steamy movie. (Yes, he's an Arian!) But they can take this exuberance to extremes. (They can take a lot of things to extremes!) Arians can step out, putting their best feet forward (all four of them – well, they are animals!) and sinking up to their best end of necks in trouble.

Luscious Libra is the polar sign of assertive Aries, and these signs have a lot to learn from each other. Librans always put others first, which is something Arians find almost impossible to do. In fact, a relationship between these two is their idea of heaven, because they both think about the Arian. (And of course, after 'Me', the Ram's favourite word is 'Ewe'!)

Sometimes, this can cause a contretemps in the course of true love. Male Arians may forget about the wife and six kids at home and gad about like a bachelor gay, with a collection of conquests. Arian women may throw their weight about too, demanding new dresses and wanting to be taken to the best restaurants, even when their men haven't got two halfpennies to rub together.

Aries is ruled by Mars, the planet that gives them that gorgeous get-up-and-go, that delicious drive and determination. (As long as they're not determinedly driving all over delicious *you!*) Mighty Mars rules Scorpio, too, when he shares the limelight with powerful Pluto. Then he can make Scorpios furtive and underhand, but when he's in open Aries, it's a very different story. Arians can be so candid and frank that it's an excruciating experience to hear them. You can meet your Martian mate for a meal, and swan in, looking sensational. (Or so you think, you poor dear.) The Arian will take one look at you and say 'That frock makes you look fatter than ever'. (How can you then say that you've just lost two stone – and a pal in the process!)

There's something rather ingenuous about Aries. Because this is the first sign of the zodiac, Rams represent the babies of the celestial sky. Sometimes they're so naive and innocent it's astounding, and they'll dash off and do or say something really reckless. (Or just plain potty!) They can also have terrible temper tantrums, like a tirading toddler, and shout and scream till they're blue in the face. Assertive Arians are so determined to get what they want that they'll let nothing stand in their way. They'll go on until it kills them.

Every sign has its own song, and the Arian's aria must be 'Let's Get Physical'. (Take that in any way you like. After all, they will!) Rams are imbued with enough physical energy to fill a whole football team (and a stand of supporters!). But, like children, they have to find positive pursuits in which to burn it all off. Arians are full of fire, fun, vivacity, verve and virility. (Quite a captivating concoction, which can really go to your head!) But they can fritter away their fantastic physical fitness, and instead of having an active social, sports or sex life, turn to violence and vandalism. (Even the meekest and mildest mutton will show a strong side sometimes, and may bop you on the bonce for no apparent reason.) Some of these Martians can be all brawn and no brain, thinking with their fists – or any other part of the anatomy that springs to mind! (Arians have powerful passions and strong sex drives!)

Arians are like medieval knights, arrayed in armour and jousting for superiority. Their Fiery natures make them compulsively competitive, and determined to do battle. They have *got* to come first. Rams, lambs and sheep hate losing, whether at Ludo, life or love. (They'll just throw the dice for a six and start again.) When they see success slipping away, they'll fight tooth and claw, frightening off folk in their flocks. Watch out, watch out, there's a Ram about!

Aries Man

G uess what! Casanova was an Arian. Need I say more? (What do you mean, yes!)

Rams have a lot going for them, because they are usually striking, to say the least. Mars gives these males muscles, and perfect physiques. (Think of Martian Marlon Brando in his tiny T-shirt.) And because of their love for the great outdoors, they're often tanned, even in the winter. Flocks of these Fiery fellows are fair, with fetching freckles too. But the greatest give-away are the Arian eyebrows, which are shaped like the Ram's horns, and meet in the middle. Sadly, some of these sheep run to rack and ruin as the years roll by, turning from charming chump chops into seedy scrag end.

Before you decide that a Martian male is just what the doctor ordered (can you get them on the NHS?), hold on to your heart-strings. All Arians should think twice before becoming embroiled in emotional encounters. In fact, any sort of partnership can be problematic for these chaps. Even as business partners, some Arian men can forget that it takes two to tango, and will want to be assertive and the one who's winning. (They forget that their colleagues are on their side!)

This is a very impulsive and impatient sign, and Arian men don't like waiting for things. *(Anything.)* If they have an idea, they want to do it *now*, not wait until next week! They think that life is too short to hang about, and they like to see instant results. Sometimes, this impetuousness can lead to trouble, and all Martian men should look before they leap!

Most Arians are in love with life, and the men can buzz about like busy bumble bees, full of fervour and fire. Their childlike enthusiasm can be intoxicating and infectious, and make the world a brighter place for the rest of us. But there's one area of their lives that provokes problems: passion. The Arian's ardour can get the better of him, making him want to get the better of *you!* But often, once he's got it, he'll move on to pastures new.

It's easy to catch a Martian man, but much harder to keep him. You've got to give him a good run for his money, even if he ties you in reef-knots. The name of the game is to keep him guessing. If you seem to always elude his embraces, he'll increase his efforts to ensnare you, because he'll want to know how you can resist a Ram. (He'll also find it a captivating change not to have a female fall at his feet at the first flick of his finger.)

However, once you've been dragged off by the dreadlocks to your ardent Arian amour's abode (not for nothing is his nickname Tarzan), you can expect to spend a lot of time in bed. (And it won't be tucked up with a good book either!) Audacious Arian men have strong sex drives, and need partners who also pulsate to passion. (It's no good saying you have a headache. Your romantic Ram will just offer you an Anadin, and then carry on where he left off!)

These men have an animal appeal and Martian magnetism which can be very attractive. Their Fiery element gives them strong egos, and they'll be very aware of themselves, and their images. (Negative Rams will prance about like peacocks, thinking they look like the cat's whiskers, when actually they're more like dogs' dinners.)

Because of his innate need to put himself first, the average Arian man needs to meet his match in both business and the boudoir. If he's a wonder at work, bursting with brainwaves, he needs a partner with a brilliant mind, who's properly organised. Then they can work in harmony, and be a true team, because the Ram won't feel threatened. And the same goes for love. A negative Arian can even reckon his romancer is a rival, and try to cap her career and her caressing.

Being Cardinal chaps, Arians don't like failures. They sometimes like to show off, too, and can see a partner as a prized possession. So they usually want women who look wonderful, and will be as pleased as punch when their girls get wolf whistles.

The Martian man makes a good dad, and will try to get his kids out and about as much as possible. (Having a six-year-old son is a great excuse for spending Sundays kicking a ball about!) An Arian father also makes a fantastic fuss of his daughters. (He's never been able to resist a pretty face!) However, dad's temper can be as terrifying as a tornado, and he'll

rant and rave. He's not the sort to sulk in silence, yet once he's stopped shouting, he'll be all smiles again, and peace will reign. For a while!

One of the most endearing aspects of the Arian man is his adoration of his amour. When he meets Miss Right, he'll worship her and plonk her on a pedestal so high she'll get dizzy. (Look at Tarzan with Jane!) As far as he's concerned, she can do no wrong. But the minute she lets him down, he'll be beside himself with grief. Some Martian males have been so dejected, distressed and devastated by being let down, that they've called a halt then and there, rather than risk picking up the pieces and then having it happen again. They can have a very childlike outlook on love and life, and sometimes run away from their problems rather than face up to them.

So the Arian man is a magnificent mixture of life, love and lust. To prove my point, one spring morning, a man was walking by a meadow, and he spied sixty sheep and one ram. When he strolled past at the end of the day, there were sixty soporific sheep and one riotous ram. And that sums up the Aries chap for you – what a saucy thing!

Aries Woman

Attractive ain't the word! Martian maidens are marvellous. They are imbued with pootchy powers and can get away with a lot more than their male counterparts. (Even so, find me a Cancerian chap who hasn't had his heart broken by an Arian girl.) Arian women can walk into a room and steal the show with their honesty and plain-speaking. Some folk will feel suspicious of them, but others will adore them. (You can always spot a Martianess because she'll be dressed from top to toe in bright red. Rather rotund Ramettes, with tons of Taurus in their charts, will look like walking pillar-boxes!)

Before bringing up babies beckons, it's very important for this woman to have a crack at a career of some sort or another. It will help her to express her boundless bounce, her everlasting energy and enthusiasm. Otherwise, once she's begun to bring up the bairns, she'll feel restricted and tied down, which will cause a crisis. She'll become a furious feminist, and begin to fight tooth and nail with her husband. She isn't a natural housewife, and no man should try to make her one. The Lamby lass is far too independent, and her marriage will come crashing about her ears, as she tries to assert herself.

She makes a good mum, although her offspring may tie her down until they've fled the flock. Then, the minute the last child has left home, she'll kick up her heels and have a whale of a time, taking off to art classes or going ten-pin bowling with the boys.

Because this is the sign of the self, the Ramette shouldn't get tied down too soon. She has got to understand herself before she can begin to fathom out a fella, and that can take several years. If she plights her troth in her teens, or early twenties, she may yield to her impulsive nature thirty years later, and mooch off with the milkman.

These women are full of verve and vivacity, warmth and wonder. Love plays a very important role in their lives and, being Arians, they will love in a very big way indeed! Make no mistake, this is a passionate placing! After all, ardent Aries is ruled by masterful Mars, which is a pulverisingly passionate planet. Arian girls (and boys) are carnal and libidinous, and have strong sex drives. In fact, it will be a very unusual Ewe who doesn't think sex is the greatest thing since sliced bread.

Sometimes, the Lamb lass will be as pleased as punch with her partner, but will still have a lot of lovers, simply for the sex. Even the most contented, married Martian maiden will have the occasional fling, especially if the spark has left her marriage. It may be that her need for sex is greater than her partner's, and she has to look elsewhere for her excitement.

When she finds a likely lad, she won't beat about the bush; she isn't backward in coming forward. And just like the male Martian, sometimes she'll strike lucky, and sometimes the fellow of her fantasies will bolt off into the blue like a bewildered bunny. (Arians aren't always very subtle and sophisticated, and may scare off sensitive souls with their bombastic behaviour.)

These lasses may appear bright and brittle, but underneath they are incredibly idealistic, and as mushy as a marshmallow on a hot day. Just like the kids they really are, they believe that things end happily ever after and that they will shimmer off into the sunset with the ones they love. The Arian lass who's discovered that her Sheep of Araby is really just a wolf in sheep's clothing will be a sorry sight to see. She's very vulnerable, no matter how hard she hides it.

Martianesses should try to get out and about, and socialise separately from their families once in a while. Unlike the Watery and Earthy signs, who have an innate need for family security, these women need to stand alone from their loved ones and rediscover themselves, even if it's only for one night a month. If the Aries girl doesn't have some time to herself, she can begin to resent her relations and will start to shout and scream, and have more flare-ups than there are in a box of matches.

Arian women are arresting to look at. They aren't a slender sign as a rule, so much as well-built. (But I'm sure I don't have to talk about mutton dressed as lamb!) Two women who are the epitome of this fantastic Fiery sign are Bette Davis and Joan Crawford. Let's face it, you only had to look at Joan Crawford's eyebrows to see what sign she was!

Aries Child

These kids never stop! They're as bright as buttons, as perky as poppers and as zesty as zips, and they're on the go from dawn to dusk. (Come bedtime, the parents are usually more tired than they are!)

Arian kids think they've had a dull day if they've dashed around in their tiny tracksuits, scored more goals than Kevin Keegan (into their gran's greenhouse), bicycled round the block and mowed their mums down with their midget machine guns! Arian energy can be so amazing that it's like watching a whirlwind whizzing about. And if this isn't enough to help you spot an Arian kid, keep a peeper peeled for the plasters. Because Ramlettes rush around at the speed of sound (Geminis move at the speed of light), they're always hurting themselves, and have to be patched up by their parents. So the average Arian will be enveloped in Elastoplast!

If you think children should be seen and not heard, and preferably sit in a corner buried in a book, you've got problems with an Arian kid. Of course, he or she will read books every now and then, because this is an intelligent sign, but most Ramlettes like to be out and about, racing hither and thither.

When you have one of these diminutive dynamos, you must make sure this astonishing Arian activity is piloted into positive pursuits. Even if you can't stand sporty things, you've got to get your kid to join junior sports clubs, climb conifers, have fun with a football, and generally unleash all that Arian energy.

By now, you might be peering at your little lamb, and wondering why he or she is always so quiet. (Quiet, that is, compared to other Arians.) Some baby Rams seem subdued, and don't rave about rugby or flip about football. They will love building things instead, and are as happy as sheepy sandboys (and girls) if they have Meccano or Lego sets.

At school, Arian children are more active with their feet than

15

their brains. Usually, they excel on the sports field rather than in the classroom, and can become heroes (and heroines) of the hour, winning races and collecting cups for cricket.

The best bet for a Ramlette is to give him or her a playroom. Then your kid can make a mighty great mess, but it won't matter. Even as tiny tots, these children have competitive spirits, and will love staging races with their mates. They'll also love plastic guns (most Martian!), toy forts and dolls, and will adore playing cowboys and indians, or cops and robbers. (Some of them will have a go at doctors and nurses, too!)

Life can be one long laugh with these little lambs. They have a fabulous feeling for fun, and can clown around to get you giggling. One Ram called Robert used to have his sister in stitches when they played football. In between each kick he'd toss himself on to the turf, then leap up, still laughing, and biff the ball with his bonce! If you can encourage this lively side of your little lamb, you'll bring up a radiant Ram. But if you suffocate and stifle your sheep, or restrict your Ram, you'll be in danger of acquiring an aggressive, argumentative, antagonistic Arian. Mishandled minor Martians can be mini monsters. (And sometimes that's putting it politely!) You must show your kid what's what, and exercise discipline when it's demanded. After all, you don't want to bring up a brat, do you, when you could have an adorable adult Arian!

Aries in Love

Romance, to a Ram (or even love to a lamb), isn't always a tender scene from Romeo and Juliet. Sometimes, it's more like a torrid ten minutes from a Swedish sex film.

Arian amour is active, and Rams often prefer to give their emotions a physical outlet. (Reinforce your bed before you bring a Ram home for a night of passion. You don't want it to snap under the strain.) This is a very sexy sign, and few Rams go to bed just to sleep! (And when they do drop off, you can guess what they dream about!)

And now for the bad news. The Arian attitude of 'Me first' can turn into the Martian mating call, making some of the sign supremely selfish between the sheets. They can forget that their partners in passion should get any pleasure, and will get so carried away that everything's over in two ticks. (Well, two somethings!) Some of them want to be overcome with ecstasy every ten minutes. (While their partners are overcome with fatigue!)

Arians love the thrill of the chase, and some Martian men can develop tender traits which make even Fishy fellows look like first-timers. This chop – I mean, chap – will woo wonderfully, and court charismatically, drowning his paramour in posies and perfumes, taking her out to the best joints in town and spouting sonnets like Shakespeare. However, the minute she shows signs of succumbing to his sexual shenanigans, he'll cancel the Interflora order, and drag her back to his dwelling! (Then he'll show her where the saucepans are and hint that he's hungry!)

Rams can be rather too rampant and rumbustious when it comes to romance, and they need to be coaxed into showing more love and less lust. But once you've succeeded, you'll be glad you bothered. One of the most endearing and enthralling things about Arians is that, although they like to be leaders, they're putty in your hands if they love you, and will do anything for you. But don't go mad! Remember that Rams are completely honest and childlike, and that what you see is what there is. (This is a very straightforward, simple sign.) Just as they're the babies of the zodiac, so they are babies in love, trusting you totally and willing to do anything in return for your love.

Rams often put their loved ones on pedestals, believing they can do no wrong. But the minute the paramour topples off the perch, like a parrot that's passed on, the Ram will be broken-hearted. Arians are especially agonised by deceit and duplicity in their loved ones, because they're so open and honest themselves.

However, they can be a wee bit hypocritical, because they often flirt and play the field, even when they've tied the nuptial knot into a beautiful bow. The reason is that they need someone at the centre of their lives, who loves and understands them, but doesn't stop them having delightful dalliances and exciting encounters. But they always return to their true loves. (And if you're lucky, that could be you!)

However, you may still be at the starting-post, with a Ram who just makes sheep's eyes at you. Even if the sight of your Aries amour makes you go weak at the knees (you're not a Capricorn, are you?) or makes your head swim (Pisces?), and all you want to do is grab 'em and get on with it (must be Taurus) – don't! Play hard to get, even if it kills you. (That would be enticingly elusive, but a bit drastic.) If the Arian is interested, he or she will pursue you up hill and down dale. (Better put your running shoes on.)

Arians are used to getting whatever they want, and are fascinated if the quarry doesn't want to be caught. So if a Ram wants *you*, but you're one step ahead of the game, he or she will be intrigued, and try extra hard to catch you. Only surrender when you're absolutely sure that you've won the heart of your Arian amour. It'll be worth the wait, I promise!

Aries as a Friend

If you're a stodgy stay-at-home you don't want a Martian marvel for a mate. If your idea of a good time is a quiet night in front of the TV, your Arian pal will drag you off to the sports centre or down to the pub quicker than you can say 'What's on next?'

Arians make fantastic friends. They can transform your life, turning a dull and dreary day into something bright and breezy. These folk will try anything once, and will get you to have a go, too. (And they won't stand for you being weak, weedy and wimpish, saying that you'd rather stay at home with a good book than drive a dodgem for a dare.) In fact, Arians can be like a walking bottle of Sanatogen, making you bounce and bourrée about, as if you'd just had an injection of iron. There are a lot of wilting wallflowers who've become pepped-up pansies, simply because an Arian has watered them, dusted their leaves and given them a new lease of life, with their very own brand of Baby Bio.

Now, hold on a minute, before you gallop off to grab a whole farmyard of lively lambs. Arians don't like competition in the sheepstakes. If you're the mate of a Martian, you can't be a rival to your Ram. He or she may love you dearly, but will hate it if you forge ahead in any way.

Some Arians pick pals they can pounce on passionately when the fancy takes them. But many Martians choose chums who are inferior in some way, and perhaps just content to sit on the sidelines and watch them showing off.

You must be prepared for an active social life when you've got an Arian friend. If your Martian mate rings you up and asks you out, try not to say 'But I'm washing my hair'. (Well, you can, of course. Then you'll either be a challenge to your chum, who'll think 'I'm going to drag Doreen – or Dorian – out of that place if it's the last thing I do', or the sheep will shrug, say 'I can't be bothered' and waltz off to find a new friend.)

19

But usually, once you've attracted an Arian, as a friend or a lover, he or she will devote a lot of time to you. But let's not kid ourselves. This is a Cardinal sign, so the Ram will always have one mince pie on the main chance, and think it's worth their while having you as a mate, because you'll be of help somehow. But the other peeper will be pinned on your pootchy personality – or your perfect posterior! And that's when the Ram will help you, and cheer you up when you're down in the dumps. (Any excuse for a cuddle!) In fact, if you've just lost something, whether it's a loved one, your bet on the 2.15 at Aintree, or all your marbles, one of the best signs to have around you is Aries.

Most Martians have a plethora of pals, but there's always a central cast of cherished chums that doesn't change. Others may come and go – especially if the Arian fancies them and lures them into bed! Sex often plays a part in a palship for this sign. Arians can get fun and friendship mixed up, and sometimes ruin everything in the process. If your pal suddenly pounces, remember not to show any signs of attachment, or you won't see the Ram for dust.

But you can have a grand time with a Martian mate if you keep your wits about you, and are full of fun and frolics. You have only to think of Rupert Bear taking his pals on adventures to see a Martian mate at his best. There's never a dull moment with a Ram. Can you stand the pace? (But with Tarzan about, does it matter?)

Aries at Work

Is it a bird, is it a plane? No, it's an Arian at work. Gosh, these Martians can be real balls of fire once they get going. They whizz around, exuding energy from every pore, until you feel exhausted just watching them. Do they *ever* slow down?

There's no getting away from it, Arians need to be top dog. (All right then, top ram!) Whether they're little lambs in a fabulous flock, head of their department, or just head of the tea trolley, they have to be able to give the orders somewhere along the line. (Even if it's decreeing no one can scoff more than two custard creams in one tea break.)

Arians need to be leaders, so it's very important that a woolly worker should leap up the ladder of success as quickly as possible. Otherwise there will be many flare-ups along the way, as the Arian attempts to be assertive over the powers that be. (And no one wants to work with a Ram on the rampage – it's too traumatic.)

There's an old saying that you have to speculate to accumulate, and a positive Arian will agree wholeheartedly. Rams make great bosses, because they crave challenge, are inspired innovators, and are always ready and willing to have a go at something new. (That could be a brand-new deal or it could be a brand-new secretary! You never know with a Ram!)

The other side of the coin is that Arians want everything to happen *now*, and won't hang around and let the grass grow under their feet. They will join the firm as a junior in January, and expect to be manager by March! (And they'll think that's slow-going!) Like children, they just can't wait, and will seethe with impatience. (And then throw a tantrum!)

Remember Aesop's Fable about the tortoise and the hare? Well, if Taurus is the tortoise, guess who's the one with the floppy ears! With their love of competition, Rams want to beat everyone to the winning-post, but are sometimes too clever by half. (If only they could slow down and hold their horses – or horns – they'd stun everyone into silence with their dynamic, daring dreams and vivacious vitality. Patience, Aries!)

A positive Ram will excel in almost anything he or she puts a hoof to, work-wise, especially if it's an active occupation. Being ruled by Mars, Arians make smashing soldiers, are amazing at adventure, and stunning at sports or something similar. Their brawny biceps also mean they excel at jobs requiring mighty muscles, such as being a village blacksmith or a steelwelder. (And, of course, they love working – and playing – with fire!)

Some Arians don't have much sticking power when it comes to boring work. They're geniuses at coming up with new ideas, organising everyone to execute them and taking the credit. But they're not so keen on seeing something through to the end. They'd rather rush off to the next great idea, and leave the donkey work to someone else. But don't think they're all flash and fire at work. Many Martians will burn the candle at both ends, and in the middle, when they're working on something they believe in. They can be incredibly industrious when they want. Arians will gladly put their backs into their jobs, their noses to the grindstone, and their whole hearts and souls into their work. Gosh!

Rams don't take kindly to being pinned to a desk all day, because they're too restless. (They may create a few fireworks just to show how unhappy they are! And I don't mean just sparklers, but whole Catherine wheels and Roman candles.) Arians who like to get out and about enjoy jobs like journalism, when they can be roving Ram reporters in Rotherham one day, and Russia the next.

In fact, the worst way to knock the stuffing out of Rams is to ignore them. Because they belong to the Fire element, they have well-developed egos (some would say enormous) and like their achievements to be applauded. But let's face it, they're never ignored for long. You can't keep a good Ram down!

Aries at Home

Forget 'olde-worlde' atmosphere, chintz curtains and roaring log fires with this sign. Arians have no time for tedious things like that. They're too busy having fun. (Some of them are so focused on fun that they're rarely at home.)

The Aries abode is a base, but it may not be the centre of the Ram's universe, as it is for a Cancerian or Taurean. Think of all the Rams you know. How many of them own their own homes? Now think of your Crab and Bull mates, who probably all own their own places. See what I mean? Lots of Arians are content to rent their dwellings for years and years. (They love to know they're not tied down, and could scoot off to Siberia or Senghenydd on Sunday if they wanted to.) Martians with mortgages have usually been brow-beaten into them by their spouses.

Have you ever wondered how other people live? (Nosey, aren't you?) Well, a typical Sunday for an Arian is to lie-in till twelve, reading the papers and being passionate with a partner. Then it's down to the club or out for some grub. Back about three or four, just in time for a quick kip on the couch, and then he or she can stroll out again in the evening for a meal with some mates, or a liaison with the latest in a long line of lovers. You may not even see a Ram for the rest of the weekend, as he or she will be out all the time. (Of course, married Martians will be at home much more. Unless they're up to no good!)

What does an Arian abode look like? Well, because this is a wacky sign, it'll be a fairly modern joint. (Rams aren't bothered about tradition.) The most important thing is that everything in it must tick along nicely, like Big Ben. (Arians are usually too busy to be bothered to mend things.) Rams aren't keen on fuss either, but will try to make the place smart and functional, with plenty of labour-saving devices dotted about the dwelling. (The last thing an Arian wants is for the homestead to be a chore, because most Rams are out and about a lot.) So, as long as there's a telly to watch on the rare nights that the Ram's at a loose end, he or she will be happy. There are also likely to be 101 phones, because Rams like to ring up their chums, and keep in constant contact.

There are bound to be plenty of pictures on the walls, and several will be of the resident Ram! Mirrors often abound, too, because Arians like to know they're looking their best. (You never know who might pop round!)

If you've been paying attention, there are no prizes for guessing which is the most important room to a Ram! There's no doubt about it, the bedroom wins hands down every time. And pride of place will be the biggest double bed in the world. (A really rich Ram will blow the boodle on a bed that moves up and down, tilts from side to side and even vibrates, all at the touch of a button from the control panel in the headboard! Yes, honestly!)

Arians who live with someone let their partners decide the decor and be the real influence on the place.

Most Arians don't spend enough time in their homes to even glance at the gardens. (For a lot of them, a front garden is the green stuff that lies between the garden gate and the front door.) If the spouse doesn't go for gardening, the Arian will splash out and pay someone to do it for them. Many Rams can't stand doing the dusting either, and will pay someone else to do it for them, if they can afford it. (Astute Arians choose Virgos.)

Rams don't like living in little homes, and will move out when they feel cramped, and buy or rent something bigger to roam about in. Being a Cardinal sign, they enjoy status symbols, and a large house can be just the job. They'll puff up like proud peacocks when people admire their abodes.

They may like to live in a wide open house, but they're not so keen on the wide open spaces of the countryside. Like Gemini, they love the hustle and bustle of the city, and can't stay away from it for too long. Anyway, who can they show off to in the middle of a field? Cows can't clap, can they?

Aries
Health and Relaxation

Vincent Van Gogh was an Arian, and look what happened to him! That doesn't mean that every Arian is about to lop off a lughole, but this sign does rule the head, and that's where things can go wrong for a Ram. For example, lots of Arians are as blind as bats without their glasses or contact lenses, and you'll find others who are as deaf as posts.

A very Arian ailment is pains in the head (no, not in the neck, or anywhere else, for that matter!). Nearly every Arian you'll meet gets mind-boggling migraines, or horrendous headaches at the very least. Some severely stressed sheep can suffer from a series of hefty headaches, and may polish off painkillers the way other signs swallow Smarties.

The Arian head does seem to come in for a lot of trouble, one way and another. What starts off as a simple cold, for example, can end up doing dreadful damage. Rams can go deaf in one ear, making them bellow like tetchy town criers, or their teeth can become ultra-sensitive to cold air, hot drinks and knickerbocker glories, making them entrechat about as if they'd just sat on a wasp's nest.

So, sensible Arians should make sure they have regular check-ups for their gnashers, peepers and lugholes if they want to avoid any trouble. (Mind you, this may be the sign of courage, but try getting a Ram to a dentist!)

Although their polar sign is lazy Libra, this is definitely active Aries! Rams have mountains of Martian motivation, making them bound around and exude exuberance. Just like the kids that they really are, the best way to make a Ram relax is to wear him or her out first! Sport is one of the best ways. Arians like indoor sports best of all, but that's not always possible. (Their partner is positively pooped, or the neighbours keep complaining – what can those Rams get up to?) The next best thing is a sport played outdoors. (And I don't mean chasing someone down the garden and into the coal shed, either!)

Arians enjoy aggressive activities, such as football (they like being centre-forward in everything they do), rugby (how they love a good scrum) or squash (well, you know how cramped it can be in a cupboard). (They like to leave the gentler pursuits, such as tatting or tiddly-winks, to less sporty souls.)

If the Ram can't play a sport, he or she will love being a spectator, whether on the terraces or in front of the TV. Even when just watching *Grandstand*, Arians will be swathed in scarves, and waving rattles. They'll then go off to get pie-eyed in the pub when all the fun's finished.

Although Arians think of themselves first and foremost, they're very gregarious, and enjoy being with their mates, when they can let off steam. In fact, it's very important for an Arian to burn up that endless energy in a positive way, whether it's darts, dancing or drinking. Otherwise, if their energy is not used properly, it can turn the Ram into a mixture of Mount Etna and Vesuvius on a bad day. It may metamorphose into a migraine, or it could erupt into a volley of violence, and end in game, set and match to the Martian. And while we're on the subject, Arians have tempestuous tempers. They flare up in a matter of minutes, but once the tirade is terminated, they forget all about it. (In the meantime, though, they'll have shouted and screamed like a rabid Ram.) And that's the lovely thing about this Fiery sign. They may make you feel like last night's left-overs one minute but they'll turn you into a peach melba the next – all gooey and gorgeous!

Taurus

21 April — 21 May

What Makes Taurus Tick

Taureans are very easy creatures to understand. They have very basic needs: male Bulls love grub and girls, and females of this sign adore food and fellas. Simple, isn't it?

Being the first of the Earth signs, Taurus symbolises rich, rolling fields of very dark brown earth waiting to be cultivated. The Sun sits in the sign of Taurus at Maytime, and so Taurus is linked with the ritual of Mayday, the maypole, young maidens, and earthy, pagan customs and folklore.

Taureans are governed by their love of sensuality in all its forms, and some of them can go a mite mad and over-indulge themselves, whether it's with sex or a simmering stew with delicious dumplings.

A lot of Taureans have very expressive, often deep-set eyes, that can put across their message better than a million Gemini words. I know one normally sensible, sane Capricorn girl who was reduced to a gibbering wreck when one of these Bulls looked at her across a crowded room. He didn't have to say a word – his eyes did all the talking. (I'd wondered why she suddenly blushed like a beetroot.)

Bulls hate change. They need to know that tomorrow will be the same as today, and that the day after tomorrow will be the same as a week next Wednesday. This is not a sign that is moved by challenge, but Bulls can show tremendous endeavour, patience, persistence and resoluteness.

I have many Taurean chums, and what I absolutely adore about them is that when you go to visit them, you will have barely opened the garden gate before they've offered you a cuppa and asked you if you've eaten. (Say no.) They can be wonderfully warm and welcoming, really making you feel at home, and wondering what they can give you that is theirs. (More stew?)

Ownership is very important to Taureans. Seeing a room full of furniture they've paid for, or a freezer full of food, makes them feel secure. However, negative Taureans can be so possessive and narow-minded that they can class wives, husbands, kids and pets in the same category as the couch and the cooker and feel that they own them lock, stock and barrel.

To give you an idea of the good and bad sides of the Bull, a country said to be ruled by Taurus is the Emerald Isle. Think of the simple, relaxed way of life there, those glorious greens and beautiful browns of the Irish countryside; then think of the widespread bigotry over religion with both sides refusing to compromise, and you have Taurus at its worst.

In fact, one description of Taurus that you will hear time and time again is 'stubborn as a mule'. Certainly, Taurus is a Fixed sign, and Taureans can be as hard to shift as a sack of soggy cement, but I do think this so-called stubbornness is a wee bit over-emphasised. Of course, there is a diabolical dose of dogged determination in the Taurean character, but these Bulls are not always as obstinate and obtuse as they are portrayed. In fact, if used positively, this steadfast streak can lead to persistence and determination. On the negative side, it can lead to rumbustious rows because of the Taurean's intransigence and inability to see another person's point of view.

But make no mistake. If used in the right way, fixity can be a wonderful thing. If Bulls want something slightly out of reach, they will put their heads down and charge (slowly) straight for it, eventually achieving their goal, even if it kills them in the process!

As you might expect from a sign that symbolises the countryside, often Taureans aren't very happy in the city – unlike Air or Fire signs, who like hustle and bustle. Taureans, on the other hand, need to live in a place where they can commune with nature, feeling the ground beneath their feet and seeing the sky above their heads. Bulls will be at their best in a verdant village, or a comfy crofter's cottage. City Bulls will have stacks of window-boxes crammed with leafy flora, to give them that 'at home' feeling. Bulls' abodes will be warm and welcoming, unless they are going through a desperate disruption or change in their relationships.

Taureans rarely do anything quickly, choosing to take their time. If they're negative, they may prefer to pretend that their position, passion-wise, is pootchy, when even the fly on the

wall can see that it isn't. Eventually the world will crumble around their ears, when their amour ambles off with another. Everyone except the Bull will have seen exactly what was happening, and not be outraged at the outcome.

Taureans find it especially difficult to accept change in their emotional relationships, because fidelity and loyalty are paramount to them. But whether a Taurean likes it or not (probably not), changes of some sort or another will be inevitable in their lives, and the sooner they get used to the idea the better. The more they can make themselves cope with change, the less heartache they will have in the long run. I know many Taureans who have resisted an upheaval that was inevitable, and gone through hell and high water as a result.

Venus rules Taurus and Libra, endowing both signs with a love of beauty and a need for harmony, although they seek these ideals in different ways. When ruling Libra, Venus is lighter and more sanguine, but she's much deeper and richer in Taurus. Librans love Rodgers and Hammerstein, while Taureans will opt for opera. They love the beauty of flowers, the earth and all the good things in life, and with their classical, traditional outlook, can teach a lot of the more restless signs quite a lesson or two. So don't fall into the trap of thinking Taureans are simply bull-headed. They can be obstinate, though they would call it being strong-minded!

Taurus Man

Taurean men can be so saucy! You should never stand too near a Taurus man on a crowded bus or train, because he'll probably have an uncontrollable urge to pinch your bum. Taureans have a very strong sense of humour, but it tends towards slapstick, with lots of custard pies and banana skins thrown in for good measure. (Anything that features food is fine for these fellows.) These Bulls can be a barrel of belly laughs (sometimes literally, if they've overdone the food and drink), and they always remind me of Shakespeare's Falstaff, bawdy and so, so Bullish.

Trust and loyalty are priorities for the uncomplicated Taurean male, who will expect to find these qualities in everyone he knows, from the window cleaner to his wife. In spite of (or because of) that, Bulls can be manipulated very easily by a clever woman. The Taurean is the sort of man who will happily marry his secretary, or his housekeeper. (Whoever she is, she'll know a good thing when she sees it.) He needs a wife or partner who can cook well (this is of prime importance to any Taurean man worth his salt), and keep the house running smoothly. It's not that he wants to show off, because he couldn't care less about what his chums think, but he does need to know that when he brings them home, the place will be cosy, a meal of meaty magnificence will be waiting, and his wife will be welcoming in the lads.

Unlike some of the other signs, he won't pick his partner principally for prettiness. Being ruled by Venus, he's not going to go for someone who cracks mirrors just by looking at them, but he will usually fall more for the figure than the face, especially if it's one that goes in and out in all the right places. He likes women to be curvaceous rather than emaciated.

Both male and female Bulls need time to adapt to change, and therefore to any new situation that may arise. So, the longer a love-affair goes on for these sensual subjects, the deeper and deeper it gets, until it makes Loch Ness look like a puddle! And the deeper it becomes, the more difficult it will be for the Taurean to climb out of it, should he ever want to. The more negative Bulls will cling on to an affair long after it should have ended.

As my fellow astrologer, Liz Greene, has said, for every year that a Taurean is in a relationship, they will need seven to sever it: it can be a real wrench for a Taurean male to cut the ties. To make matters worse, the longer the relationship lasts, the more the negative Bull will feel he owns his partner. He will forget that she is a woman in her own right, and just think of her as part of the furniture, and a piece he has paid for. He will think of his living, breathing amour as an inanimate object. So much so, that if he has a vestige of Virgo in his chart, she may wake up one morning and find herself being covered with best bees' wax. He'll have forgotten she's a damsel and decided she's the dining-room table instead!

On a positive note, though, the Taurean man can be gloriously generous, willing to give you his last crust of bread (probably smothered in strawberry jam), or the shirt off his back (and it will be soft and silky to the touch). I would always invite a male Bull to a party, because he will be one long laugh, and will always bring something with him. Taurean men really are very generous creatures (though that stops when you grab their girls), but will be mostly so with material goods, not money. But the more 'well-hoofed' ones will be bounteous with their boodle as well as their booze.

The negative Taurean man can be cripplingly jealous and possessive. If his partner pops out unexpectedly, or is five minutes late home, he'll demand to know where she's been, imagining all sorts of sultry scenes. But it's all part and parcel of his ceaseless search for security.

Taureans of both sexes draw attention to their necks (which is the bit of the body ruled by the Bull), and they all tend to be thickset round the throat – and often everywhere else as well! Some male Bulls can be very bulky indeed, but nearly all of them will be attractive with it, thanks to their ruler, Venus. Some of them will be skinny, of course, but even those will have the distinctive Taurean broad shoulders and straight backs.

Male Bulls tend to have dark curly hair, expressive dark brown eyes and slightly sallow skins. And it's a strange thing, but a lot of them have an unruly lock of hair that always flops on to their foreheads. The sports presenter, David Icke, has a typically Taurean face, especially since it's topped with that curly hair.

Taurean men can be wonderful once you've got them going, but arousing their interest can be a laborious business. The Bull will take a long time to make up his mind about you, but once he has, it'll be like bonfire night! The trouble is that you may have difficulties in getting him to calm down again. (Fancy stopping a Bull in full charge? No, I didn't think so!)

If the male Bull falls in love with you, I should send all your pals postcards, telling them you won't be seeing them for a while. You'll be far too busy, and it won't be just for a week or two, either. When this man finally decides that you're the one, he doesn't mess around. Don't look to him for a quick fling, if that's all you want. The Bull means business. However, try to get rid of the more persistent Taurean man once you've gone off the boil, and you may find it impossible. That's when the Bull can become a bore.

Taurean men are full of ardour, but their passion takes a long time to build. The same goes for their temper, which you will only see once in a blue moon, if you're lucky. Unlike Aries, who will huff and puff and blow your house down, Taureans will huff and puff slowly over a year, and when they finally blow your house down they'll take the whole street with it!

Taurus Woman

Go to a Women's Institute meeting, and look at the lady who's in charge. She's probably clutching a couple of crates of her own chutney, or a magnum of marmalade. She's also a Taurus.

How do I know? Well, if you think of Venus as the bringer of good things, the bearer of luxuries, and the provider of provender, you have the Taurean woman. She is a home-maker. Cancerian women are home-makers too, but are concerned with their families. Taurean women are literally home-makers, preoccupied with putting down permanent roots and providing a solid foundation to their lives.

Permanence is an extremely important word for Taureans. Anything that seems to be the tiniest bit temporary, and isn't going to be there forever, gives them the collywobbles.

Taurean women are like acorns, growing into huge oak trees (though they don't always weigh twenty tons), and putting down roots that will be there for life. Sometimes the Taurean lass won't even move away from her own home, and will continue to live with her parents until she gets married herself. This won't be through laziness or lack of imagination, but simply because she is very attached to her family, and won't want to wander far from them.

The female Bull believes that if something is tangible, then it must be terrific. It's odd, then, that a lot of our most brilliant mediums are Taureans, but put that down to their earthy intuition. This is the Earth Mother of the zodiac, and the true Taurean woman is the jolly farmer's wife, living off the land, and spending her days totally in tune with nature.

These lovely lasses long for a solid, strong life, but if they can't find it, or are negative Taureans, they will become doxies and real flirts. Physical desire is heightened and intensified by this sign, and Taurean women need the sort of sensual stimulation you only receive between the sheets. (They're not very keen on making love on the mat, or canoodling in the closet.)

This is not a flirtatious sign, because Bulls consider life too short to be coy. On the contrary, they can be blunt to the point of blushing, saying 'We both know what we want, so let's get on with it.' They can see no reason to linger over a lemonade when they could be having fun frolicking. The Taurean woman can be very slow and seductive, though, and will always have silky smooth sheets on her bed, and sumptuous-smelling soaps in the shower.

Once the Taurean girl has the ring on her finger, her husband, her home, her kitchen and her offspring will all be vitally important to her. She will do her utmost to be the perfect wife and mother. Being such a physical sign, the Taurean woman will love with her whole body. Fidelity is all to her, and she will expect her man to love with his whole body too, and not lend it out to other people on the nights she's at her Townswomen's Guild.

These are all positive personality traits but, negatively, she can leave most other signs, with the exception of sizzling Scorpio, standing when it comes to envy and possessiveness. She's too phlegmatic to behave in the same way as a Scorpio, ruled by emotion, who will send someone to their peril with impunity. Instead, like that other bulky beast, the elephant, she'll always remember. Don't expect the Taurean gal to forgive and forget, because it's not in her nature. She won't want to get even with whoever has wronged her, but she will calmly choose never to have anything to do with the offending person ever again. It's as simple as that (after all, this is a very simple sign), and it's her way of protecting herself from being hurt in the same way in the future.

Just like her male counterpart, she can take people for granted, and especially her nearest and dearest. A Taurean lass will never be cold, but she can be bad at expressing her emotions, because she'll forget that her partner needs to hear how she feels about him, and that she loves him. Somehow the fact that he's made of flesh and blood too will slip her mind. Sometimes she'll only learn her lesson when it's too late, and her lover is leaving. She will have gone on month after month, year after year, not giving anything of herself and thinking how great life is. Then one day, her husband, who has received rather less attention than an old Christmas card, will announce he's leaving her. He'll berate his bemused and bewildered Bull, accusing her of never saying how much he meant to her. Truly Taurean, she'll reply that she didn't have to. Surely staying with him told him everything he needed to know? But she'll be talking to thin air, as he marches out of the door.

Sometimes the Taurean lass has to make mincemeat out of her marriage before she alters her attitudes. But hopefully she will realise the error of her ways before it's too late, and any frost can easily be melted with a little love and affection.

Taurean women are extremely attractive. Selina Scott has a truly Taurean face, though not the fulsome figure that besets some Bulls. The Queen is a wonderful example of a Taurean woman, combining a desperately demanding duty with a harmonious home life. She's at her happiest in the country, clad in her green wellies and a headscarf, talking to her horses and hounds. Her hair is also particularly Taurean, changing little over the years and ears. Taurus, of course, rules the voice, and two famous singing Bulls are Ella Fitzgerald and Barbra Streisand.

Being the Earth Mother, the Taurean woman will make an excellent mum to her children. She'll dote on her kids, never neglect them and instead envelop them in a warm welter of love. She can be too possessive, though, and be reluctant to let them leave home and spread their wings. She may find it hard to chastise them, but will have no problems showing her love.

And that's what makes her one of the warmest signs in the celestial sky.

Taurus Child

If you fancy taking up weight-lifting, but don't feel like joining a gym, find a baby Bull instead. A couple of hours spent bathing it, burping it, and putting it to bed should do marvels for your muscles.

If you have just had a Taurean child, reinforce the pram before you take it on its first promenade. The bouncing baby Bull can look like a dumpling on legs, even if you do put it in a blue bonnet. Its cot will need steel girders beneath the mattress, and its highchair may need to be specially strengthened. Of course, it's up to the small Bull's parents not to pander too much to his or her demands for food and to teach the tiny Taurean the art of moderation.

As the Taurean child grows (in years as well as inches), he or she will rely much more on the family than a lot of other kids. It's of vital importance that the home life should be as safe and secure as possible, and offer that much-needed security and permanence. Having parents who get divorced can be devastating for a lot of children, but a small Bull will be affected more than most. The more bitter the breakup, the more emotionally scarred the Taurean kid will be, and the memory will linger long after everyone else has settled down into their new lives. Even a tiff or two carried out within earshot of a little Bull can upset and worry them.

The Taurean child is often artistic, so make sure you cultivate this side of your kid's nature as much as possible. Encourage them to learn to play an instrument, so you can bring out their Venusian love of music, even if it's only a triangle or a tin drum at first. (Buy some ear-plugs if necessary.)

However, whether your small Bull chooses castanets or the cello, don't be too impatient if he or she takes a long time to learn. Taureans don't have the quick and ready wit of Air children (although Mercury in Gemini should liven things up), and it takes a long time for them to absorb information. Remember that your child may be slow on the scales, but it doesn't mean he or she is stupid. Don't push or nag, or you'll give your child a complex. Just bear in mind that things sink in slowly, and Taurean children have to ruminate like cows chewing the cud.

Sometimes, of course, your little Bull is just being lazy. So, if you suspect your child isn't doing something because he or she can't be bothered, administer a verbal boot up the backside. (If you really do kick, you'll be kicked back.)

The Taurean imagination sometimes needs a bit of a boost, so get your kid's mind working at an early age. The Taurean love of routine will be present in your Bull from birth, but try to introduce a few gentle changes every now and then. Don't move house every six months, or change your hair colour every week, or your kid will grow up an emotional wreck. Remember that the solid foundations of a Taurean's life must remain constant and unchanging.

Equally, if you always go to Benidorm for your family holidays, try Blackpool instead, or Eastbourne instead of Estartit. Even if the coast has changed, make sure that nothing else has, or your Bullette will have a nervous breakdown before you're off the coach. Pack their favourite teddy, bring their best bucket and spade, and make sure they are reassured by being surrounded by lots of familiar things.

Whatever you choose, do it gently, and don't force your Taurean kid to do something that's not in his or her nature. But do encourage them to enjoy a change sometimes, because otherwise they'll become solidly set in their ways.

They will be happier venturing off into the great unknown of the local Cubs or Brownies if their home life is as secure and happy as possible, given their parents' position. Even if you are a one-parent family, your little Bull will grow up hale and hearty if he or she can depend on you, and skip home from school sure of a warm welcome and a terrific tea!

Taurus in Love

A Taurean in love is truly a sight to behold. These Bulls don't fall in love very often. As the song goes, 'When I fall in love, it will be forever'; these words could have been written about a Taurean. They long with all their bovine hearts that when they do fall in love they will trot straight to the altar. Taureans love the very thought of marriage and all that it entails, because it seems so safe and secure, so comfy and cosy.

The positive Taurean will love wholeheartedly and completely, leaving their amour in no doubt about their feelings. They will pay out pounds on providing their partners with presents, posies of pansies, and practically paralyse them with pleasure.

Negative Taureans, however, will view their loved ones as pieces of property. When they are murmuring endearments into the amour's aural orifice, and saying in that velvety, Venusian voice 'You're mine', they're not joking. They will firmly believe that you really do belong to them, body and soul. And that can be when the problems start.

A Taurean in love is supremely sexy; unfortunately, though, sex can become as much of a routine as putting out the milk bottles. This doesn't mean that they don't enjoy it anymore, it's just that everything has a time and a place for a Bull, and sex may be relegated to Saturday nights. In addition, unless the Bull has an inventive partner, they may play the same sexual games every time.

If your Taurean isn't exactly earth-shatteringly inventive in bed, try to introduce a few changes gradually. If you suddenly swoop on Taureans when they're doing the ironing and suggest an adventure in the airing cupboard, the poor things won't be able to cope. You may even put them off their food (which would be a real shame). Bear in mind the tactile tendencies of the Taurean, and give him or her a massage with aromatic oils, then go for the jugular (in the nicest possible way, of course). The neck is the Taurean's most erogenous zone. Then see what happens!

If a Taurean loses their partner, whether through divorce, death or daffiness, it will be unusual for them to marry again. They will be content to live with their memories of their one true love, and will get a dog for a companion instead.

If you want a Taurean to fall for you, it's easy to do, my dears. The way to that titanic Taurean ticker is through that titanic Taurean tummy! You can't fail, unless the Bull is on a diet and has his or her jaws wired together. (When you could always give them some soup through a straw.)

Invite them round for a meal, make yourself look as attractive as possible without going over the top, (plenty of time for that later), and lower the lights. You could pop over to the pub for a quick Campari, but then get straight back so the Bull can wallow in your home-cooking.

Show them you can cook good food, but make sure you try tasty, traditional things. Don't tempt a Taurean with a tangerine, turnip and tapioca tart. Instead, serve them a succulent stew, or a pootchy pie, with piles of potatoes and gallons of gravy.

Taureans love touch, so make sure you touch them a lot throughout the evening, maybe ending up with a gargantuan grab! But don't maul them about like a lump of dough.

Remember this is a sign that doesn't go for pomp and circumstance, so save the Beluga caviar and your tiara with toning trinkets for your Leo and Libran pals, and make a jam roly-poly instead. Be careful, though, not to show off too much (jam roly-poly on a silver salver), show yourself to be too unconventional (jam and Brussels sprout roly-poly), or be too secretive (jam and Brussels sprout roly-poly which is divine, but you won't disclose the recipe); these things will all count against you.

But if you demonstrate your natural flair and ability, you could go a long way with your Bull. Gosh, you lucky thing, you!

Taurus as a Friend

Taureans make very good friends, but they will always be much better lovers. A lot of Taureans can devote so much time and emotion to their partner and family that their friends become very few and far between. Those friends they do have are likely to have been chums from the cradle, or pals from the playground. Being such faithful old Bulls, they stick to what they're used to, so are happier around people they've known for years, rather than acquaintances they met the previous week at a party.

To a Taurean, loyalty and faithfulness are qualities that are equally as important in their friends as in their lovers. If they commit themselves to a chum, they will stand stolidly by them through thick and thin, and if the pal is going through a bad patch, no matter what the problem is, Taureans will give of themselves totally, providing food, money, a roof over their heads – whatever is needed. You will never want if you have a chum who's a Bull.

I have always believed that the more Taureans I have as friends, the better. If you are privileged enough to be the pal of a Bull, try to do gentle things together. Taureans like to follow peaceful pursuits, when they can be like a cow plodding through a meadow, taking things slowly and doing what comes naturally.

Bulls enjoy social interests that don't demand too much energy, and preferably where the most they're expected to do is chat idly, eat and drink (but not so idly). Neither are they the night-clubbing, disco-dancing ravers of the zodiac. In fact, many young Taureans adopt a somewhat sedentary lifestyle quite happily.

To give you an indication of how energetic Taureans can be (outside the bedroom), their idea of hard work is playing bowls on the village green! They also love pottering around their garden, but may prefer to leave the digging to someone else, such as you. After that, they enjoy eating, and will always go out with you for a meal. Trying to get a Taurean to stop eating is like asking a fish not to swim. (But don't make the mistake of thinking that Taureans stuff their faces all day long, because they don't.)

If you want to give your Taurean mates a treat, and I expect they deserve it, take them off into the country for an outing. The minute they clamber out of the car, or trip off the train (clutching the picnic basket as if it contained the Crown Jewels), they'll rush into the nearest field, and sit in the long grass, surrounded by daisies and poppies, letting the sun shine on them, smelling the rich brown earth and hearing the birds tweeting and the cows lowing in the distance. Sounds idyllic, doesn't it?

Take them to a county show if it's raining, and have a look at the biggest carrot in the county, or the tiniest tattie in the tent. They will adore anything of a countrified nature. Have a ploughman's lunch and a pint of best bitter in a lovely old-fashioned country pub and watch them unwind.

Taureans should make sure they're always doing something. If they don't do anything at all, they slump like a sack of spuds. There is a tremendous danger that the less strong-minded Bulls could contentedly meander through their lives without doing or achieving anything.

All in all, if you have a Taurean friend, you will not want for much. Just don't let them stagnate, or slump like a cow in a field before a rainstorm. Help them, as I am sure they will have helped you in the past.

Taurus at Work

A Taurean with even one atom of ambition can be a fairly formidable force. They will be imbued with persistence, resoluteness, endeavour and fixity. Nothing will be able to stop them climbing the ladder of their chosen career.

You see, Taureans aren't at all lazy once they're doing something they enjoy. But they'll find it hard to exert themselves when they hate what they're doing. So, it's very important for Bulls to enjoy their work; if they do, they can become a roaring success.

Taurus is the sign ruling all the things most valued in the world. (Note that I said 'world' not 'heaven'. Taureans have their feet fixed firmly on the ground. You will never catch a Bull building castles in the air.) Money matters in general and all things material are governed by this sign, so it's no surprise that there are a lot of Taurean millionaires about! And a lot of those Bulls will have made their boodle through property, antiques (which is when you get a Bull in a china shop), or works of art. So put a Taurean and all the good things in life together, add a telephone or two, and you will have a slow but sure success.

Bulls should use the fact that theirs is the sign of money to their best advantage. A Bull working in a bank will go far. In fact, any profession concerned with money, whether it's in a building society, with unit trusts or the Stock Exchange, will be positively profitable for Taureans. They show themselves at their most reliable, and their steadfast, straight-as-a-die stability will shine through. They seem to have a Midas touch with money: whether a barrow boy or a banker, it's most unlikely that a Taurean with a drop of drive will ever be poor.

Unlike Leos and Capricorns, Taureans don't see a career as a way of achieving public acclaim or recognition, but first and foremost as a way of ensuring continued security, keeping a roof over their family's heads, and enough food in the fridge.

But they do like to live in the style to which they are accustomed, like Leos, although the two signs have different reasons for doing so.

So, a Taurean at work is not after applause, just the boodle. That doesn't mean they won't work hard, because they will, but in their own time. They are the tortoises, rather than the hares. Their reward can come through spiritual satisfaction at what they are doing, but principally it will be when they examine their bulging bank balances. With Venus as their ruler, Taureans need harmony at the very centre of their lives, and this is how they can achieve it.

As I've told you before, Taureans thrive on routine, because they need to know exactly where they are, and what they will be doing on each day of the week. It is vital that the Bull chooses a job with a definite working pattern. They need to know that if it's Tuesday, they will be having a late lunch, or that if it's Thursday, they can leave work early. Never mock a Taurean for loving routine, because this ability to settle down into a discipline is a trait that a lot of other signs could happily adopt to their advantage.

Obviously, if a Bull finds a job that has a completely concrete schedule, this will be bad for them, as they will stagnate like an old dew pond or cowpat!

Another suitable career for a Taurean (and a Capricorn, too, for that matter) is being a madame in a brothel. You'd have all the Scorpios lying upstairs, ready to receive the clients, but it would be a practical, money-minded Bull who sat by the door and took the loot! (They're not daft, these Taureans!) They also make marvellous masseurs, because of their great sensuality and love of touch. Go into the country and you will find acres of Taureans farming the land, sitting on tractors, and leading the cows home from pasture. In fact, any activity connected with farming and the land is perfect for a Taurean. You will also find them in the arts, when they can use their sense of the ridiculous to become crazy comedians, such as Terry Scott, Victoria Wood and Eric Sykes.

So, Taureans should go for jobs that offer a certain amount of routine. Add to that a solid, safe salary and you will have a happy and contented Bull worker!

Taurus at Home

C ancerians may be the best home-makers of the zodiac, but Taureans come a pretty close second in their ability to create a harmonious household.

Taureans are basically shy and introverted, but they become much bolder when they're sitting safely within the security of their own four walls. You will notice the difference when you take them away from their haven, because their confidence will ebb, and they may be slow to react to their new surroundings.

Don't imagine that these Bulls are winsome wee wallflowers. Every so often they love a rollicking good knees-up, bawling out 'Roll Out the Barrel' and 'Daisy Daisy' at the tops of their voices, and getting roaring drunk, though they will enjoy themselves best if the party takes place somewhere they know well.

You won't find anything more comfy than a Taurean's abode. It will be terribly traditional, large and luxurious, in a quiet, steady sort of way. When you go to visit, you'll be able to collapse into big comfy armchairs and sink into sofas shaped like ships. Every stick of furniture in a Bull's home will have been built to last, and to accommodate at least fourteen folk at any one time.

Taureans often think that the bigger something is, the better it must be. They will have as large a lair as they can possibly afford (and they don't mind scrimping and saving to get it), normally preferring a house to a flat, because it seems more permanent, and will probably be larger, with a garden. Taureans need room to move about, you see, and you can't keep them cooped up in a bedsit without them becoming unbearably unhappy.

It is a very rare Bull who won't want to own his or her own home as soon as possible because Taureans like to know that their hard-earned cash is being spent wisely and productively. Once they have their own home they can nurture, cultivate and care for

45

their relationships in the way they would a sunflower seedling or a sycamore sapling.

When you are asked to eat with a Bull, make sure you haven't had any food for a couple of days beforehand, so you've worked up the appropriate appetite. If you're going to Sunday lunch, you'll have a rib of beef with plenty of roast potatoes and lashings of rich gravy. (Taureans don't go for fancy food.) There is a Taurean lady I know who always helps her guests to their grub and, if they blink, their plates are heaped so high they have to take half their food home in their handbags. Desperate Dan, whose favourite dish was cow pie, must have been a Taurean!

Nearly every Bull will have a record-player. Even if they're tone-deaf and can't sing a note, they will still love music. They will prefer to stick to the tried and tested, ten-year-old turntable, which they know works, than to bourrée out and blow the boodle on a new stereo system that has flashing lights and can tell you the time in Abu Dhabi.

Taureans like animals, and will probably prefer a pooch to anything else. Of course, if they live in the country they may well keep a pet cow, or a goat for its milk, if they have a Capricorn ascendant. But wherever they are, they'll want a typically domestic animal.

Navy blue is a tremendously Taurean tone, but they will probably prefer to save it for their clothes. Instead, their homes will look like leafy glades, as they will surround themselves with colours that suggest nature at its nicest. They will go for rich, country colours, such as greens, russets and browns, and their homes will always have a hint of the countryside, even if they live in the heart of the city.

The most important part of the house for a Taurean won't actually be a room at all, but the garden. They will love to be out in the flower-beds, surrounded by nature, tending their plants and breathing the fresh air. Failing that, if they don't have a garden, or have surrendered to sloth, they will adore the sitting-room, which will be filled with comfy chairs, melodious music and a lovely log fire. It will also be packed with pot plants. And after that, Taureans love their larders and care about their kitchens. And I'm sure you don't need me to tell you why!

Taurus
Health and Relaxation

The best way for a Taurean to relax is not propped up at the bar in the nearest pub, but to get out to the garden and into the potting shed. There they can mull over life while pruning the privet. City Taureans should caper off into the country and stay with chums, or find a cheap bed and breakfast place for a few days. Then they can walk through the woods, collect leaves and acorns, gaze across the fields and commune with nature. (One Taurean I know loves to touch the bark of trees, as she says she can hear their hearts beat.)

Those Taureans who are clever enough to live in the country already will probably be pretty relaxed anyway, especially if they enjoy gardening and are members of the local horticultural society, or musical appreciation society. A nice change (whoops, wrong word for a Bull), *treat* for them would be to take a loved one out for a good meal in an old country inn. Alternatively, they could hold a little soirée at home, perhaps serving their home-made wine and home-cured hams.

Generally speaking, Taureans find it easy to unwind, because they won't have got very tense in the first place. This is a very relaxed, easygoing sign, and if the Bull is doing all the right things, he or she won't have much to worry about.

The best way for Taureans to relax is simply to follow their instincts and do those things which feel best. They really are so simple, and are not like the Air signs who need calming down, or the Fire signs who need slowing down. Both Water and Earth signs find it far easier to take things slowly; Bulls are some of the most relaxed people you can ever hope to meet.

However, a lot of Taureans will have big doses of Aries and Gemini in their charts, especially through Mars and Mercury. If so, they would do well to calm down, stop rushing about in three directions at once, and find their true Taurean soul, which will be lurking latently beneath that lively exterior.

If you know a Taurean who is normally placid and

phlegmatic, but is charging around as if they're in the bullring and have just seen the matador, sit them down for a soothing chat. You'll find that they're bottling something up inside, so help them to get it off their chests, and then they'll feel much better.

Taurus, of course, rules the neck, but the famous Taurean voice is often hampered by the equally famous Taurean sore throat. If a Bull is going to be ill, you can bet that most of the time the throat will be affected in some way. Children's wards in hospitals are full of little Bulls having their tonsils taken out.

Being the polar sign of sexy Scorpio, they will be afflicted with that sign's problem area which, not surprisingly, is the genitals. So, if the Bull has been overdoing things in the bedroom. . .

Some Taureans can have a terrible time with their weight, if they don't watch what they eat. In fact, I know a lot of Taureans who are diabetics, and they certainly have a sweet tooth. Taureans are renowned for gobbling up half a gross of sweets at one go, and being unable to walk past a *pâtisserie* without shuffling in to sample something. They must be careful to keep their diets well balanced, otherwise they will go for stodge every time, and put on pounds. A lot of them love meat, but they should try to eat more fresh fruit and vegetables.

Some Bulls should cut down on all their food. A lot of them heap their plates so high that all you can see is a tuft of hair over the top of their tatties! They may not care if they put on weight, but they should realise it can endanger their health, and put a strain on their hearts. (And hearts are very important to red-blooded Bulls.)

Taureans also like rich red wines to wash down all this grub, with a couple of whisky chasers for good measure. Pisceans may drink to escape from the harsh realities of life, but Bulls booze because they like the taste!

As you can imagine, you won't find too many Taureans tearing round the tennis courts, or sweating through a game of squash. (Not the sort that's played at sports centres anyway. Games of a different sort of squash played in private are another matter.) They aren't very enthusiastic when it comes to exercise, so the best thing for them will be to take their dogs for brisk walks in the country, after a large lunch. It will be an excellent excuse to work up an appetite for tea!

Gemini

22 May – 21 June

What Makes Gemini Tick

If you want to know how a Gemini ticks, sidle up to the one you're trying to puzzle out, start up a chatette, and then listen very carefully. Above the twinkling tones of the Twin twittering on, you may hear a weird whirring, combined with a couple of clicks. Yes? Well, congratulations, my dears, you have just heard the Gemini brain cells in action. And they are what make every Gemini tick.

The more astute Twins will actually admit to being aware of their Mercurial minds working. They can *feel* themselves thinking. Just imagine all those neurons neoning away inside their noddles. Geminis think so quickly that they leave some of the other signs standing. Everything they see and hear will pass through that brilliant brainbox and be stored away for future reference in the Geminian filing system.

If you're meeting a Gemini for the first time, you'll notice how nervously and quickly he or she moves. Even if the Twin is sitting talking to you, his or her eyes will be taking in everything in the room, and everything about you. Even the egg stain on your tie and the fascinating fact that you're wearing odd socks.

Geminis have a very low boredom threshold, and you'll soon know if you've made them cross it. Their peepers will be poring all over the place and rarely popping back to you. (Apart from your egg stain, of course, because they'll be dying to ask you if it was boiled or fried.) Their fingers will begin to tap out tunes on the table, their feet will jiggle up and down, and they will become fantastically fidgety. This is a danger sign, and unless you can suddenly turn the conversation on to a different, more scintillating subject, to ignite their interest again, you may as well give up and go home. Otherwise you'll be written off as being too boring to bother with.

All Geminis have an elfin appearance, and look like potential pixies. It's rare for them to look like hobgoblins, because this is a very attractive sign, both mentally and physically. The typical Twin – male or female – is incredibly pretty in a boyish way, with alert, shining eyes and fine features.

Most Twins have a very fast way of talking, and may even start to stammer when excited. That may sound strange when you consider that Geminis are so glib and garrulous, and graced with the gift of the gab, but actually sometimes their minds move faster than their mouths, and you get a right old scramble coming out! Geminis love puns because it means they can play about with their favourite toys – words.

Every sign has its good and bad side, and Gemini is no exception. Positively, Geminis are incredibly lively, witty people, extremely articulate and natural communicators. But the reverse of that is the Twin who uses communication in the wrong way, and tells terrible lies (like Matilda's, they make one gasp and stretch one's eyes). Some Geminis like to bend the truth into real reef-knots: they can be real Uri Gellers with words.

A lot of Geminis say to me 'Oh, I'm two-faced, because I'm a Twin', but I think they've got it wrong. The popular myth is that all Geminis are raving schizophrenics, or Jekyll and Hyde characters, being sweet as sugar one minute and ravening beasties the next. You have to look at Gemini's ruling planet, Mercury, to work this out. As it spins about the solar system, one side of it is always in darkness, and the other is always light. And it's the same with the Twins. When we talk of dark and light in a personality, we can mean a true schizophrenic, with two personalities in one mind, or simply someone, like a Gemini, who experiences a tremendous variety of emotions within *one* personality. Geminis can certainly have extremes of character, and on one level be alert, bright, chatty and chirpy, and on another, be so depressed they can't even find the words to describe how miserable they are.

Very often, Geminis can be desperately disappointed with the world. It can be such a dull place, full of such dreary people that Twins have to invent their own, brighter world to cheer themselves up. Geminian memories of events are always a slightly different version of what really happened!

If you understand this it'll help you to appreciate the Twins you know better. You should even feel a bit sorry for them, if you think about it. People who live in their heads that much are bound to be lonely, at least some of the time.

Gemini Man

Well! He can make you feel really dizzy. If you get involved with a Gemini man you can feel as if you're dancing the World Ice Skating Championships with Torvill and Dean.

Gemini men, you see, are fatally attractive. Whether a friend or a lover (and many Gemini men will be both – they're not daft!), a Gemini man is irresistible. And what's more, he knows it. He will concoct a cocoon of charm around you until you're a quivering chrysalis, waiting to be transformed into the beautiful butterfly you know you are underneath. But once he's got you where he wants you, your Gemini man may decide he doesn't like butterflies any more. He's seen a much more mysterious moth and off he'll go, butterfly net waving in the breeze. You have just seen a Mercurial mirage. So, the way to avoid being left with one of his pins stuck through your heart, is to play him at his own game. Keep him guessing. Are you a ravishing Red Admiral or a cool Cabbage White?

The best way to attract a Gemini man is to ignore him. If you're at a party, pretend he's invisible, and he'll scoot over to your side in two ticks. He will have noticed everything around him, but most of all he'll have noticed you, *not* noticing him. However, your problems are about to begin, because he'll chat you up as you've never been chatted up before. The trouble is that he'll chat you up even if he doesn't fancy you. He's frightened that his fatal powers of attraction are fading, and will keep testing them out. (Keeping his hand in, so to speak!) But they rarely, if ever, fail.

It's an unfortunate fact of love that a lot of Gemini men have a Casanova complex. You may pick one who had so many notches on his bedhead that it fell apart, and now he has to use the doorjamb. (Have a look next time you get the chance, and see if you can find the scores on the doors.)

Even when a Gemini is married, he may still be something of

a philanderer. He can ring up his wife to announce he's going on a trip to Turkey when actually he's off on a shopping spree (testing out the bedding department or gazing at a floppy disk). (Don't think he's meeting his mistress – remember, Gemini men don't just have affairs with women but with computers too!) He can't shake off his need for variety, and if his partner can't supply it, he'll look for it elsewhere. Often, even if he is fantastically faithful, he'll still flirt like a – well, like a Gemini! I know one Gemini man who's very happily married, but still walks around telling women that he loves them. And he means it. He loves them all, but in different ways and for different reasons.

Most of these Mercurially motivated men have preternaturally perceptive peepers. A lot of them will have luxurious long lashes too, and beautiful eyes combined with an attractive face can be a pretty powerful proposition. Proceed at your peril! His Mercurial mentality and metabolism means that he'll probably be quite slim, unless he has important planets in Taurus or Cancer, when he may be a trifle on the plump side.

If he's a businessman, he'll be a walking library of credit cards, because he adores gimmicks, and those pieces of plastic are perfect. His office will be oscillating to the latest push-button cordless telephones (so he can walk and talk at the same time), and be crammed with calculators with computer print-outs. But his favourite toy will be a word processor or two. Preferably two, so he can have different dealings with each one at the same time. He's also likely to have a sexy secretary, but that's another story!

Most Gemini dads are made, not born. Gemini is the sign of communication, but the Mercurial man finds it complicated and confusing to communicate with a bawling baby. He will twitch away until the new addition to the family starts speaking. That, for a Gemini man, is when the fun begins.

For his wife, however, it could be when the headaches start. The Mercurial dad will play with his kids until the cows come home, while his wife is moaning about a migraine. His kids will love him for it, though, because he'll behave like their big brother, rather than their dad. After all, every Gemini man is really a child at heart no matter what year is written on his birth certificate!

Gemini Woman

Polish off a plate of pilchards, pronto! They say that fish feeds the brain, and you'll need to nosh it by the netful if you're hoping to keep a Gemini woman interested. Some of them are so bright they make a rainbow look dull.

Gemini women spend pounds on postage. They could keep the Post Office going single-handed. If you have a Gemini woman as a pal, you're probably the happy recipient of piles of postcards, numerous notettes (life is too short, and she is too busy, to write letters), and countless calls. It's her way of keeping in touch. Her diary absolutely abounds with arrangements, appointments and assignations. If you want to see her, you often have to book two weeks in advance. She'll love to see the new plays, the latest films, read the newest books and will happily join you for a jaunt, whether artistic or academic, amusing or athletic.

Some people say they can see the Gemini woman leaning over the wall having a good gossip, and while I must admit that she does thrill to titillating, terribly tantalising and transmogrifying titbits of topicality, she isn't usually a trite tittle-tattler. But don't trust her with a secret, unless she has a strong Scorpio somewhere in her solar scenario, otherwise no sooner have you told her than she'll be traipsing off to make a cup of tea and phone a friend to break the news.

Gemini women love to leap around in slacks and separates. They are feminists at heart, and believe totally that they are equal to men in every way. They have no need to demonstrate their femininity with frills, frocks and flounces, and will flit about in fusty old things to prove their point. They want to be known and loved for themselves, and their brains. A Gemini girl will therefore be much more interested in your mind than your body, and if you plan to bowl one over, you'd better brush up on your brainpower before you begin.

Some sage said that a little learning is a dangerous thing,

and that is true of the Gemini woman, because she can be more than a match for any of the other eleven signs. She loves discussions and debates, and will tie you up in knots intellectually, even if she's making it up as she goes along.

Most Gemini women are incredibly popular, and some might even say shallow, but they aren't really. Just because she knows, and is liked by, so many people, doesn't mean that there is little depth to her. A Gemini girl is just amazingly adaptable, and being a Mutable, Mercurial sign, can switch from subject to subject as she scampers along the highways and byways of conversation. All of her pals, if asked to describe her character, would come up with a different description of her. She's like a chameleon, changing her colours according to the characters and circumstances around her.

A lot of Gemini women are outrageous flirts, but only after you've got to know them. At your first meeting, a Gemini's outwardly cool, calm and collected manner will mean that you have to go easy on the flannel, but once you know each other better, she will unbend and flirt like fury. But don't fall into the trap of thinking that all Gemini girls are just funny flibberti-gibbets. A lot of them may appear so, but they do have a serious side too.

Even if you know a Gemini girl who's the sizzliest thing on two legs, don't let her know you see her as a sex symbol. She will raise an elegant eyebrow, clock you with a look that will make you wish you'd never mentioned it in the first place, and quote a large lump of Freud or Jung at you. (And don't say to her 'Who's he'!)

Although she is generally very pretty, one of her best features is the one you will never, ever see – her mind. Even if you hold her head up to the light and peer through her ears, you won't spot it. You'll only be aware of it working twenty-four hours a day, seven days a week. Whether she's awake or asleep, it will be ambling away, assimilating facts, amassing future knowledge. If you share your life, or just your living-room with her, you'll be constantly confounded by her chirpiness at all hours of the day or night. She is the woman who wakes up in the morning and instantly begins a conversa-tion about conservation, a chat about Chad. (It's in Africa, dear.) You'll be trying to consume your cereal, while she'll be replying to the radio, and completing the crossword over the cornflakes, at the first tra-la-la from the lark.

Judy Garland was a typical Gemini woman, both to look at, and in the way her moods were either up or down. She had the elfin prettiness which is so Geminian, and she always looked as if she knew exactly what she was about.

I don't think the Gemini woman makes a very good mother, in the accepted sense, unless the maternal sign of Cancer was hovering about the heavens when she was born, in which case she'll be much more broody and will want her own children. Like her Mercurial male counterpart, she much prefers kiddiwinks when they're old enough to talk, and she may opt to adopt or foster a child rather than have one herself, and spend a year or more mopping it up and putting it to bed every three hours.

She won't behave in the way mothers are meant to, either. Her children can consider themselves very lucky indeed if she feeds them food regularly – especially if she cooks it herself first. She's much more concerned about feeding their minds than their mouths, and will lead her children off to the local library, read them stories and encourage them to think intelligently for themselves, to discover the diversities and wonders of the world at first hand. If her children want a cuddle, they may be disappointed, but if they want good advice, then she'll be more than able to help them.

Gemini Child

Just what *is* a Gemini child? Gemini kids go from cradle to coffin, and a Twin will be a child at heart whether aged eight or eighty.

Geminis are at their best in their teens. It is when their brains are working like clockwork, and very often those child prodigies who go to university at thirteen are Geminis. The teenage Twin will have an extremely open and receptive mind, and will be constantly learning.

Gemini kids can be really naughty. They can easily play one parent off against the other, and look as innocent as the day. They can also come out with whopping fibs – and get away with them. The kid will believe any story he or she concocts, and so can carry off any flight of fancy. Piscean children have the same ability, because of their fertile imaginations, but Gemini kids have the added benefit of being wonders with words.

Not surprisingly, Gemini children like to have a free rein to do whatever they wish. At school they will very often be more clever than their teachers, and may answer them back. If a Gemini child is taught by a Gemini teacher, all will be well, but otherwise the teacher will either love or hate the Gemini pupil. Gemini kids are often one step ahead of everyone else, either academically or simply by being aware of their surroundings, such as the fact that the teacher is about to walk into the wastepaper bin.

The Gemini child will often be head of the school debating society, because he or she can argue for almost anything. Sometimes, the Gemini won't believe the case he or she is defending, and will have adopted a standpoint just for the fun of it. The more mischievous among them will choose a topic which they know will get the fur flying.

As a child, the Gemini will love playing with colouring books, will be an avid reader, and love making things (such as a mess). Lots of Gemini kids like puppets too, and will subject

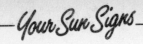

their parents to endless hours of puppet plays from behind the sofa.

It's important that things should be of use if they are to be of interest to Gemini children. If they've been given something to assemble themselves, they'll give up half-way through unless it will be useful when it's finished.

These kids like to be treated as adults, and will try to join in adult things whenever possible. If they aren't allowed to, you may find the thwarted Twin listening at the keyhole to the grown-ups, or with a glass tumbler pressed to the wall.

Often a Gemini child will get on as well, if not better, with a beloved aunt or neighbour than with his or her parents. But Gemini kids love having brothers and sisters, so if your only child is a Gemini, have another kid quick! If you have twins, and they really are Twins, then you're laughing (when you're not crying with frustration, tearing your hair out, and secretly reading their copy of Pears Cyclopedia so you'll have the right answer next time they ask you if Darwin's theory of evolution is scientifically correct, that is).

Gemini children need friends too, of course, and will like their mates to enjoy doing the same sorts of things as they themselves. But give a Gemini an idea or suggestion and, if he or she likes it, that Twin could run riot. So, if you're the parent of a Gemini kid, make sure he or she doesn't have any pals who could be a really bad influence. (A worse influence, that is, than your kid will be on the others!)

Gemini in Love

Geminis will even admit it themselves. They're always falling in love, whether for five minutes or fifty years. But it's not really their fault: they just adore other people. Although they might find it a teensy bit difficult to fall in love with the Hunchback of Notre Dame, their amour doesn't have to be the double of Romeo or Juliet to get those Geminian hearts pounding extra ecstatically.

When Geminis are in love they watch their romantic p's and q's constantly. They are scared of sounding or seeming silly, so they can appear a mite chilly to their partners. They can even be icy, leaving their loved ones covered in hoar-frost. But such is Geminis' dual nature that although they can seem as cool as a cucumber on the surface, underneath they may be feeling as red-hot as a radish. (You see, they're as perplexing as a pomegranate – often to themselves as well as others.)

Generally, when a Gemini loves it is in an Airy way, and quite different from that of a sensual Taurean or a sexy Scorpio, both of whom make no bones about grabbing what they want. Geminis, on the other hand, would much rather grab their amour's brain, not their body.

Possessive partners will turn Geminis off in a trice, and passionate declarations of love, even if they are what a Twin most wants to hear, will make him or her panic. You see, Geminis hate to be tied down in any way. Remember that Gemini is an Air sign, so Twins need a lot of space in relationships, or they will suffocate.

Many Twins march down the aisle twice, or have two incredibly important affairs. The first love-affair or marriage will be important because through it they will discover what not to do next time. Then, when nuptial number two comes along, they will have learnt a lot and won't make the same mistakes twice, and may even allow themselves to be more tender and less rational.

Geminis are renowned for having a butterfly attitude to love, but that's because, on a superficial level, love is a flirtation to them. They know many people and will say that they love a lot of them, but they don't always mean it in a romantic way. Some Geminis can easily have four or five relationships on the go at the same time. But each of them will be for a different reason and won't necessarily all involve sex.

Variety is definitely the spice of life for a Gemini, and the partner must make sure he or she has plenty to offer the Twin in the spice rack of life. Geminis need the delicious feeling of never knowing what's round the corner, if their love-affairs are to survive.

If you think you've got something to offer a Gemini, invite your Mercurial mate round to your place. But first, make sure that you put a complete set of the relative theories of Einstein, or the Shorter Oxford English Dictionary, in the loo. And leave an album of your school photographs lying around. The Gemini will notice it, because those Mercurial peepers miss nothing, whether it's dusty skirting boards or your new designer socks. Call the album 'Me at Eton' or 'Me at Roedean', and cross out 'Me at the comp'. The Twin will think that because you went to such a good school you have the upper hand intellectually, and be fascinated by you.

If you're serious about the Gemini you're in love with, you have got to come up with enough interesting things to keep him or her occupied for the next forty-seven years, give or take a decade. Whatever you do, don't put all your cards on the table at once, because Geminis love to be kept guessing. Keep a few aces up your sleeve to play when the going gets a mite dicey, and then you'll be on to a winning streak!

Gemini as a Friend

Well, it's a funny thing but these gyroscopic Geminis make much better friends than they do lovers. Friendships are less restricting than love-affairs. Geminis are likely to have millions of mates mooching about, culled from all walks of life, and will be just as palsy-walsy with a politician as a painter, an architect as an aardvark expert.

But all those friends, no matter how old or young they are, must have one thing in common. They must be bright, breezy and bursting with brilliant brainwaves, because Geminis will cast aside the dozy, depressing dullards in the twinkling of an eye. They can be very sympathetic if a friend is feeling under the weather, or down in the dumps, but you won't catch them saying 'Oh, you poor thing' for long. If a Gemini knows people who are naturally miserable, they'll be way down their Christmas card list (bound to be a long one, by the way), if they don't actually fall off it altogether. (Negative Capricorns, like Eeyore, would get short shrift from most Geminis.) Loyalty is not one of their shining virtues, I'm afraid.

A Gemini's idea of a fun friend is one who rings the doorbell on a sunny Saturday morning and suggests an expedition to Exeter, to see if the cathedral has fallen down yet, traipsing off on a trek to see if there really is a town called Timbuctoo, or popping off on a plane to Paris.

Geminis like their pals always to be coming up with new, good ideas. After all, *they* are! (It's a rare Gemini who wants to check on the state of Exeter Cathedral two Saturdays running. Unless they've fallen in love with the person who purveys the postcards, of course. Otherwise Notre-Dame will be the preferred place in another week.)

They absolutely adore adventures and like to have a companion to take along on a trip. The Gemini's idea of adventure can be anything from capering off to a crochet class together to skipping off to do something slightly shady, at

which point the pal will become a partner in crime. They love doing things that are rather risqué, niftily naughty, or absolutely against the law! But unless they have a severely afflicted natal chart, they aren't out-and-out law-breakers. Geminians just love new ventures, like Noddy and Big Ears (who must have been born under this sign).

Twins are always going off at new tangents, or on new levels – even if geometry wasn't their best subject at school! One of the best points about a Gemini is that he or she is very receptive to new ideas, and will go in any direction a friend suggests. Who knows where it will lead?

Predictability breeds contempt for a typical Twin. Geminis like their friends, as well as their lovers, to keep them mentally alert, and physically on their toes. Tennis is one of their favourite games, and if you have a ferocious forehand, and your Mercurial mate has a vicious volley, you're in clover. It's love all!

One of a Geminian's ideas of bliss is to browse in a bookshop, new or second-hand. A perfect place for all book-loving Geminis must be Hay-on-Wye (surely a Gemini town), which abounds with bookshops. The Twin could go there for a day trip with a chum and end up spending the weekend! There are so many shops to see.

Geminis don't like buddies they can boss around, as they need to respect their pals rather than dominate them, and what they will most like in a mate (or anyone else, for that matter) is the mind. If they can find someone who echoes their vitality, versatility and variety, they will have found a true starmate.

Gemini at Work

If you work with a Gemini you have probably already considered going out and buying a pair of ear-plugs (or fur-lined ear-muffs if you've got Leo or Libra rising) to protect your sensitive shell-likes from the Gemini's noisier moments. The Gemini will have been wondering why all his or her colleagues have been sticking things in their ears and have apparently gone deaf!

These children of Mercury are really busy bees at work, but in a lively, not a leaden, way. Geminis are able to do at least forty-eight different things at once, and frequently do. I think of them as the octopus of the zodiac, doing different things with each digit. They would love to be able to write or draw with their feet, because it would leave their hands free to do something else at the same time. But sometimes the Geminian tendency to do different things with each hand means that the left hand doesn't know what the right one is doing. (Most Geminis are ambidextrous, anyway!)

I always think that a Gemini working in an office should be on flexitime. The Twins' time clocks may mean they do their best work between ten at night and two in the morning, when most mortals are tucked up in bed asleep. But Geminis may be raring to go, simmering with stunning schemes, and frustrated at being unable to ring their pals (unless they're Geminis too) to tell them all about their latest million-pound brainwave.

Geminis make good workers because they need to express their thoughts and not their emotions. They should choose jobs where their lively imaginations and special spiel are used to the full, and in which they can be in constant contact with others. Among the best professions for these Mercurial marvels are door-to-door salesmen (let's face it, Geminis could sell fridges to Eskimos), telephone operators (they can listen in to the calls), writers, journalists and teachers. Geminis are natural communicators and will become frustrated and un-

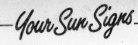

happy if their jobs don't allow them to use this skill. The worlds of television and the media in general are bursting with brilliant Geminis.

Ideally, the Gemini should have at least three different jobs, and you will find many of them actually do have two jobs on the go at the same time. Mercurial minds need the constant stimulation of having dozens of different dealings to dabble with, and the variety helps stave off the boredom which all Twins dread. Even if they have just one job, it will keep their minds as fresh as fuschias, as perky as petunias, if they can work on one project in the morning and another in the afternoon. Negatively, though, they can flit from project to project like a butterfly, and never get anything finished. (Remember that Jack of all trades, master of none, is a phrase which applies to a lot of Twins.)

An easy way to spot a Gemini in an office is to look for the person talking on two telephones at once. (Geminis love the telephone and think it was invented for them. It probably was.) As well as carrying on two telephone conversations at the same time, this child of Mercury will be cutting his or her nails, taking notes, gossiping to a colleague on the other side of the room, noticing what's going on in the corridor, waving to a friend, and scanning the pages of the magazine propped up against the typewriter. What's more, the Gemini won't have got a single wire crossed or messed up any deals. It's enough to make some of the slower signs sleepy just to watch a Gemini in action.

But five minutes later, when the telephone calls are over, the gossiping has stopped and the corridor is empty, the Gemini will be fidgeting and wondering why it's such a dull day! Nothing exciting has happened for hours! But none of the Gemini's colleagues will care – they'll all be too busy swallowing sedatives!

Gemini at Home

Talk about a tip! Most Gemini homes are in a shocking state. Geminis will tell you they have better things to do than tidy up, flick a feather duster about or polish a piece of furniture.

Every now and then, when the place is too much of a pigsty, the Gemini will finally notice the mess, and try to clear it up. But don't expect the Gemini's idea of a tidy house to be the same as other people's. Geminis think a room is tidy if most of the things have been put away (which means crammed into already overflowing drawers or pushed into bulging bookshelves), leaving only three tottering towers of books and magazines on tables and the floor. Even when fired with enthusiasm to tidy up, Geminis will take twice as long as any other sign, because they will be side-tracked at least eight times before they give up, and hide the last of the rubbish under the sofa and behind the cushions. But no matter how tidy the place will be, two days later it will be back to normal.

The typical Twins' home will be a Mercurial mirror, reflecting the tastes and interests of the Gemini who lives there. It will be full of books, telephones, writing materials, and masses of gadgets, and will have a busy, bright atmosphere. When you go to a Gemini's home for the first time, you'll be able to tell at a glance exactly what he or she is like, because everything will be scattered all over the place, in a positively pandemonic profusion, for all and sundry to see.

In fact, you are very lucky indeed if you are invited to a Gemini's home. Unless there is a more domestically-orientated placing in the chart, the typical Gemini will much prefer to see pals in restaurants or pubs – anywhere that is full of life, with plenty to look at in case things get boring.

The Gemini needs to live in a house or flat which is airy, with lots of windows. Geminis also love birds, and like to have them as pets, or perhaps an independent cat.

A lot of Geminis think they'd like to live in the countryside away from it all, but actually most of them need to live in a city, or at least a large town, which is full of life, and where they can feel in the thick of things. A Gemini who feels cut off will dread going home, and will arrange endless evenings out instead.

A favourite pastime of a Gemini is to rearrange the furniture. If you're nipping off to the shops and your Gemini partner is pacing up and down, looking restless, make sure you go to a supermarket which doesn't have long queues at the check-outs. Otherwise, you could come home, laden with the week's groceries and the birdseed for the pet parrot, and find everything's been changed around. Geminis seem to be blessed with superhuman strength at times like these, and will happily hump hefty houseloads up and down stairs, making Big Daddy look like a seven-stone weakling. (But ask them another day to help you get the coal in, and they'll talk about their war wounds!)

If this happens in broad daylight, at least you're safe. Never take a Gemini for granted, and always switch on the light before you enter a darkened room. Quite apart from the ever-present dangers of stubbing your toes on the iron castors of the sofa as you walk into the loo, or falling nose-first over the budgie's cage when you go to hang up your coat, there are even worse perils that could befall you. Whatever you do don't get into bed in the dark if you live with a Gemini, especially if you usually fling yourself into it from the door. You could find yourself lying face-down on the floor of the dining-room, while your amour slumbers peacefully downstairs in what used to be the sitting-room. Living with a Gemini can be a danger to the health as well as a delight to the heart.

Gemini

Health and Relaxation

It can be almost impossible for some Geminis to relax, since they hate inactivity. It makes them nervous. But it's vital for them to force themselves to unwind, to allow some time for the Mercurial batteries to recharge, before they rush off again into the world, with their brains buzzing, chattering away nineteen to the dozen. If Geminis don't relax, they get nervous collywobbles, a complaint they share with Virgo, the other sign ruled by Mercury. Although Geminis can become ill if they find themselves in an environment that is too peaceful and quiet, they must cultivate the self-discipline to retreat from the world every now and again.

They don't naturally enjoy their own company, and often find it difficult to live with themselves. They'll hate it at first, but should learn to set aside a couple of days a month when they can be alone. They should grit those Geminian gnashers, and take the telephone off the hook, lash up the letterbox, and disconnect the doorbell. (Digging up the front path is probably going a teensy bit too far.)

It's also good for Geminis to cultivate what they call 'naff' pastimes, such as gardening, or even just growing mustard and cress on their Noddy face-flannels – any run-of-the-mill, restful recreation will be beneficial, as long as it's interesting enough so that they don't give up half-way through. (*Again.*)

Gemini rules the chest, arms and hands. When a Twin is talking (when aren't Geminis gabbling?), he or she will look like a tick-tack man (or woman). Those arms fly in all directions at once and even when the Twin is on the telephone (something which happens a lot), the hand not holding the receiver will be waving about, performing graceful arabesques to emphasise a point. With all that waggling about, the arms and mitts are bound to come to grief quite often, and Geminis who operate machinery of any kind should be doubly careful. Getting a finger trapped between the keys of a typewriter is one thing, but having your hand converted into a string of sausages is quite another.

The lungs and chest can cause problems for Geminis if they aren't taken care of. I'm always astounded when I see Geminis smoking. They have so much nervous energy that the nicotine certainly calms them down, but it does terrible things to their lungs. A lot of Geminis don't breathe properly anyway. They should practise breathing deeply and slowly, and will soon notice the difference. (If they breathe too deeply and slowly, they'll really notice the difference, because everything will go black and they'll pass out.)

It's an odd thing, but Geminis, who are known as the butterflies of the zodiac, can have terrible butterflies themselves. It's all part of their sensitive nervous systems, and if things get out of proportion, they can become nervous wrecks. They'll smoke six cigarettes at once in an effort to calm down, and get out the Wrigleys at the earliest opportunity.

The Twins should ensure that they get enough kip, too. A lot of them see sleeping as a waste of time, and would love to be able to function on as little sleep as possible. However, they should be disciplined and turn out the bedside light before beginning another chapter of one of the many books they are always reading. Many Mercurians are prone to insomnia, because they can't switch their brains off the way they can that bedside light.

Geminis love doing several things at once, such as reading, watching the telly and chatting on the telephone, but every now and then should take things one at a time. They'll feel much better for it. (So will you. Why's it gone so *quiet?*)

Cancer

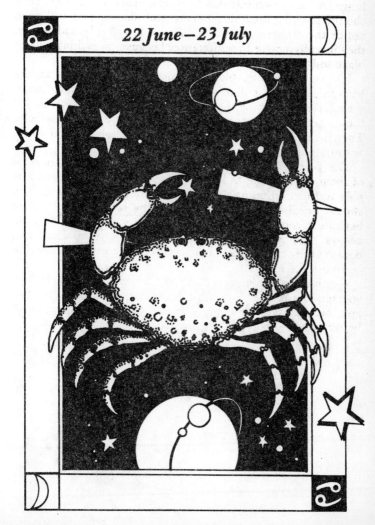

22 June – 23 July

What Makes Cancer Tick

Cuddle and caress a Cancerian you know, today! Crabs need to feel safe and secure, and to know that they are adored and amoured.

This is the sign of Moons and Junes – literally! Leo is led by the Sun, but Cancer is ruled by the other leading light of the zodiac, the Moon. Throughout history and legend, the Moon has always represented motherhood, and she rules the tides, menstruation, and everything else associated with the 28-day cycle. (No, it's not a new form of transport!) The Moon is the peaceful, passive, defensive drive within us, and in the natal chart she shows our maternal instincts, habits and childhoods. And whether we love or loathe our mums.

Generally speaking, Cancerians are ultra-protective, and that can mean they protect themselves as well as others. (Well, aren't crabs encased in shells?) A very good friend of mine says that if you think of a rocker, clad in chain-mail and leather, looking fearfully ferocious, then try to imagine taking all that chain-mail off, you'll find a very ordinary person underneath. And you can say exactly the same thing about Cancer the Crab. There they are, with that solid shell, that concrete coating, waving their pincers about provocatively, and pretending to be pugnacious. But get out the crab cracker and you have the main ingredient for a rather nice crab sandwich – sweet and soft! (Slap two slices of brown bread around them, quick!)

When you first meet a Cancerian, you will sense a hardness, tetchiness, and moodiness, as Crabs are always on the defensive! These are the folk who rush into the room and slap you round the face, just in case you're going to be nasty!

On a positive level, this is a devoted sign. Crabs have a fierce family feeling, can get quite clannish, and put their kith and kin at the centre of their universes.

Many Cancerian men tie the nuptial knot, but can't untangle the apron-strings that bind them to their mums and dads. This can cause fantastic flare-ups within their marriages, because their wives feel upstaged by their mothers-in-law. And lots of Cancerian women spend almost all their weekends at home in the bosom (what a nice Cancerian word!) of their families, even when they've got a husband and six kids at home. (Maybe that's why!)

Crabs can remember what they had for breakfast on their second birthdays, but they can also remember when you last let them down. They will hurl back past slights, which happened many moons before, in the middle of a row. They also like to live in the past (ever seen a Crab in a crinoline?), and they're very traditional, and tremendous collectors of bits and bobs, especially if they are full of memories. (They call them mementoes. Other people call them tat.) And they hoard letters like mad! (A true Crab will have kept all the letters he or she has ever received from the age of six months onwards.)

You see, they hate to throw things away. (Just in case they come in handy.) A Cancerian friend of mine once went whizzing off to a jumble sale at eleven in the morning loaded with the memorabilia (another good Cancerian word) she was chucking out. At half past three she bought the lot back for ten bob. She couldn't bear to part with a single sock!

Being a Water sign, and ruled by the Moon, Crabs are powerfully psychic, and they will have incredibly intuitive instincts. (When they say they're tuning in, they're not talking about the radio!) Crowds of Cancerians can walk into a room and instantly pick up an atmosphere. (And I don't mean the sultry scent of Saturday's supper – sprouts and stew – either.) Their superb sensitivity also means they can be hurt far too easily, and often over nothing at all. Some of them are hypersensitive, and should realise that when they are told something, it's not always meant as a criticism, or an out-and-out rejection.

Cancerians should try to toughen their soft skins which sit beneath their shells, and not harbour hurts or supposed slights. When they do take umbrage, they become changeable and crabby, mean, moony and moody, huffy and hostile, and almost unapproachable at times. They should use their highly-developed instincts in a positive manner, and trust them and live by them. (Very intense Crabs will tune into their teapots, saying at about four in the afternoon, 'I feel I should put the kettle on'. If you're there, try saying you can sense a custard cream hovering in the biscuit tin.)

Security is of vital importance to Cancerians; often if they feel down and depressed, and are doddering about in the doldrums, it's because they don't have a real base to go home to. They need the emotional security of having their own four walls about them, whereas Taureans need nests for material security.

If you're married to a Cancerian, or have a chum who's a Crab, you have to behave like a cuckoo clock, and at every half hour pop your head round the door and say 'I love you!' (You must mean it, though.) Then they'll feel safe and secure. (Go on, give 'em a kiss!) They can be so gruff that they take you by surprise sometimes. So, if you know a Cancerian who is being crabby, just remember the rocker with the chain-mail. (If you're a Bull, you'll remember the crab sandwich!) Underneath that hard shell shimmers a heart of pure gold, which is just waiting to melt as the first words of love cascade from your lips!

Now, of course, there are some cantankerous, cross and cranky Crabs about. They'll be mean and moody, and will scowl like scallops. They'll click away with their pincers, sounding like a couple of castanets on a package holiday, but they will still be soft and sweet underneath.

Cancerians really do need to be needed, and know that they're loved. Otherwise, they can't function fully. Remember this is the polar sign of Capricorn, and most Goats are frightened of rejection. Crabs can be just the same. If they do have particularly firm filial feelings, especially for a matriarchal mum, they'll prefer to hide at home than go out into the big wide world and face whatever it may have to offer them. And when they do scuttle out from under a rock to test the waters of life, if they're used and abused, they'll sound a furious fandango with their perpetually pirouetting pincers, and then rush back to the boulder as fast as their pins can propel them.

Babies are a must for this sign. Whereas procreation is important for Leos, who love children and like to be proud of their own cubs, with Cancer it is much deeper, and more a case of carrying on the family name. Cynthia Crab. Cyril Crab. . .

Cancer Man

What a sweet sign! I like Cancerian men because they're such cuddly crustaceans beneath their crusty coatings. Whenever you consider a Cancerian, you must recall the crab, which walks sideways into trouble, or sideways out of it, depending on the sort of crab it is! (Never judge a Crab by its cover!)

Most male Crabs are really soft and sentimental, and lots of them will cry at the drop of a tissue. (It's awful if you've got a cold.) They're very domestic, and a lot of Cancerian men adore being in their kitchens and cooking. Take my boss at Breakfast Time, who is strongly Cancerian (although he's got the Sun in Gemini), and spends virtually all his weekends in his kitchen, cooking enough grub to feed an army. (Even the programme's called after a meal!) Cancer rules the tummy, and the old adage that the way to a man's heart is through his stomach will apply to just about every Cancerian man! (Don't believe what he says about going on a diet!)

Cancerians are very changeable crustaceans, and these moods – motivated by the Moon – can plumb the depths of despair, or soar way beyond the bounds of rationality and logic. (Two words Cancerians don't understand.) Both men and women born under this sign let their hearts rule their heads, because they have such pulverisingly powerful passions. Cancerian men can let their feelings rule their lives, and find it easier to express their emotions than the men in any of the other elements of Fire, Air, or Earth. (And that's good news for anyone in love with one of them!) In the Watery wonderland, Scorpio men tend to express their feelings sexually, and Pisces men express them romantically, but Cancerian chaps express them emotionally.

The main problem with the Cancerian man, actually, is going to be his mum. He will have a tremendously strong link with her, and that can mean love or hate. Some Crabby chaps

can loathe their mothers so obsessively that they destroy every other relationship. Every woman becomes an extension of the odious object, and is abhorred also. Alternatively, they will love their mum munificently. Sometimes, these sentiments can be so strong that a Crab's mate feels left out, and resents her mum-in-law. And unless this 'other woman' is a cool Air sign, she'll become like the mother-in-law of countless music-hall jokes, who's always dropping round to keep an eye on her little soldier, even when he's forty-five! (She'll also appear clutching a cake tin in case 'she's' not feeding him up!)

Before getting totally tied up to a Cancerian man, it wouldn't be a bad idea to find out exactly what his relationship with his mum is, and whether he's cut the maternal strings that bind him. If she was the doting sort of mum who mollycoddled him all his young life, you could be in for trouble. You'll wonder sometimes if he's a man or a mouse, a chap or a crab. (Put down a trap and see what happens!)

As you might have gathered, Cancerian men tend to look for mates who remind them of their mums, though sometimes they shouldn't! Very often, because they are a Water sign, this will be a subconscious search. But whether they realise it or not, they may provoke a rivalry between their mothers and their loved ones, which will be hard to resolve. (It can also be very awkward when they get the names mixed up!)

It's incredibly important for the Cancerian chap not to develop a lot of bad habits, because it's very difficult to teach an old crab new tricks. (When did you last see an old Crab balancing a plate on his nose? There you are, then!) Old habits die hard. An evening of edited highlights, featuring his bad behaviour and boyhood every now and then won't go amiss, because if he's positive, he'll be able to shrug off some of the shackles of the past. (Crash!) He's very good at carrying on family traditions, but sometimes doesn't realise that what was good in the fifties doesn't work so well in the eighties. (Here, he's not a Teddy Crab, is he?)

Roots are all-important to Cancerian men, and often they'll live and die in the town in which they were born. Some may even try to live in their childhood homes, either by hanging on to them through the years, or buying them back when they're up for sale years later. They hate to rip out their solid foundations, unless they have an ascendant which gives them some get-up-and-go. (Then you'll see a Crab with a knapsack on his back.)

Usually, the male Crab is a creature of habit, never straying too far from his beginnings, and needing a mate who will mother him. But this is getting on to dangerous ground, because if he can't find someone to fit the bill, passion-wise, he can lapse into an emotionally entangled connection with his kith and kin, which may elevate a few eyebrows!

One man who looks truly Cancerian is Eddie Large, with his round face and curly hair. He was also born under a Full Moon, which accentuates his Cancerian qualities. This sign is said to have the best sense of humour in the zodiac, and other naturally funny Cancerian men include Tim Brooke-Taylor and John Inman.

It goes without saying that the Cancerian man will make a delicious and doting dad. But even so, he will be more maternal in his feelings than paternal. For example, he can go home after a hard day at work, put on a pinny, and cook for his kids without a murmur. He'll look after his family, take the kids out at weekends, and his life will revolve around his home and all who sleep in it. (He'll even care about the canary.) He's a natural dad, and will find it very hard to come to terms with not having any offspring of his own. If that's the case, he'll adopt colleagues or pals, and consider them as his kids. Don Revie used to do the same with his football teams and call them his little families.

All Cancerians live in the past, and the best-known book full of one man's memories is *Remembrance of Things Past,* by Marcel Proust. And yes, he was a Cancerian! Now do you believe in astrology? (You're reading this book, aren't you, dear?)

Cancer Woman

What a fulfilling sign! This is one of the best signs to be born under if you're a woman. Mind you, it may be too much for some Crabettes to cope with!

The Cancerian woman is endowed with almost mystical powers of sensitivity. In the Tarot, she's the Enchantress, because of her incredible emotional energy. Selina Scott has got the Moon in Cancer, making her vulnerable and defensive, and that is truly Crab-like. Sometimes the Cancerian lass can be too sensitive for words, so it's vital for her to be organised and aware emotionally. Otherwise she can be tossed about on the sea of life like a piece of flotsam and jetsam, with bits torn off in all directions.

On one level, this can mean that she falls in love with love, because her emotions don't tell her when to stop. (*Why stop?* she'll say.) She can gush forth her feelings in such a torrential way that she'll frighten everyone off for miles around. And she can become so protective and possessive of people, pals, kids and cousins, that it's difficult for them to escape her Cancerian clutches. She's terribly tenacious. Whereas on a professional level that's lovely, because tenacity can help ambition along, on an emotional level it can be a disaster, because she won't know when to give up and stop clinging. (Her little claws can clutch and crush until she's squeezed all the love out of a liaison.) She won't be able to see when a relationship is over and out (Roger), and even if she gets an inkling, instead of admitting it's ended, she'll carry on clinging – just in case there's a chance – and love will turn to hate, on both sides.

Her emotions are so highly developed, perhaps even to the point of excess, that in the end they can wreak havoc, rather than make her an amorous, affectionate, docile, devoted, protective and passive person. (Phew!) Other people may misunderstand her motives, and see her as a grasping, scheming, over-emotional woman whom everyone tries to avoid. Her feelings and desires can be too powerful, and far too strong for her to handle.

When she's being positive, the Cancerian woman can be superbly sympathetic, sensitive and supportive. If she channels these emotions properly, and devotes herself to her partner in a controlled, constructive way, then everything in the garden will be lovely. But if she's negative, she can pulverise everything in her path with her phantasmagorically potent passions. Then she'll weep and wail when she's reduced everything to ruins around her. The old adage 'It'll end in tears' must have been created by a Crab. (Where's the Kleenex!)

Cancerian women who have organised their existences are excellent, and they'll protect their partners, and fend for their families, and anyone else they care for, devotedly, but with discipline. Positive Crabettes won't be reluctant to reprimand when it's required, whereas the negative Nellies can feel too timid to tell anyone off. Of course, after a tirade or a ticking off, the Cancerian woman will go away worrying if she's done the right thing, and have a wonderful weep. But at least she'll have said something, and probably she'll have acted wisely.

Size-wise, most Crabettes are comfortably, cosily curvy. (Look at Gina Lollobrigida – you did?) They can even be delightfully dumpy, and often have big breasts, which are a part of the body ruled by this sign. Cancerian women usually smile a lot, and are a joy to be with, because they have such warm, homely and motherly auras. They will always be trying to feed you up. And Crabettes *love* having children! The Princess of Wales is going to have lots of kids, but she would anyway, even if she weren't married to Prince Charles, because she needs to live out that maternal role. Other very Cancerian women include Fern Britton and Molly Sugden. (Aren't they cuddly?)

Don't make the mistake of thinking that Cancerian women must be terribly unliberated, being so devoted to domesticity, because that's not true at all. They can be feminists, but it will be with sympathy and sense, and they won't come across as furious and fanatical as some of their more strident sisters.

If she hasn't got kids of her own, the Crabette will keep a pet. Some signs, such as Sagittarius, adore animals, but remember that they're four-legged friends. If Cancerians keep pets, they can become child substitutes. For example, a dachshund will

stop being a dog and become a daughter.

These women make the best mothers of the zodiac, without a shadow of a doubt. But they can be ultra-possessive, and if they're negative, they can be very complex about their children indeed. The thought of their kids leaving the nest can send them into terrible tizzies, and can make some mixed-up Crabs suicidal. (It won't be 'Fly away Peter, fly away Paul', but *'Come back*, Peter, all is forgiven'!) But if they have their heads screwed on and their emotions flow forth fluently, they will command real respect from their kids. Their lovely warmth will then flood out without them being clinging and claustrophobic. And that's when they'll be wonderfully warm, lusciously loving, captivating Crabs. But they must watch the tendency to mollycoddle their kids and not let them out of their sight. (Otherwise, it'll be a real case of smother love.)

Cancerian women find it hard to separate themselves from their families and, even as adults, they often spend as much time with their folks as they did when they lived at home. A prime example is my caring Cancerian manager, Jacque, who spends most of her spare time with her family. And, like most Cancerian women, when you ask her to name her friends, she can count them on the fingers of one hand, because her life revolves round her relations.

There are tremendous tie-ups and lots of links between Cancer and Taurus, and it's super to see these signs together. They can be so alike, both needing security, but in different, complementary ways. Another pootchy pairing is Cancer and Capricorn. Put these two together, and you get the real Darby and Joan of the zodiac!

Cancer Child

Unless Fate is against them, and they have an upbringing purloined from the pages of Hans Christian Andersen, childhood is a happy state for most Cancerians. The Moon rules the life up to puberty, which is a very Moony manifestation indeed. Until you achieve adulthood, you are protected by your parents, and you'll have no real responsibilities. So childhood can mean heavenly halcyon happenings for most Crabs, even if it's just in retrospect, when they've forgotten the trials and tribulations of those tiny times. Children's emotions are usually carefree, and it's only when they become older that they get more complex and convoluted.

Crabs will be even more cheerful as kids if their parents get on well together and have made a happy family. But if the mum and dad have difficulties, the worst thing they can do is use the kid as a parental ping-pong ball. They'll end up with a very confused little Crab, who'll be distrustful of folk in the future. So as far as a Cancerian kid is concerned, life will be much rosier if the home fires are burning with love and not loathing. Crabs can't protect their peepers with their pincers perpetually, and they can usually uncover any uncomfortable undercurrents, which will upset and undermine them.

If you have a Crablette for a kid, you must show lots of love, reams of reassurance and crates of caring. Read your child bedtime stories, cover them with cuddles, dress up their dolls, and show that you care. Then the Crablette will feel that delightful, delicious devotion flowing from the family. But remember that once is not enough. Crabs need constant caring.

Crabby kiddiwinks won't wander very far from home – in fact their parents can have a terrible time trying to get them to scamper off to school. They can have tears and tantrums, and grab on to the garden gate, because it'll be the first time they have to leave home.

In fact, leaving home for a Crab of any age will be a

tremendous trauma. Parents should plan the proceedings like a military manoeuvre. Even Crabby kids commencing kindergarten should be prepared six months ahead, so they can get used to the idea. If this is a parental problem for you, tell your Crablette how much fun school will be. (OK, lie a little!) But, most important of all, say that being sent off to school doesn't mean that you don't care for your Crablette any more. (Don't laugh – Cancerians worry about these things.)

Make no mistake, the period up to puberty will provide the pattern for the Crablette's life ahead. If he or she was emotionally brow-beaten, bashed and battered in this important interlude, the scars will stay till senility sets in. They may be thinly disguised but they'll be lurking just beneath the surface. (They can convert a Moon maiden from Gentleman's Relish to crab paste.) If the childhood was happy and harmonious, you'll have an adult Crab who is extremely organised. But if it was a nasty nightmare, the demons won't disappear, and instead will invade every aspect of the Crab's existence. But most affected will be emotional entanglements.

The meanderings of Mercury in the Crabby kid's chart will indicate his or her intelligence. For example, Mercury in Gemini will add an extra snap, crackle and pop to the Moony mind. But if you were to ask me if Cancerians are clever, I could only reply that they aren't logical enough. (Which is an excellent example of an Aquarian answer!) Emotions are what make these Crabs click and tick. No sign is daft, but some are quicker at picking things up than others. So, your Crablette won't be blessed with the brilliance of the Twins. But, instead, this kid will have vistas of vision a lot of other signs are short of. What you lose on the swings you gain on the roundabouts! But for Cancer, once seen and experienced, never forgotten. And who could forget a captivating Crab!

Cancer in Love

Crumbs! When Cancerians care, they go the whole hog. (Or, if you prefer, the complete crab!) This is doting and devotion time, with lots of billing and cooing, though Crabs aren't love-birds like Librans.

It's incredibly important for Crabs who care not to let themselves go immediately. But, quite honestly, that's like trying to hold back a team of wild horses! (You carryell 'Whoa!' till you're blue in the face, but the Crab won't take a blind bit of notice.) Once a Cancerian has latched on to someone with those prehensile pincers, it's very difficult for him or her to remember that anyone else exists but the object of affection.

That's all very well, and a Crabette can still be in love with her husband thirty years after she did arabesques down the aisle, but she won't know anyone outside her family. Cancerians in love like to wrap themselves and their partners up in cocoons, and stay in the cosy chrysalis, away from the outside world. But this can cause terrible trouble and traumas if the Crab has a pash for a person who doesn't want to be restricted in this way. Once the affair is over, the Crab will feel rejected, rebuffed and repulsed. Some signs could shrug it off, but the Cancerian will go home to mum. He or she can even refuse to go out with anyone else ever again, just in case lightning strikes twice. (Ever wondered why many Cancerians wear rubber-soled shoes? Well, now you know!)

The classic sign of a Cancerian who's in love and getting nowhere fast (or slowly), is that he or she will become stroppy, slink back into that shell, sulk and be silent. When asked what the matter is, the Crab will find it difficult to spill the beans, but may finally turn on a torrent of tears. (Tears are the ultimate, secret weapon, which every Crab will use to gain a heart's desire. Does that sound familiar? I thought it might! Pass the Kleenex again!)

A Crab in love can be the most angelic of amours, warm and

wonderful, or an emotional tornado and a crabby crustacean who dissolves into weepings and wailings at a moment's notice. It will all depend on how much control the Crab has.

These are very affectionate creatures, and they'll nuzzle you with their nippers. But unless there is a focus for their feelings, their highly sensitive Watery intellects may make them imagine things that don't exist, though they will never be as fantasial as Pisces. ('You don't love me anymore' they'll say, if you haven't canoodled with your Crab for a full five minutes.)

Once a Cancerian settles down to a committed relationship, it will usually be for life. But Crabs rarely recover from the guilt ingrained from their first love. (And they'll keep all their old love-letters, tied up in a pink ribbon, to agonise over in secret. 'If only...' they'll sigh.) Cancerians have gallons of guilt, which they get from their opposite numbers, the Goats. They can even suffer from real persecution complexes. Crabs can replay scenes time and time again, on their mental videos, wondering if it was all their fault. They'll revel in recriminations, while howling into hankies.

All Water signs have a sensual side, and Cancerians like sex, often because of the cuddly closeness it can bring. Crabs can get really carried away over sex, but if they screw for the sake of it, they should see it as such. They're only asking for trouble when they think that a one-night stand will automatically lead to nuptial bliss! Because when the flingette floats off, without so much as an 'I'll call you', the Crab will be completely crushed. 'But this was *It*' they'll scream. 'The minute I saw him, I *knew* he was The One.' (Don't say 'But you said that *last* time'!)

If you want to make a Crab go crazy about you, be kind, considerate, and chat about your family. Mention your mother. Casually drop into the conversation that all you want is to live in a cosy little nest with the one you love. If you give your Crabette a Mary Baker Sponge Mix, a whisk and a pinny on your second date, she'll rush you off to buy the ring the minute the shops are open, then rip down the net curtains to use as a veil!

One word of warning. If a Crab you care for starts singing 'I'm getting married in the morning' it's not an edited highlight from *My Fair Lady*. It's a heavy hint! (Well, what about it? You'd look terrific in a topper!)

Cancer as a Friend

Y ou're on to a good thing here. Crabs make cherishing chums and marvellous mates. If you become a buddy, you'll automatically also become part of the family. Everything that applies to your friend's brothers and sisters, uncles and aunts, will apply to you, too. For good and bad.

That means you'll have to behave in the same way to your mate, being kind and caring. You can tell him or her when to go home, when to leave you alone, and when to stop sympathising, or interfering. But do it gently. Cancerians, bless their crabby cotton claw coverings, can ring you up and say 'How *are* you? All alone? I'll be right round to keep you company' when you really want to be by yourself. If you say, in best Garbo style, that you want to be alone, your sweet, sympathetic Cancerian will instantly be replaced by a cranky, crusty, crabby crustacean, who will take it personally. (Cancerians are *always* taking things personally.) 'Oh, OK' they'll say, and slam the phone down, nearly deafening you.

They really are fantastic friends, but they often take things too much to heart. Crabs don't stand aside from their fun friendships enough, turning them into embroiled and emotional experiences. Many Crabs will have platonic palships for a couple of years, and then suddenly get an urge to jump into bed with their buddies, and they can destroy the relationship as a result. (And then out comes yet another box of Kleenex.)

Cancerians love to look after the people they care for, and one of their favourite pastimes is getting all their pals together under their roofs and giving them a good feed. They like to socialise in their own homes, and though they'll have the odd drink-up down the pub, they'll be the first to say 'Everyone back to my place'. Crab chums are also devoted, and will defend you to the hilt, as they will defend anything they care about.

Your Cancerian pal will be delighted to dash round and dole

out tea and sympathy when you need it, and hold your hand over the chocolate cake. (Which could be messy.) He or she will like to have a good natter, and lots of Cancerians indulge in the teeniest of small talk. They can have great gossips about the shelving systems in supermarkets, which is all right when you don't fancy discussing whether the chicken or the egg came first. They like rather prosaic pursuits, such as going shopping with a close chum, and they adore their little habits.

Cancerians don't expect too much razzle dazzle from their friends. (Just a lot of love.) They like cosy, comfortable carryings-on, and adore going to jumble sales, winter fairs, summer fêtes, spring bazaars and autumn bonfires – any season is a reason to rummage through a lot of old junk! And they love weddings. (Especially their own.)

A treat for your Cancerian pal would be a day out with you, ambling around a lot of antique shops, because most Crabs collect old things of one sort or another. (Exactly when *were* you born?) Just don't expect your pal to want to do anything too engrossing or enterprising. A Crab's energies are all directed towards the family and fireside. So when it comes to friendships, the Cancerian simply needs someone to chat to, and have a good gossip with.

As this is a Water sign, the Crab may enjoy messing about on the river, especially if you've packed a picnic basket. This is also the sign of mountain streams and lakes, so why not brush up on your yodelling and amble off to Austria together!

Don't forget that Cancerians absolutely adore history, so they'll enjoy going to see old edifices such as Stonehenge or Edinburgh Castle. (Or Aunt Dolly.) Their lunar sensitivity means that they'll be able to absorb the atmosphere to the utmost. They also love old films, and some Cancerians start sniffling the second the credits commence for sentimental old stuff like *The Wizard of Oz*. It may not be because they are sad, so much as the fact that the film will remind them of their childhoods and how happy they were. In fact, anything that reminds these Crabs of their pasts will be bound to be a big hit. Just remember to take along a hanky for when the floodgates open!

Cancer at Work

Don't be fooled by a Cancerian. You may think it's all tears and tirades, smiles and snuggles, with Crabs, but they know exactly what they're doing, and can be very ambitious when they want to be. They're a Cardinal sign, after all, along with Aries, Libra and Capricorn, so are absolutely sure of what they want and how to achieve it.

In fact, Crabs can be insatiable for success. In astrology, the Moon represents a powerful public persona, and prominence in the public eye. This is why you'll find many Crabs in public-orientated professions, whether it's meeting the public as a hotel receptionist, or *maitre d'*, dinner lady or top chef. All of these things appeal to Cancerians, who are tremendous helpers and more than liberally endowed with total sympathy. (A sad story can have them sobbing themselves silly.) Whatever position they have, whether it is catering (a very Crabby career), generally helping the poor or improving social conditions, Cancerians are adept at picking up and analysing the feelings, emotions and atmospheres around them. Then they can help to the best of their abilities and capacities.

But mark my words, an ambitious Crab isn't going to be docile, or sit on the sidelines. He or she will want to get to the top, and can be quite envious and angry when other people seem to be getting the acclaim the Crab craves.

Although Cancerians may want public positions, and success, that doesn't always mean they want to be in charge. Ideally, Crabs should do work in which their egos and names aren't at stake, even though they will still want to reign supreme in some way. Because of their lunar links, the more they can be with others and do things for them (though not necessarily in a charitable, voluntary, Piscean way), the happier they'll be. They aren't absolutely altruistic, because they want to bring in enough boodle to be able to afford the possessions and nice things they enjoy. (Antiques and arty artefacts, especially.)

Many Crabs work from home, and are very happy to do so. Sometimes, it will mean they can work and be with their beloved families at the same time, and they'll feel soothed and safe by being within their own four walls.

Ideal occupations for Cancerians to do from home include running a catering service from their own kitchens, providing grub for banquets or barbeques, crocheting or knitting jumpers, or embroidering old-fashioned samplers and selling them. (They like loot. And while Leos go for gold, Moony Crabs save silver.)

Often the hardest choice for a Cancerian to make will be between family and career. Some of them, of course, never make it that far, having opted for the family very early along the line. But a lot of Crabettes are quite happy to turn their clan into their careers, and make being a housewife a profession.

This will most often be a difficult decision for Cancerian men, although some high-flying female Crabs can have the same problem. But unless the high-powered Cancerian is self-employed and works from home, he or she can find it difficult to fulfil that maternal, protective side of the crustacean character. (Don't think that men can't feel maternal. Cancerian men can, and do. You've only got to see one in a pinny to realise that.) And if the Crab is married with kids, he or she can feel guilty at spending too much time working away from home.

Crabby chaps will use their protective personalities in a very positive way by treating the folk in their office, factory, or wherever they work, as part of the family. For this reason, Cancerians would make very good trades union leaders, shop stewards, or personnel officers. But whatever they do, they'll try their hardest to be liked and respected, and can make a lot of money at the same time. Now that can't be bad, can it? Of course not!

Cancer at Home

C rabs at home will be on top of the world, even if they live in basement flats. Whenever they're away from them, they long to be back in their little nests, safe from the ravages of the world.

Crabby chums will scuttle home at the first opportunity. You can ask them in for tea, but they'll refuse and say they want to have a cuppa in their cosy cocoons in Crouch End.

Many Cancerians will go out for the evening, and even before they've started on the soup they'll slope off home! Some Crabs can even go on holiday, and be so homesick after a few days that they'll take the first train home again! Everything will revolve around the homestead. There is one girl who's strongly Cancerian, and she actually walks around saying goodnight to all the rooms in her flat before she goes to bed! (Must be Moon madness!)

As you might have guessed, the Cancerian home will be the very characterisation of cosiness. Crabs like old, traditional things and will often copy the furniture, decorations or colour schemes of their childhood homes.

The kitchen will be the Crab's idea of heaven, because that's where he or she can bake cakes, biscuits, make stews, roast dinners, and have a whale of a time. Every Crab is bound to have a family of one sort or another – real relations or close chums who seem like part of the clan – round for Sunday lunch, or dinner on Saturday night.

A Cancerian's home is a fortress against the world, a little cocoon he or she can crawl into at the end of the day, and pull up the drawbridge. If the Crab is in tune with those intense lunar intuitions, he or she will have chosen the nest because of its atmosphere. (Cancerians can sniff out a good or bad atmosphere in two seconds flat.)

If you were rude enough to open a drawer in a Cancerian's home you'd never get it shut again. It'll be overflowing with letters, strands of string, perished pens, crunched crayons, and lots of other things the Crab no longer needs but can't bear to part with. The loft will have to be specially reinforced to take the wondrous weight of all the bits and pieces the Crab will have collected over the years, from a thousand rummage sales or hand-me-downs from great-grandmother Kate, which they feel is their duty to keep in the family. Spare rooms will be crammed with collections left by dead aunts, which the Cancerian can't possibly give away. It can cause trouble if the Crab is married to someone who hates the hoard, and craves to chuck it all out. 'Aunt Ada made that in 1950!' the Crab will cry, as you unearth a hatstand made out of an aerial and two fish slices. (That's right, Aunt Ada was an Aquarian!)

Crabs like lots of little rooms, rather than the great big barns that Arians and Leos love. And if they possibly can, they'll have roaring log fires, so they can toast crumpets in front of the flames, and roast chestnuts round them in the winter, while playing 'White Christmas' on the stereo (Bing Crosby *was* the best), and sobbing sentimentally into a Scottie. (Paper hanky, not handy pooch.)

You can never really tell what colours a Crab will choose for decor, because it will depend on what he or she grew up with. Astrologically, though, Crabs choose the colours of the Moon and the stars – silvers, blues, whites, blacks and greys. A lot of Crabs paint the outside of their houses black and white, with pebble-dashing – which reminds them of the seashore!

Cancerians may continue their hankering for happy homes to the grave. One Crabette chum has already chosen the plot of land where she'll be buried, because it's got a nice view. Having been content in her cocoon during her life, she wants to be equally delighted when she's dead! So try to make sure Crabs push up the daisies in a homely, pretty place. (A church they used to go to in the good old days.) Otherwise they'll come back and haunt you, with sounds of ghostly, Crabby crying!

Cancer
Health and Relaxation

There's no getting away from it. Nearly every Cancerian I know lives on Rennies and Setlers, crunching them up the way other signs scoff Smarties. So many of them suffer from indigestion, it's uncanny, and it will either be through bad eating habits, being het-up, or both. Cancerians have such big butterflies in their stomachs they're almost vampire bats.

Cancer rules the stomach, and Crabs can have terrible trouble with their tummies. They can get upset stomachs, gripes, wind, heartburn or indigestion. Very often, these attacks are brought on by a build-up of *brouhaha* about them. Ulcers are almost an occupational hazard for Cancerians, and the poor things can writhe around in agony as their tummies tie themselves in tangles and their abdomens do aerobics.

Now, before we go any further, let's get one thing straight. If you're born under this sign, it does *not* mean you're going to contract cancer. You aren't more vulnerable to it than anyone else, because it can attack anyone born under any sign. So don't worry, dear.

This motherly sign also rules the breasts, and I've noticed that Crabettes always believe in breast-feeding their babies. Mumsy old Cancer is the sign of childbirth, and the reproductive system. Some Cancerian lasses can have worries with their wombs, and when they're pregnant they should do everything by the book to avoid any trouble. Cancerian men have problems with their tummies, and can often become quite podgy and cuddly as the years progress. (Humpty Dumpty, though an egg, must have been born a Crab!)

Most of the Water signs have a tendency to go through a boozy binge at some point in their lives. Negatively, they can drink to drown their sorrows, and harm their health as a result. It'll be no good at all if gallons of gin are poured into those Cancerian tummies, only to clash with all the medicines and remedies already swishing about trying to relieve the agonies of indigestion.

The best way for a Cancerian to dispel all this tummy trouble is to cut down on drink and rich food. Crabs should stick to regular habits, and not eat a mountain one meal and a molehill the next. And the women should have regular check-ups of their breasts and reproductive organs, to make sure everything is as it should be.

You can tell a Fire sign to relax by going out and burning off some of that excess energy, but you can't do that to Crabs, because they exist on such an emotional level. You can only tell them to hold on to their hats and their horses, and lead very stable lives.

Very often ulcers and similar stomach sufferings are the results of an emotionally nasty nuptial, an agonising affair, a cheerless childhood, and the like. So when a Cancerian is facing a furore of ferocious feelings, you can't tell him or her to trot round the block and then to forget all about it. The problem is often far more deep-rooted and complex than that, sometimes going back for years. The only cure for the Crab may be to break up the betrothal, forget the family or walk out on the wedlock. Prevention is the pootchiest policy for a crustacean, if he or she can use those insights and instincts and look into the crystal ball of love, before jumping out of the fire to become a Crab fritter in the frying pan of life.

Leo

24 July – 23 August

What Makes Leo Tick

Inside every Leo is a king or queen waiting to jump out. (In a little Leo it'll be a prince or princess.) But whatever the rank, Leos do like to wear the crown, hold the sceptre, and be in charge. It's a Leo who will lead a little old lady across the road, even when she doesn't want to go! (You try arguing with a Lion half-way across a zebra crossing!)

Leos aren't going to like this, but what makes many of them tick is acres of applause. They like to be the centre of attention and know that their public – whether it's 5,000 fans or the boy next door – appreciates them.

There are some very colourful Leos around, but there are some very grey ones too. Think of a Leo, and you'll see someone blond and blue-eyed, with a magnificent mane of hair. The men always look like Apollo, who is associated with this sunny sign. And the women are stunningly striking, and have long golden tresses (even if they are out of a bottle!), which shimmer every time they toss their heads in a majestic manner. However, there's another sort, too. This breed look a little like moles, not lions at all, with black barnets, piggy peepers and a rather shifty air! It's very hard to believe that they belong to this splendid sign, but they do!

But whatever they look like, there's no doubt that positive Leos will offer you the earth and give you their hearts. (Gold-plated ones, of course). There is a gorgeous grandioseness about Leos, but sometimes they can be all mouth. It's only when it's too late that you realise the Lion was just out to impress you.

There was a Lion I used to know, who would offer everyone the earth. He made you feel there was nothing he wouldn't do for you, and promises, offers and assurances flew from his mouth like bees from a hive. The trouble was that those bees never made any honey! It was all hot air, and that's very disappointing indeed from a Lion.

You must never forget (as if the Lions would let you!) that Leo is ruled by the Sun, the centre of the solar system. This star controls almost everything and we'd die without the heat from its rays. So, a lot of Leos can live their lives with a Sun complex. The modest wee beasts feel that as the Sun is the centre of the solar system, so they are the centre of the human race!

As a result, of course, they expect people to put down the red carpet for them. Everything has to be done in a stately, stylish way, as if entertaining royalty. When a Leo comes to tea, he or she won't want to be fobbed off with just one fairy cake, but will demand a three-tiered Victoria sponge. This is a regal, dignified and imperial sign, and the Leo will be either an Emperor Nero or Good Queen Bess. But whatever part he or she is playing, it has to be one that doesn't go unnoticed. Leos don't like to be just one of the crowd, like an extra in a scene from *Gone With the Wind*. They want to be Rhett Butler or Scarlett O'Hara. (Lions with strong Cancerian links will want to play Tara, the O'Hara home!)

In astrology, the Sun is our creative core. So Leo is said to be the most creative of the signs. Leos may portray this by playing Annie in *Annie Get Your Gun* at the local amateur dramatic society or by painting their self-portraits on a 40-foot canvas. If they can't be creative themselves in an active way, they'll do it passively, taking off to the theatre, or burying themselves in a book. (Why not start with this one?)

Make no mistake, Leo is the sign of the Hollywood musical extravaganza. It may be a bit brash, but it'll have a massive orchestra, and you'll be spellbound by the majesty of it all. And that's what Leos love most. Neptune was tripping the light fantastic through Leo during the great age of Hollywood musicals, which is why they were so lavish. And believe it or not, lots of film producers and directors are Leos – Sam Goldwyn, Alfred Hitchcock, Busby Berkeley and Cecil B. DeMille were all born under this splendid sign of the silver screen. (Leos certainly know how to do things in style.)

There's a fantastic feeling of leisure and pleasure about this sign. Leos love enjoying themselves. (And that's not as obvious as it sounds. Virgos and Capricorns sometimes feel guilty when they have a good knees-up.) They also adore being seen with the right people. (Upmarket Leos will be the people the other Leos want to be seen with!)

What makes most Leos tick, though, is very simple. It's the biggest heart imaginable – a sort of titanic ticker. Positive Lions can be wonderfully warm and lastingly loving. And as if that weren't enough, they have a rich sense of humour running through them that will surround you and make you feel safe and secure.

Some Leos aren't lovable Lions at all, but are cheetahs, literally. This sneaky side of the sign comes from the Leonine lust for power. These crafty cats won't have the personality or warmth of the positive Leo, so will have to achieve their ambitions through underhand acts. Don't expect all Leos to want to be centre-stage, because some of them will prefer to wait in the wings, looking on. But most Leos love the limelight, and are happier playing the main man or leading lady. (They may even stick gold stars on their bedroom doors at home.) These Leos aren't concerned with the chorus; they want the bright lights and all that goes with them. Their love of luxury means they can look and dress the part to perfection. But very often they'll behave abominably, and treat everyone as if they were their servants. Don't let a Lion make you his or her skivvy!

Just because a Leo chooses *not* to come on like a Hollywood hotch-potch of Mae West, Cleopatra (don't let her get the needle), and Napoleon Bonaparte, doesn't mean he or she is negative. Sometimes, it's quite the reverse! All you need is a peek at a pirouetting and preening prima donna to see what produces a positive Leo. Some Lions will convey their creative concerto in a quieter, more controlled way. (A Moonlight Sonata rather than an 1812 Overture!) But a positive pussy cat will always be the sunshine of your life.

Leo Man

He's an Adonis! And usually he's got the personality (and the photographs) to prove it! Like the starlet he is, the Leo lad cascades like a fantastic firework, attracting admirers from all around to come and see the show. But he can have more than a suspicion of swank. Big talk can be all too easy for him, especially if he's carving out a career in a competitive cosmos.

Leos are great show people, and they don't do things by halves when they can do them by seven eighths. Some Leo men can be down to their last Luncheon Voucher, but will borrow £500 from the bank just to throw a pootchy party for their pals. They might want to show off with champagne and caviar, or just be jolly with jelly and jam butties. (But they will be the best.) One of the loveliest things about Leos is their passion for pleasing people. (Yes, even platonically!) Making people happy makes them feel warm all over, and beats wearing a woolly vest any day.

Usually, the Leo man looks good, with his long, lavish hair constantly combed. You can always tell a Leo lad by his locks. Even if they're cut quite short, and he looks like a shaving brush on legs, his barnet should bear a real resemblance to the most long and lustrous paint brush. (Be careful you don't mistake him for a broom, and sweep the floor with him. You'll regret it.) And to add to the attractions, he'll have oodles of oomph.

Just think of some famous Leo men. Reading from the reasonable to the ridiculous, they include Robert Redford, Mick Jagger, Peter O'Toole, Sir Freddie Laker, George Bernard Shaw, Mussolini, Fidel Castro and Napoleon – none of whom you could say seemed shy! They are all imbued with pounds of power and considerable charisma; even Bert from Bognor, if he was born a Leo, will appear assured and assertive.

Leo lads love doing things in style. This is one of the two

signs of love, along with luscious Libra, and he can really sweep you off your pins. (Back to the brooms!) He'll flabbergast you with flowers, provide you with posh nosh, and take you to the theatre and bung you in a box. (And hand you a huge box of chocs!) In fact, he'll treat the one he loves like a queen.

Dad-wise, he can be brill. After all, the Sun represents fatherhood, so he's got a head start! Kids will mean a lot to him, and he'll want his own collection of cubs. So it's no good tying the love knot with a Leo if you never want kids. He may say he's not bothered at the moment, but just you wait and see!

Leo is one of the Fixed signs, so this man will be loyal and faithful – two traits which will be very important to him. The law of the jungle decrees that although the lion has a pride of lionesses (and proud of 'em he is!) he'll stand by them all till he is surpassed by one of his siblings. And the law of a Leo lad is that you must be loyal, and not betray him in any way.

Being part of his own pride will be incredibly important to him. He'll want to be the breadwinner, fending like fury to feed his family. With his little sunbeams as his satellites, he'll provide for them and protect them when necessary. But he needs his partner to be loving and loyal.

Now, before you throw this book down and dash out of the door to look for a Leo, wait a minute. It's a shame to say it, but sometimes this man can be a hypocrite. If he's the sort of Lion who travels around a lot, he'll probably have a lioness in most locations. But that doesn't mean that what's good for the goose is good for the gander, so don't go finding yourself a fellow. Your Leo love sees himself as ruler of his own regal realm, and will want the respect he feels is due to him from his loyal subjects. And that means you and the kiddiwinks! (Curtseying over the cornflakes may be going too far, though!)

His need for loyalty doesn't stop there. He'll expect respect from his colleagues at work, too, and his pals in the pub.

It can be a bit frightening at times, especially if you're feeling a mite meek and mild. My Leo grandfather was literally larger than life, tipping the scales at twenty-five stone! He'd sit in his chair as if it were a throne and his merest miaou sounded like a resounding roar. Although he was really just a gentle pussy cat, he looked like a large lion, because he had such an awe-inspiring aura.

If used in the wrong way, this superb strength can turn a

likeable Lion into a bullying bossy-boots, who's bursting with bravado, puffed up with pomposity, and swanks, struts and swaggers, till you long to stick your shoe out and trip him up! The Leo man can use you as a puny pawn in his game of imperial chess, or he'll consider his kith and kin to be a collection of courtiers. If he gets his own way often enough, and is rather negative in the first place, he can turn into a true tyrant, a despot, who will constantly abuse his power. This won't be in a psychological, Scorpio way, or an argumentative Arian way, but in a very haughty, grand way. There's definitely a dowager duchess feel about negative Leos, even if they are men!

Because he is a Fixed sign, the Leo lad will want permanence in all the primary parts of his life. This fixity will also give him a degree of stubbornness. He won't give way easily on things, because he can't. It's not in his nature. But if you ever want to get round a Leo man, and make him see things your way, there's just one thing you have to do. Flatter him. It never fails!

Leo Woman

When you want to waltz through life, look for a Leo lass. She'll already be out there on the floor dancing the night away. Swallow a couple of iron pills, or swig down some Sanatogen, and off you go!

Leo is the sign of the Hollywood superstar, the leading lady of the zodiac. In fact, a lot of Leo ladies would love to be superstars, although most of them will only get as far as playing Calamity Jane in the local dramatic society production (or sometimes just at home!). Nevertheless, inside nearly every Leo woman is another Ethel Merman, a revamped Mae West (gosh!) or a new Lucille Ball, waiting to burst on to the scene and take the world by storm with a song and a dance. (If you see a woman in Waitrose, dolled up in *diamanté* and doing the carioca by the cornflakes, she's a Leo!)

Leo women are drama queens in many ways, and see the dramatic side of any situation. They usually look good (and even if they don't, woe betide you if you say so), and flowing locks and big hats (look at the Queen Mum!) are part of the Leo woman's image. Ginger Rogers, for example, was born in the last days of Cancer, but she looks lusciously Leonine, with her red hair cascading down her back.

The Leo lass loves to love. She adores being flirted with, being made a fuss of, titillated and chased. But no matter what you see on the surface, inside every Leo lady is a pussy cat who wants to be caressed and adored. The lioness will do her duty by going off for food, and looking after her cubs, but her reward is being kissed and cuddled by her mate.

One lesson you'll learn early on in your liaisons with Leos is that you can't ignore them. Remember to say 'Didn't you do well' when your mate merits it. (Then watch your pal preen like a peacock.) Never drown your chum with a diatribe of defects from A to Z. Your Leo won't be able to cope.

As a mum, this lass loves her children, and very often they'll be the be-all and end-all of her whole existence. The Leo mother is easygoing, and allows her cubs lots of freedom, while keeping a protective peeper on each bonny bundle.

She'll like the high life, with plenty of social gallivanting and parties to attend, but she'll want her mate by her side. When a Leo lady goes to a do alone something's up on the marital front. Unless, that is, there is a cast-iron reason for her mate not being there, such as the fact that he's lying low in the lair with lumbago.

Leos are said to be the narcissists of the zodiac (no, it's not a plant, dear) and the women love to watch the effect they're exerting on others. Very often, a Leo lass will go to a gathering with her guy and end up as the star turn, caught in the spotlight of adoring men. As long as she doesn't play that game too hard and too often, this can delight her husband, especially if he's a Leo too. But she should watch it with one of the more possessive signs. (If she tried it with a Taurean she could have problems!) In fact, if you're involved with a Leo lad, it's quite good to show him, without going too far, that other men are interested in you. But it won't work quite so well the other way round, when it's the Leo woman who's having the point proved to her! (Sometimes she loses her sunny sense of humour!)

If you want to impress a Leo woman, you've got to do the right thing. Send her Chanel No.5, or orchids, and take her to the best restaurant in town. If you're a meanie or a miser, a Leo lady is not for you, simply because, in her own inimitable way, she'll bleed you dry. Of course, every sign has its gold-diggers, but you'll find a lot of them born under Leo. (They will tell you with a dazzling smile that gold *is* their colour, after all!) So there's no point in being stingy with a Leo lady because she will want and expect the best from you.

There's no getting away from the fact that Leos are snobs. They really want to keep up with the Joneses, but often in a flashy, get-rich-quick way. Of course, some of them will be Joneses themselves, and then they'll go for big status symbols, such as a gold Rolls-Royce, or, at the least, two cars. The Leo woman is the lass who staggers down the street in the most ferocious heatwave, clad in a mink coat, and showing off her jewels! (You may be dazzled to death, too, as the sun reflects off the rocks in which she's arrayed. There'll be a diamond here, a ruby there and a sapphire somewhere else.)

Now, Leo, of course, is the sign of royalty, and it's no coincidence that the Queen Mother, Princess Anne and Princess Margaret are all Leos, and that Prince Charles has a Leo ascendant. Princess Margaret epitomises the Leo character, being a lover of theatre and ballet, and the Queen Mother has got that wonderful Leo dress sense, with all her bright colours, fluffy feathers and frivolous hats. This is definitely the sign of caviar, champagne and ostrich feathers. *'Daahling!'* is the Leo lady's war-cry, and as soon as you hear it, run for cover!

The Leo woman really does like style, and does her best to have as much of it as possible. (But a glamorous Goat will tell you that style doesn't always mean taste!) She'll insist on patronising the most expensive emporium she can find, and have an account there, just so she can buy baked beans with the right label. (Her husband may have a heart attack when she brings him the bill!) But if you appreciate a woman with style, a Leo lady's certainly got it!

Leo Child

L ion cubs can be such sensational sunbeams. Most of them are bundles of fun, and a source of tremendous pleasure to their parents and everyone else around them.

Nearly every Leo child has a tremendous sense of humour, and is full of fun and frolics. But some of them can be precious and precocious, always wanting to show off. They're the children who play the piano for you when you go to tea, or pirouette about the place in a pink party frock. (Remember Bette Davis in *What Ever Happened to Baby Jane!*)

If you have a Leo child, you may have already heard that little voice saying 'I want to do this' and 'I want that – *now!*' You may have a battle of wills with your child, because he or she will want to be in control and command. A little Leo can find it very difficult to take orders from you, or will find it hard to accept that he or she is under your thumb, and you're the one who's in charge.

You can get the best out of your Leo child by settling him or her down with a pad of paper, a paintbox or pencils, or lots of books: watch that creativity shine through. And almost as soon as your child can stand, send him or her off to the local drama school, or to take dancing lessons of some sort, whether tap or ballet. If your little Leo has more of an athletic aptitude, he or she should be encouraged to go to youth centres or sports clubs.

The sooner your Leo child begins to mix with other people, testing out that powerful pussy cat's personality on others, the better. If you mollycoddle and smother a Leo child, you may risk bringing out the sign's overbearing side.

So don't spoil your Leo kid. (Give one of these Lion cubs an inch and they'll take a yard.) You should bring him or her up on a mixture of love and discipline, in fairly equal doses. (Leos need both; it's no good just giving them one without the other.) Help your Leo to learn that things don't always go the way one

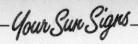

would like. And don't allow yourself to be bossed about as though you were the butler or maid. Encourage your Lion cub to help with the washing up, the housework or cooking. And make sure that your little Leo tidies up any mess or muddle he or she might create. Otherwise, your potentially adorable cub will grow up into an egotistical Lion who roars and expects other people to do his or her dirty work.

If you encourage your Leo child to be creative from an early age, you could bring up a budding, brilliant entrepreneur or creative director. You will also have the sort of child who really does brighten up your life, and is the apple of your eye. (A real Golden Delicious!)

There's a sensational sense of warmth, loving and giving in this child. Even at an early age, a little Leo will know the right thing to do to keep you happy. For example, your child may bring you breakfast in bed one day, or pick a posy of pansies for you when you're in the doldrums. In return, encourage your little bundle of joy to bring home lots of friends. It's very important for Leos of all ages to mix with other people. But if you see your Leo child being bossy or bad-mannered, domineering or dictatorial with other small kids, you must put your foot down. Children born under this sign should be disciplined, and though you shouldn't clout your kid, don't forget the old adage, 'Spare the rod and spoil the child'. Then you'll turn your kitten into the nicest Leo around!

Leo in Love

Leo in love is a lion in ecstasy. This is amour, amour, all the way. Leo love is like Paris in the spring, and once Cupid has loaded up his little bow and arrow, taken aim and fired, it will be all liberated passions and desires, with a distinctly French flavour. (Crumbs! Or, should I say, croûtons!)

This is love on the impulse, ships that pass in the night, or a delightful dalliance in Doncaster. (Love can transform even the most unromantic joint.) To look at it on another level, it may be a one-night stand, or a fling. (Leos who live North of the border will have a Highland fling!) However, the one-night stand won't necessarily mean sex, which is rather more Scorpio's style. Instead, the Leo can drift off feeling very much in love – until the next time!

Leos who aren't in love are like fish out of water. They can't work properly. They get tetchy, and they'll growl and roar like an out-of-sorts lion, and whisk their tails around madly. In fact, they'll be very, very sad pussies indeed. Nothing in their lives will go right, or so they'll tell you. (A frequent flirtation is essential!)

But Lions who *are* in love will hop, skip and jump through life. They'll feel frisky and kittenish, with a chronic case of spring fever. They'll do soft shoe shuffles and brisk buck and wing dances as the fancy takes them, and tie pretty little bows in their tails and manes.

Actually, love doesn't have to be a grand passion for these pussy cats. It can just mean being noticed, wanted and cared for. Often you'll find that if your Leo pal is down in the dumps, it's because his or her marriage or partnership is in trouble.

The most important thing of all for a Leo is to be in love with another human being. Leos love and need that warmth and touch. But if that's not possible, Lions can derive almost as much satisfaction from being involved in a creative concept or hobby that tantalises them in some way. Being in love with what they're doing is just as splendid, and keeps the strings of their childlike hearts in tune!

Now, don't get the wrong idea and think that Leos shun sex. They are an animal sign, after all, so passion will be part and parcel of the package. Leos certainly don't find sex off-putting, and they take it in their stride! (Sometimes, the more they get the better they like it!) But love must be there first, or at least some form of appreciation. They aren't like Scorpios, who can't sizzle without sex. Instead, they are idealists, like Librans. When Leos do leap into bed with a lover, it's with a stunning style. They may not be able to run to satin sheets, but a sheepskin hearthrug is just as sensual!

Let's suppose you've met a Leo who makes you go funny all over, but you're not sure that your feelings are reciprocated. Well, as with Aries, you've got to convince your Lion that you're a jolly good catch. You must also look luscious. (So you might as well forget the whole thing if you've got a face that could turn milk sour!) However, if you've got power and charisma, you're laughing. Leos love a bit of glitter to land on them, and really stunning Leos will go charging off after the ugliest of creatures, just because he or she is a starlette. The Leo won't be in love, but that powerful position can make up for it.

Sometimes, meeting a Leo's high standard can be a tall order, but luckily there are some Lions who don't have such great expectations. Even so, you must be faithful and funny, and appeal to that tremendous Leo vanity. Just say 'Darling, you're wonderful' every fifteen minutes or so, and you've got a pussy cat who'll purr happily for the whole of your life together.

Leo as a Friend

L ife with the Lions can be a ball, whether it's caviar-flavoured crisps at the Dog and Duck, or getting involved in the general carnival of life. They don't like being alone, and adore other people's company.

Leos make good mates, but they often choose chums they can boss about a bit. (Leos do like to take the lead.) Sporty Leos will want to be team captain, and will give out commands even if they're not!

Lions will put their love first, but friends come next. With their Fixed and faithful natures, Leos often keep the same pals throughout life. So the pussy cat and their pal will start off as youngsters, and go through life together, getting married at about the same time, having their children together, and so on, until they end up as a couple of geriatrics down at the Bingo.

You'll never want if you have a Leo pal. Some of them will be generous to a fault, giving out gifts left, right and centre, and spending lots of loot on little luxuries for you. And all they want is for you to be pleased. They don't expect you to rush off and go silly in Selfridges, spending all your salary on a present of preposterous proportions. (Though they won't say 'no' when you hand it over!)

There's a grand camaraderie between a Leo and a chum, and they can go off and paint the town gold together. (You don't expect a Lion to do anything as commonplace as paint it *red*, do you?) You can traipse off to the theatre, cinema, night-clubs, discos or pubs together, sit in the sports club for a snifter, or any centre of recreation or entertainment, leisure and pleasure. Leos, of course, are great sun worshippers. They adore lying on a sandy beach during the day and showing off their tans at night while dancing in a disco. So pack your towel, and off you go together!

You must remember one thing, though. Don't step out of line. Your chum will want to be in the limelight, and it's not big enough to take two. But would you want to spoil their moments of glory?

Leos' faces light up when they come across kids, because they adore them. These Lions have an enormous affinity and affection for children, though not in the same way as Geminis, who see kids as intellectual and intelligent. Leos consider kids to be cuddly, clowning creatures, who they enjoy being with. So, if you have any children, you can be sure your Leo pal will get on with them like a house on fire.

Lovely Leos will be staunch and sincere, and will want you to be the same. And if you do treat your pal properly, you'll have a friend for life. But let your Leo down in some way, and be prepared for the consequences. Usually, Lions have a good growl to keep you on your toes. They don't mean it, and quickly start purring again when you pat them on the head.

You incur the wrath of one of these beasties at your peril. That purring pussy cat will suddenly roar and rampage, full of fire and fury, and send you running up the nearest tree. But rather than snap and snarl, Leos will love to laugh, and especially with their pals. They don't have a dry sense of humour like Capricorns, but prefer belly laughs. So you can be sure that he who laughs loudest is Leo! What do you expect from a barrel of fun?

Leo at Work

'There's no business like show business' is the Leo theme song. Entertainment is in a Leo's blood, and if he or she can actually earn money from it – *well!* For instance, thousands of theatres and countless cinemas are run by Leos, to showcase the other Lions who are up there on the silver screen, or spouting speeches in the spotlight. Leos also excel in creative careers, and will be designers, painters, and film and television directors. And half the pubs, clubs and cabaret spots in the world are led by Lions. In fact, you'll find Leos anywhere that is glittery and full of spectacle. They add razzmatazz to almost anything.

Even if Leo is organising the most sober and sedate soirée, he or she will hang tinsel everywhere, hire a big band, bring on the dancing girls, and really brighten up the dullest do. (Don't let them organise a funeral, whatever you do!)

Leos need to work in a profession that caters to their sense of style, if they are to be truly happy. If a Leo has a job that is a mite mundane, such as working in a tea warehouse, counting the packets, he or she may take on the role of amateur theatre director in the evenings. Anything to add zip and zap to their everyday existence.

There's no doubt that a Leo will be happiest if he or she can follow in the paw prints of Busby Berkeley in some way. I suppose getting five bathing beauties to leap out of the tea urn during the office coffee break, wearing swimsuits made of tea bags tied together, is a bit much. But put it down to the Leo's natural high spirits and sense of occasion! (One lump or two?)

The polarity between Aquarius and Leo will come to the fore when you compare their attitudes to the arts. Leo represents the theatre, cinema and night-club side of show business, whereas Aquarius is more concerned with the latest technical advances in television, video and all things futuristic.

Lions really do need to work in some sort of creative

profession, if they are to feel fulfilled. They aren't academic like brainy Virgos and clever Capricorns, as alert as Geminis or as practical as Taureans. Instead, Leos like to direct things, and be the ones in charge (hopefully holding large loudhailers). Of course, it goes without saying that Leos make smashing stars of stage and screen, and will love being the leading lady or handsome hero. But they can be at the forefront of almost anything and everything they do.

A Leo may have a dreary job, but he or she will run the firm's dance, collect for the Christmas knees-up, or organise a trip to the seaside with fantastic flair. Or it could be that your Leo is a budding Brown Owl or a mini Baden-Powell. Lions really are outstanding organisers; 'I'm in charge' is their motto. (As you probably already know!)

Equally, if a Leo can't be creative career-wise, he or she will be so at home. One Leo chum had a tedious time at work, finding her considerable creativity blocked. But her hobby was photography, so she submitted some snaps in a national competition and won! Now that's a positive, creative Leo for you!

They don't make terribly good politicians, because they can't bear to be answered back! Usually they know how far up the ladder of success they want to clamber, and once they've reached their chosen rung, that's where they'll stay. Leos in the world of big business usually aim for positions such as honorary president. (They love the word 'honour'!) They prefer to be the figurehead on the ship of commerce, rather than the captain steering the vessel to victory.

Lots of Leos will slog away for years, and their only incentive will be the thought of a knighthood or being made a dame (yes, even the panto type will appeal to them!) at the end of it all. Lions know they can't be made king or queen, however much they may dream, so they'll settle for the Order of the Bath and the House of Lords instead. (You'd better practise your curtsies, quick!) One thing's for sure – a Leo will add lustre to any profession.

Leo at Home

There are no two ways about it. The Leo lair has got to be a palace, even if it's a one-roomed residence in Rhyl.

But whatever it is, it'll be spectacular rather than cosy. The Leo is quite likely to use it as a way of entertaining pals and showing off. There's bound to be the odd gold-plated *objet d'art* scattered about somewhere. (But not so scattered that you can't spot it.)

If a Gemini has a family heirloom, it will probably be buried under a mound of magazines. A Capricorn will lock it away in case it gets nicked, and a Virgo will wonder if it harbours any germs and douse it in disinfectant just to be on the safe side. But a Leo will build a special case for a family heirloom, and give it pride of place, so no one can fail to notice and comment on it.

There's bound to be a swanky feel to a Leo's home. If the Leo has the loot, it'll be bursting with all the latest appliances. And they'll all be arranged so you can't fail to notice them!

Leos love to entertain, so the most important room in the house for them will be the dining-room. They'll have the best china, goblet-sized wine glasses, and a couple of candelabras for good measure. (Eat your heart out, Liberace!) In fact, the whole dwelling will be geared for gregarious gatherings. (Leos make wonderful hosts and hostesses, and when you go to their homesteads, you're bound to have a good time.)

The Leo colours are all shades of the sun, so the home will be decked out in golds, oranges and yellows. Lions are also fascinated by fire, and will have gas fires with artificial flames and a gold surround. (Flashy Lions will have ones that play 'Keep the home fires burning' when you switch them on.)

Leos love the sun, and rich ones will have their own sunbeds, so they can get a tan even in the depths of December in Dorking. (Leos who are low on loot will rub fake tanning lotion into their limbs and emerge the next morning looking like streaky mandarin oranges.) You'll see mementoes of their holidays about too, which will remind them of long sunny days in Spain, and take their minds off the rainy British weather.

Some Leos will have just the odd knick-knack, but others can go mad. Sometimes, the residence can resemble a cheap bordello, with leatherette love seats, mock-marble tables with fake filigree, and wall lights with red and gold tassels on the shades. Bits of ghastly gadgetry will abound, such as musical ice buckets and mirrored cocktail cabinets with neon lights, which flash on and off and give you a headache. One Leo home I once visited was filled with the most noxious pong in the world. It smelt as though a Virgo had gone bonkers in there with a couple of crates of air freshener, and sprayed everything in sight. (Actually, the asphyxiating smell was from some plastic roses which had specially perfumed petals!)

The positive, more polished Leo, with a bit of boodle to blow, will get an interior decorator. They won't care how it looks, as long as it looks good.

But however the Leo decorates, he or she will be very generous, and as you enter the Spanish-style hall, you'll be offered lots of food and drink. If they serve you a sarnie, it'll be on the best plates, so you can see how expensive they are. And your drink, which should be on the large side, will probably have paper parasols floating in it, so that the minute you take a sip, one will get stuck up your nose.

This is a sign that adores animals, and Leos often keep pets for company. But whether it's a cat or a canary, it will have to be pretty. A lot of Leos will choose to keep cats, because they understand them, but a surprising number go for dogs, too. Leo lads love labradors and dote on dobermans.

Leo
Health and Relaxation

As you might expect from a sign that loves to love, Leos can have tons of trouble with their tickers. (In fact, Leo rules the heart.) Not only are they apt to lose their hearts to all and sundry, but they are also more prone than any other sign to having them go on strike.

Leos should be extremely careful not to overload their hearts by putting on too much weight and scoffing too much rich grub. If they don't take it easy, they can become very overweight pussy cats indeed, and will be likely to strain their hearts. With their love of all things romantic, they can also break their hearts in two, and will mope about like miserable moggies when their feelings are trampled over by a loved one. With Aquarius as their opposite sign, Leos have to keep a close eye on their circulatory systems. Otherwise, they can be prone to problems like hypertension, or anything akin to heart ailments, such as hardening of the arteries and blood clots. They may also get varicose veins, and chilblains in cold weather. (Knit them some woolly bed socks.)

Most Leos aren't such home birds that they need to scurry back to their nests a lot. Even during their working week they will want to socialise, meeting friends for lunch and scampering off at night to the pictures or to an evening class. In fact, all in all, Leos don't find it difficult to relax. The only occasion a Lion will get into a rut, a fix, or generally all het-up, will be if he or she is alone. Remember that this is a Fire sign, so that like their Arian and Sagittarian cousins Leos can let off steam by being active, whether that's through sports or socialising.

Leos aren't loners, as a rule, and they like to be with other people, so it's incredibly important for them to have a sizzling social life. A lot of Leos like joining (and then running) clubs and societies, where they can meet new people. Even if the Leo doesn't fancy doing anything like that, he or she could become a friend of the local theatre, and sell tickets, or ice-creams, on the night. Leos have such radiant personalities that they easily make lots of pals. Usually, the only time Leos come unstuck is if they just plonk themselves down in front of the telly, and don't stir all night. Even a pint down the pub once a week is better than nothing for a Leo.

One of the best ways for a Leo to relax is when the Lion is surrounded by a pride of pals. This social sign loves unwinding by entertaining at home, so if a Leo you know invites you round for some grub, make sure you go. You'll be given the best that boodle can buy, and lots of fattening, but fantastic, food.

Virgo

24 August – 23 September

What Makes Virgo Tick

N ow, before we go any further, think about the Virgos you know. (They're the ones with the neat hair-dos and shiny shoes, who make you feel as if you've just been dragged through a hedge backwards.) One of the wonderful things about Virgos is their tremendous talent for organising everything under the sun – starting with themselves. And they really come into their own when they can organise others as well, whether as a cleaning lady or as Home Secretary.

Vestal Virgos of all shapes and sizes are only too pleased to give you a helping hand; their Mercurial motto is 'Service with a smile'. What's more, they really live up to it. You can phone your friend when you're in a fix, and the Virgo will zoom round in ten seconds flat, looking as neat as a new pin. (How do they do it?) If you're feeling as if you've been slung on the scrapheap of life, a Virgo will interrupt your tale of woe with a hundred handy hints and then try to find you another job.

The next thing to remember about this sign is their ceaseless search for perfection. And because they're ruled by Mercury, the planet of the mind and communication, they do this analytically. Geminis spend a lot of time thinking too, but in a swifter, more superficial way. Mercury is more practical in Virgo, restrained by the Earthy element of this sign. This quest for all things perfect means that Virgos don't suffer fools gladly; they like everything to be of the best, both materially and mentally. Sometimes this can go too far, and a Virgo will become fussy and finicky to a fanatical degree. These folk can pick holes in everything, because nothing matches up to their ideals. (But take heart, because the faults they most often find are within themselves.)

Before you've spent five minutes with vestal Virgos you'll have noticed they're naturally neat, and like things to be spick and span, and in apple-pie order. This is the sign of cleanliness, both inner and outer. With most Virgos, this means they just keep everything hunky-dory, but others can go overboard. You'd think they had disinfectant swirling through their systems, they're so obsessed about their health. (A vulnerable Virgoan will moan 'If health is wealth, then I'm broke.')

Now, you may think this sounds a bit much, and that your Virgo pals aren't like that. But they are, even if it's just in a weensy way. Next time you meet a Mercurial mate, listen carefully to the conversation. There'll be at least one reference to keeping clean or tidy, I promise, or you'll hear about their health and hygiene. (This is the sign of hypochondria!) Still not convinced? Well, next time you have a chat in a café with your chum, do a bit of brow-clutching, or seize your stomach and sigh. Say you have a headache, or that you'd better steer clear of the sausage surprise, in case it gives you one later. Your Virgo will come over all concerned, burrow into a bag or briefcase, and produce just the pill guaranteed to get you going again. (They're *that* well organised!)

When it comes to keeping their surroundings sparkling, Virgos beat everyone dusters down. If they visit you, they'll even do your tidying up, not even noticing what they're doing. There was a Virgo girl at school who was invited to more parties than all the debs in Devon, because her idea of a good time was frolicking with the Fairy Liquid in the kitchen. Put your shandy down for a second and she'd have whizzed in and whisked it away, then given the glass a good going-over in the suds in the sink. (Invite a few Virgos to your next knees-up, and you won't even have to clear away a cup – it'll all be done for you! But you've got to pick the right sort, because some of them are unutterably untidy.)

Because Virgos are usually tidy-minded and orderly, they can be somewhat sceptical and suspicious of anything they don't understand. For them, seeing is believing: they're innately inquisitive, and like to find things out for themselves. That means it's hard to pull the wool over their eyes, because they can see straight through any fast-talking. Anyone who's a fly-by-night won't stand a chance once those Mercurial minds get moving.

Virgos who make the most of their mental mastery and organisational ability can go a long way at work. (And I don't mean they make lovely long-distance lorry drivers, either!) But you might not hear about that almost certain success. Virgos are very modest, and hate blowing their own trumpets. Even when they win accolades and awards they'll prefer to keep quiet.

Unfortunately, Virgos sometimes carry this ravishing reti-

cence into other areas of their lives. Not only will they be coy professionally, but they'll be retiring romantically, too. Their heads usually rule their hearts and Virgos can be quite cool, undemonstrative and unemotional. One Virgo relative of mine married purely for tax reasons.

This is definitely a sign that finds it hard to slow down, and Mercury makes Virgos move about like maniacs – busy bees! They can have dreadful difficulties relaxing, and will always find something to do, even if it's the dusting – for the third time in a morning. Which reminds me. I was chatting to a Mercurial male one day, and we were discussing what he'd done during Christmas. He said his girlfriend had gone to Glasgow, and left him at home. Did he mind? 'Oh no!' he grinned. 'It meant I could tidy up my flat. And I got the tops of the plugs clean. It was wonderful!' Obviously he got thirteen amps of joy from Santa that Christmas!

Virgo Man

Now here's a funny fellow for you. Sometimes this Mercurial male leaves a lot to be desired in the charm stakes. He can be a bit too blunt, and come over as cool and clinical, making you wonder what you've done wrong. But before you pen a protestation to me, remember that not all Virgo chaps are like this. Anyone with lashings of lovely Libra or leanings towards Leo in his chart will be much better at charming the birds off the trees.

But charming or not, these chaps usually look a treat. Lots of them have skins as smooth as silk, and as clear as a mountain stream, with not a spot to be seen or a pimple to be peeked. Being a Mutable sign means they're usually on the tall side and, as Mercury keeps them slim, they can be the epitome of tall, dark and handsome. These men have lovely eyes, too – usually hazel, they twinkle away like stars in the sky.

Clothes are important too, and the Virgo man likes to cut a (discreet) dash. He's often rather conservative, even when he's being trendy, and doesn't like to stand out like a sore thumb. It makes him feel uncomfortable. So he's likely to lavish his loot on simple, sophisticated suits, in sedate shades. But he'll liven them up with a terrific tie. (Lots of Virgo men go nuts on natty neck-wear, and wear ties smothered in spots.) If unconventional Uranus is strongly emphasised, the Virgo vestments may bedazzle and bewilder you, as he turns up in the quietest tie you've ever seen and a sizzling suit!

Most of these Mercurial men appear slightly cool and some of them are decidedly distant. Virgos find it hard to commit themselves emotionally, because they're frightened of losing control. They aren't nearly as sensual and tactile as their fellow Earth signs of Taurus and Capricorn, because they express their emotions in a more moderate and measured manner, and Mercury makes sure they feel more from their minds than their hearts. (They feel safer if they always adopt a logical approach.)

This can make them so frightened of emotional entanglements

that even sex suffers, and becomes clinical. At times he will have sex just for the sensation. It's the only way he can cope. He'll trot along to a brothel, be whipped into submission, tickled to death, or trussed up like a turkey at Christmas (and we all know what happens to *them!*), then amble out later, having forked out a few fivers. (After all, it is said that Virgo is the kinkiest sign of the zodiac!)

Very often the Virgo man can't get, or give, sufficient satisfaction from an amorous affair, because he find it difficult to allow his affections to flow properly. He's got to find a wonderful woman, full of fervent feelings, who can coax the caring out of him, and make him see there's nothing silly in sounding sentimental. (Something he worries about.)

Normally, it's success all the way for a Virgo chap, where work's concerned. This is an incredibly industrious sign, and a Mercurial man will always work hard to get where and what he wants. But that isn't necessarily right to the top, because he's not instilled with the astounding ambition of some of the signs of the zodiac. Instead he'll be content to be a right-hand man, and will do best as a second string to someone else's bow, rather than being the virtuoso Virgo in an orchestra of underlings.

Like all Mutable signs, this chap needs change and contrasts in his life, if he's to keep his agile and alert mind firing on all four cylinders. Sometimes he can carry that to extremes, changing his mind as if he's just out to spite you.

Because demonstrations of affection don't come easily to him, the Virgo fella finds it difficult to be a good dad. He want to be, but it's hard for him to unbend. (He's too much like a taut spring.) Sometimes he can be too disciplined a dad, and make a fuss about his kids not doing enough homework. But it's only because he wants them to succeed. Exams can assume monumental proportions and his children will dread him reading their school reports! (They'll pretend they lost them on the way home, if they've sneaked a look at the contents and cringed!)

Sometimes a Virgo dad will forget he's not a headmaster (unless he really is one, of course!). He's got to realise that education isn't everything, and that emotions matter more. And once he's learned that lesson, and put it into practice on every level of his life, he'll be a far more fulfilled and feeling fella.

Virgo Woman

This, as anyone will tell you, is the sign of the maiden, and that's certainly what the Virgo lass is. The main thing about this Mercurial maiden of astrological mythology is that she's a virgin, and every Virgo girl in the land, from Galway to Grimsby, will have been teased about this at some point or other. The funny thing is though, even if she's had so many amorous affrays and delightful dalliances that she makes Don Juan look like a beginner, she'll still be a mite mystified by her attitude to amour. It's not that she doesn't like sex – it's just that she's not very keen on it. You can find out exactly how much she can stand by peeking at her natal chart. Mars in Leo, for example, will enliven the proceedings no end, and inject a little lasciviousness into her, while Venus in Libra will make her more openly affectionate and gregarious. But even if it's just in her heart of hearts, the Virgo lass will find the sexual side of life something she could well do without. She will also find it difficult to let herself go in bed, because she tries to be in control at all times. So, this vestal virgin has got to learn to unleash her powers of passion; make no mistake, they're seething away under the surface.

There's a fantastically fresh feel to these lasses, and to look at them, you'd think they'd never behave like other humans at all – never get all hot and bothered, and certainly never disappear off to the loo like other folk.

Many Virgo girls like to look as nature intended. (No, I don't mean they nip about naked!) Greta Garbo is a Virgo, and look how natural she is! These lasses wear hardly any make-up, and what they do wear will be connected with the countryside, concocted from coriander and celery seeds, or something similar. Their Virgoan vestments will also be simple, made from natural yarns yanked from the hedgerows and converted into cloth, then printed with posies. (Virgo girls could keep Laura Ashley going single-handed!)

When it comes to motherhood, these maidens make

marvellous mums, once they forget trying to teach their babies Einstein's Theory of Relativity. (Or that Noddy's relationship with Big Ears had a very deep psychological meaning.) It's incredibly important for these Mercurial mums to have clever kiddies, but they've got to realise that their children need love as well as learning. Every Virgo mum should toss away the reading book once in a while and give her kid a cuddle instead.

She'll be ceaselessly searching for signs of brilliance in her babies – and may even think they're ill in an intelligent way! But because 'Service' is her middle name, she'll do everything she can for her kids, and nurse them from dawn to dusk when they're sick.

Remember that Virgo is an undemonstrative sign, so don't expect a Mercurial maiden to gush like a Water sign, or be as lusciously loving as a Leo or Libran lass. Instead, her eyes will be scanning you all the time, trying to fathom you out and wondering what makes you tick. (Countless Virgos say 'Penny for your thoughts' whenever you indulge in a delectable daydream. Taureans would say 'Pound', and Capricorns would offer you a mortgage!) Virgos are always analysing, comparing and contrasting, like human sorting machines, and will try to pin you down to a particular pattern.

Like Mercurial males, Virgo girls really come into their own at work. They make perfect PAs (that's personal assistants, dear, not public address systems – they're full of diligence, not decibels), and their bosses really depend on them. But they're great feminists and don't take kindly to having their bottoms pinched every time they bend over. They want to be accepted in their own right as intelligent human beings, and not just as sex objects on legs, tapping away at a typewriter.

The Virgo lass can be the Tipp-Ex queen of the zodiac, and I don't just mean in the office. Some Virgo women have awful areas of their lives they'd like to eradicate: they'd be on cloud nine if they could only blank out the blots on their own particular landscapes, as well as those on their letters. (Be careful! If you don't behave properly to a Mercurial maiden, it could be you who's wiped out by a white-out!)

Virgo Child

Virgo kids pick things up very quickly, and I'm not just talking about coughs and colds, either. (One snuffle and a Virgo mum thinks pneumonia's on the loose!) These children are like sharpshooters – very quick on the mental draw.

These children can be top of the form when it comes to school, because of their admirable ability to absorb facts and figures. But don't think that a Virgette will be a goodie-goodie, looking as though butter (or low-cholesterol margarine – Virgos start at an early age!) wouldn't melt in their mouth. Mercury makes these kids love practical jokes, and they can spend nearly all their pocket-money (they'll save the rest) buying itching powder and plastic spiders, which they'll tip into your teacup when you're not looking.

Although Virgos are naturally modest and retiring, it's important if your Virgette has done well, to say so. There's no need to go mad every time your miniature Mercurial marvel gets top marks in maths, by announcing it to the waiting world in the local paper. A pat on the head is much more this sign's style, and eventually your kid will be able to hear praise without going bright red and running from the room. In fact, if you encourage your Virgette early on, the kid will grow up to be more open emotionally, and not quite as cool and aloof as some members of this sign.

If you're the parent of a Virgo child, don't be a philistine! Most Virgos are creative in one way or another, so try to develop this side of your kid. If your child spends hours at the kitchen table (having cleaned it first, of course!) drawing and painting, don't send him or her out to play.

Even at an early age, the Virgo will attempt to be of service to family and friends. He or she may dash around with a dustpan and brush in those minute Mercurial mitts, cleaning like crazy for you, or bake a cake and take it round to a neighbour who needs it. This is a superb side of all Virgos, so don't let your kiddie's mates make fun of it.

Remember the nervy nature of all Virgoans, too, and keep your babe's mind occupied. Otherwise, he or she might start to imagine all sorts of ills, and go overboard about a cut finger, lying in a darkened room wearing an ice-pack for a hat! (Or Elastoplast as a necklace!)

As with every other sign, you must nip any negative traits in the bud before they become habits that are hard to forget. For example, don't let your kid's natural neatness turn into a fussy and finicky fixation. It may be like a dream come true to have a tidy kid, but you don't want to raise one who nags you about the state of *your* bedroom!

If you're thinking about presents for your precise, wee Virgo, don't buy anything too frivolous. Instead, opt for a toy doctor's bag, bulging with bandages, so the Virgette can rush around acting like an extra from *Angels*. Alternatively, you could buy some books. But whatever the present, you must stimulate that Mercurial mind, because Virgettes have budding, brilliant brains.

However, before you buzz off to buy your babe an enormous encyclopaedia, remember to lavish lots of what boodle can't buy – love – on your child. A kiss here and a cuddle there will make all the difference, and your Virgette will grow up to modify that Mercurial modesty and emotional uncertainty, and become loving and giving, warm and wonderful. There now!

Virgo in Love

I f you're in love with a Virgo, go and give 'em a hug, and whisper sweet somethings in their shell-like (and very clean) ears. See them turn pink and look surprised but pleased!

To all outward appearances, Virgos can seem matter of fact, and rather remote. In fact, there are more single souls under this sign than any other, and lots of Mercurially-motivated men and maidens enjoy living alone. It means they can get on with thinking, and pursuing intellectual objectives, without feeling guilty at ignoring their other halves. Even a Virgo who's happily married will want to explore new horizons alone, even if that's just spending every Sunday peering at paintings in the National Gallery, or driving along the highways and byways of the countryside in their car.

You must recognise and respect this intellectual independence if you're to get past the starting-post in the race of romance. Otherwise, you don't stand a chance.

When a Virgo falls in love, he or she really means it. The trouble is, though, that the Virgo knows it, but you don't! Sometimes trying to extract wooing words and courting couplets out of these folk is like getting blood out of a stone, only more difficult. Say you've set up the scene – soft lights, sweet music, the Pomagne on ice (are you a Capricorn?) and the sardine sandwiches on a plastic platter (good grief!). You've spent hours at the hairdressers and you're wearing your best frock, and have smothered yourself in scent. (That must be why the windows are open – your amour's asphyxiated! Tone it down a bit next time, dear.) Finally, your heart-throb hums and haws, and you think your moment of glory has arrived. 'I – I – I *like* you' mutters your heart's desire. Don't stand up and shout 'Is that *it?*,' or you'll have havoc on your hands, and a miffed Mercurial. Virgos shy away from supercharged sentimental scenes; the slightest suspicion of one makes them break out in a cold sweat. (They'll bounce off to the bathroom in a flash.)

These funny old folk really do find it an effort to express an emotion. They're frightened by feelings, and their natural reserve means they're loathe to let themselves go. And this is where you come in. (I thought you'd perk up again!) Where there's a will there's a way. Remember that your restrained Romeo, or jittery Juliet, may well love you underneath that calm exterior. As long as you lavish love and affection on your intelligent inamorata, and make it obvious you'll never let them down, love will find a way. All Virgos are intensely insecure, so you must entice their egos to blossom forth in a delicious display of devotion.

Before you set about this tricky task, though, examine your IQ. Virgos don't thrill to thickos, or dally with dunces. You've got to be a match for their mental manoeuvrings. Think you'll do? Well, on your first date, do something intelligent together, even if it's just seeing a schools' programme on the telly. Be prepared to answer a host of questions about yourself. Rock them with rhetoric and stun them with unforgettable verbal sallies. Don't lunge across the lounge at your would-be lover.

If you spout about your new Easter bonnet for too long, or your moggie's mange (in which case you'll be chatting to yourself – your love will have legged it, in case you're a carrier), you'll spoil any chances of getting together with this vivacious Virgo. And you wouldn't want to do a silly thing like that, now would you?

Virgo as a Friend

Have *you* passed the Virgo test? (No, it's not an exam in hygiene, though that will be important.) It's more like the Eleven Plus. You've got to show some mental magic and clever conversation if you want to be the mate of one of these Mercurial mind-bogglers!

Virgos love a good old chinwag, and can chatter away about any subject under the sun, but it's got to be with someone who speaks sense and doesn't just talk about trite topics. So when you first meet a Mercurial man or maiden, anything you say will be taken down and used in evidence for or against you. That doesn't mean you have to be a genius, with a brain as big as the Ritz, but you must spout sentences that sizzle.

Some Virgos have several long-standing friendships. Their chums will be drawn from all walks of life, as long as they've got brains. But Virgos don't fling themselves into friendships at the drop of a dictionary. At first, even if you think you are making a good impression, they can be slightly stand-offish and subdued. (You'll wonder if you use the wrong soap.) Virgos usually have a few firm friends, who are the pillar and pivot of their private lives, and an army of acquaintances they can take or leave.

Frankly, friendship is not at the top of a Virgo's list of life's priorities, but these folk enjoy their chums when they've got them. Because they're Mutable Mercurians, they like a little change and adaptability in their mates. Although they're not as flighty as Geminis, they can still get a bit bogged down and bored every now and then, and will be chuffed if you can come up with some new tales to tell and get them giggling. (Make them up if necessary, but don't let on!)

However, if you feel a crisis coming on, a Virgo chum is just what you need; you'll find with this sign that a friend in need is truly a friend indeed. These Earthy individuals are in their element when they can give good advice, or help you out. Virgos' brand of friendship involves a lot of give and take. (Very often,

they're the givers. They like to be of service.) But when the tables are turned, and kismet isn't being kind to them, it can be a very different story. Try as you might, you won't be allowed to provide anything more than tea and sympathy. Virgos like to cope by themselves.

Being ruled by Mercury, voracious Virgos move very fast. They hate hanging about, and dash off in all directions. They never stay in one place for long, because they'll learn all they can, and then push off for pastures new. Their minds are always on the go, always finding out new facts, then storing them up for future reference. So they find fun with their friends by indulging in exciting exploits. You can go to Greece together to explore the ruins (and the retsina, though that could cause digestive difficulties), or drive down to Dorset to go ghost-hunting. (Though the Virgo will be sceptical even if you see scores of spooks.) But whatever you do, wherever you go, if you keep your wits about you, and your brain cells up to scratch, make one of these Mercurians a mate and you could learn a lot. Virgos will make you pay attention. Come on, now – or it's slapped wrists for you!

Virgo at Work

Virgos at work shine as brightly as their bath taps. They really put vim into their vocations! (What else would you expect from such a sanitary sign?) They're conscientious to a degree and industrious to a fault, beating even career-conscious Capricorns in that department.

You can never have too many Virgos at work. (Well, almost never!) They're a positive pleasure to work with, and always do what they're told. (Try giving an Aquarian orders!) They're past masters at inventing their own systems, too, and a Virgoan secretary can figure out a fantastic filing system that will make her boss as pleased as punch – and confuse him completely!

Virgos do much better as part of a back-up team than as the boss. They're too modest to be the ones in command, but they truly come into their own when they organise others. Organisation is at the core of every Virgo's heart.

Although these Mercurians will go gaga over germs, doo-lally over dirt, and have the heebie-jeebies over health, the one thing they're not frightened of is hard work. In fact, some of them don't seem to be able to do without it, and will toil away like Trojans at all hours of the day and night.

Because of their neat natures, Virgos excel at any task that requires a tidy touch. They're fantastic at fiddly things, diligent in detail, and can be painstaking to the point of pedantry. And although their ruler, fleet-footed Mercury, encourages Geminis to give up half-way through a job, he endows Virgos with a self-discipline and determination to see things through to the bitter (or sweet) end. If you're a boss who has brainstorms, and forgets what day it is, hurry out and hire a Virgo at the double! Although you might not remember a rendezvous in Ramsgate, your Virgo will rush in and remind you, toss you a train timetable and then call you a cab. And while you're away, your vigilant Virgoan will hold the fort for you, skilfully negotiating and tying up contracts quicker than a Scout with a sheepshank.

Mercury makes these men and maidens captivatingly clever at anything to do with communications. They're terrific telephonists and telexers – on the day your phones are paralysed by a power cut, they'll race up to the roof and start semaphoring to all and sundry with two (spotless) scarves. Even a crisis won't catch them out!

Any job that requires intellect and industry, responsibility and resourcefulness, will be right up a Virgo's street. These folk make fantastic doctors, nurses, chemists, teachers, secretaries, Social Security workers and Samaritans – phew! In fact, they'll excel at anything that offers a service to others. And creative Virgos make delightful designers. So, if you want your firm to go with a gallop, rather than out like a light, you couldn't do better than to employ a couple of Virgos. How did you ever cope without them?

Virgo at Home

Drop round to a Virgo's residence at any hour of the day or night (well, almost), and you'll always be greeted with the same words – 'Sorry the place is so untidy at the moment.' As you step into the sitting-room, you'll expect to pick your way across the pile carpet. Instead, the room will look as though a hundred housemaids have been hoovering it, and there won't be a particle out of place.

Even untidy Virgos (yes, there are a few!) are disorganised in an organised sort of way. Whereas the neat natives of this sign have drawers carefully filled with rolled-up balls of string, and *always* have a clean shirt ready and waiting in the wardrobe, the disorganised ones will still have neat abodes, but when you open a cupboard everything but the kitchen sink will come cascading out. Virgos can't cope with clutter – it makes them go bonkers – so they always have stacks of storage space.

When it comes to decorating their dwellings, Virgos like functional fittings, not frills and furbelows, and often opt for plain white walls and just one perfectly-placed picture. (Run your fingers along the frame and you won't find the minutest molecule of muck. Some signs sleepwalk, but Virgos dust while they dream!) Virgos like to keep everything as pure as possible, and as natural as they can make it. They often choose rush matting or raffia rugs, rather than sensually-soft shag pile, and many Virgoan abodes proliferate in pine paraphernalia, and wickerwork wonders. The hues of the home will remind you of the countryside in autumn with wheat, barley and corn colours, as well as black and white. Even the soft furnishings will be natural, with hessian and cheesecloth abounding.

Now, it's a funny thing, but a lot of Virgos are fascinated by their floors, and spend hours getting them just right. (Well, the wrong one will harbour harmful germs.) The carpets and mats will be so clean that they squeak when you step on them, and the kitchen floor will be so shiny that you might mistake it for a mirror. And talking of floors, Virgos are hoover fanatics and give everything the once-over at least seven times a week. So watch out, watch out, if there's a vacuuming Virgo about, and you're sitting slumped on the sofa, because you could get sucked up.

All children of Mercury go for gadgets, and Virgos are no exception. They will have typewriters, tea-makers, word processors, food processors, VDUs and videos. Old-fashioned vestal Virgos will have very simple tastes, and may have a spinning-wheel instead of a stereo, so they can wear jumpers knitted from their own free-range wool. (And coloured with natural dyes, of course!)

Without a doubt, the bathroom will be the most important room in the house to a Virgo. Remember that this is the sign of health and hygiene; not only do Virgos like to keep clean, but they also eat more roughage than a rabbit. Cleanliness is definitely next to godliness for these folk.

Because they're ruled by Mercury, and belong to the Earth element, Virgos are clever in a practical way. They often lead busy lives, and can't spare as much time as they'd like on keeping their homes spotless. One Virgo I knew spent every Saturday morning scrubbing his place from top to bottom and disinfecting it to death; then he'd enfold his feet in gigantic dusters, and start skating round the sitting-room like Sonja Henie, while polishing the parquet! And some Virgos seem to think they live in mosques. If you enter their abode after they've had a spring-clean, it's off with the shoes before you step on the carpet!

Virgo
Health and Relaxation

Hug a Virgo and listen to them shake, rattle and roll, as a ton of tablets do the twist inside their tummies. Many Mercurians (Virgo-style) are mesmerised by their medicines, and can be martyrs to every ailment under the sun, or habitual hypochondriacs. As a result, they can crunch up pills composed of vitamins Barbara Cartland's never even heard of and swig down the Sanatogen as if they were fading fast. (Some Virgos are almost part of the furniture in the doctor's waiting-room, and will trot along, come rain or shine, whether they're ill or not. They know they must be sickening for something soon when they feel fine!)

Of course, not every Virgo is so medicine-mad, and can think of better things to do in bed than reading the latest *Lancet*, or a medical encyclopaedia. Positive Virgos will use their fundamental fascination for fitness by watching what they eat, and taking care of themselves.

Clever old vestal Virgos found out about high-fibre diets years ago, and rave about roughage. ('Bran is best', they'll say.) Virgo rules the bowels and all things abdominal, so these folk have to take care of this sensitive side of their systems. Even after a six-course supper, some of them will hurry home and bolt down a bowl of All Bran, just in case there should be a traffic jam in their intestinal tracts! (Give your Virgo a wholemeal loaf for Christmas!)

Although psychosomatic problems are the Piscean's province, the polarity between these two signs means that a little of this can rub off on Virgos. These people are the worrybags of the zodiac, always trying to get everything as perfect as possible, and that includes their bodies. The tiniest twinge can become magnified beyond measure.

Mercury makes these Virgos as jittery as jumping beans. They can flog their delicate nervous systems to death, so they should try to relax every now and then, putting their feet up and reading a good book. (I see you started with this one!)

Virgos aren't health conscious for nothing, and they should follow their feelings when feeding. (No, I don't mean goosing the *garçon!*) The pictorial glyph for this sign is the maiden clutching a sheaf of wheat, and lots of Virgos follow in her footsteps by becoming vegetarians, or at least wolfing down wholefoods. Simplicity is the key to success, and any folk who've overdone the grub will have ghastly gastric grouses.

Go round to a Virgo's abode, and have a butchers at the bathroom. When your eyes have recovered from the glare of the taps twinkling away, look at the bathroom cabinet. Is it supported by a steel superstructure and five wall-brackets? Take a peek inside, and you'll see enough medicines to keep Boots going for a year!

Otherwise, to see the Virgo in your life being actively healthy, go out to eat together. Watch your pal sit down, after first inspecting the seat of the chair, straightening the knife and fork, checking the rim of the glass for smears, and brushing a few stray crumbs off the tablecloth. Your Mercurial mate will then refuse the roll (too fattening), baulk at the butter (instant cardiac arrest), spurn the spuds (starch), pick at the pudding (too much sugar) and mix mineral water with the wine (alcohol kills off your brain cells). Make no mistake, this is a fastidious Virgo, all right! (Hypochondria rules, OK?)

Libra

133

What Makes Libra Tick

Sugar and spice and all things nice – that's what Librans are made of. Even if you get the rare one made from puppy-dogs' tails, you can bet they'll be pretty pooches and handsome hounds. So it may come as a shock to you that this sweet, sublime sign is the iron hand in the velvet glove. 'What? Our Ethel?' I can hear you saying, but read on, my dears. Libra is a Cardinal Air sign, which means that Librans know what they want, and usually have the mental mastery to be able to get it. I mean, look at Margaret Thatcher!

Libra's ruling planet is Venus, which makes subjects of this sign courteous, charming, cheerful, caring, caressable and captivatingly cuddly. Make no mistake, loquacious Librans can charm the birdies right out of the trees when they want to. (And scintillate the squirrels while they're about it.) But if you look closely, they usually have an aim for all that charm and diplomacy.

Take a woman who has the Sun, Moon, Mars and Jupiter all in luscious Libra. (Gosh!) One day she discovered that a near-neighbour didn't give two hoots about her so she moved heaven and earth until she did, but she killed her with kindness in the process! (And piqued all her pals, who felt ignored.)

The trouble is that Librans like to be liked. In fact, they can't bear to believe that someone can't stand them. Venus can bestow beauteous bounty on her boys and girls, but sometimes she can make them too sweet for words. Even when a Libran is at his or her sugariest and sickliest, you must work out what's behind it all. Librans are assertive, ambitious and go-ahead. So they always have an end in sight. *(Votre derrière,* dear.) It could be to keep the peace (incredibly important to Librans), or to get a new job, but it will be something. Of the other Cardinal signs, Arians will tramp through the rest of the zodiac, Cancerians will drown everyone in tears, and Capricorns will lumber along like a ten-ton tank. But Librans try to get what they want with a smile. (And they usually succeed.)

This is the sign of nuptial bliss, of partnerships of all persuasions, both in business and in love. (Committed relationships of one sort or another loom large in a Libran's life.) And so it's the sign of enemies, too. After all, you can have a rapport with a rival just as much as you'll have an affinity with an amourette. The strength of the emotion is the same. Although the Libran motto is 'Peace at all costs', you mustn't forget the razor's edge between love and hate.

The polar sign of Libra is Aries, and these two can have a wonderful relationship, because they balance each other beautifully. (And remember that though Librans, being the sign of the Scales, are always trying to achieve perfect harmony in their lives, their own set of scales can go up and down like Yo-Yos.) The archetypal Arian-Libran relationship is the Tarzan and Jane jamboree. There's Arian Tarzan swinging through the shrubbery, leaping about in a little loincloth, while Libran Jane stays at home being perky and pretty, probably with a little dishcloth. (Wearing it, of course, in a lovely shade of pink.) The Libran's keyword is 'You', whereas Arians say *'Me!'*. Librans can think too much of their partners and pals, to their own detriment, and can stride off through sleet and snow to minister to a mate who's ill. Some of them can be too selfless for words, although they may still be doing it for a reason – to be liked and loved!

Librans should stop being so concerned with the welfare of their loved ones, and think of themselves sometimes instead. In astrology, every sign has a positive and a negative side, and if you go to extremes in either direction it can be terrible.

This is the sign of puffy pink clouds, baby blue angora wool and pink and white icing. You see, Libra is a very pretty sign indeed. It's not as fantasial and fairy-tale as the Fish, because Librans have more of a sense of reality. Nevertheless, the Libran quest is very much for beauty, and with this love for all things bright and beautiful, Librans can't cope with anything coarse, callous or crude.

The trouble with Librans is that they can be irritatingly indecisive; you can go grey while waiting for them to make up their minds about whether to feast on a fairy cake or have a blow-out on bangers and mash. (In the end you want to bash them over the bonce with the frying-pan.) That may be why they're so considerate, and always ask you what *you* want to do, what *you* want to eat – because they know they haven't the foggiest idea. (Although lots of them *do* know, and try to coerce you into choosing their choice.)

They also like to keep everything fair and square, and if they feel they've been wronged, they'll fight like Aries or be as stubborn as the most intransigent Taurean to prove they're in the right. Justice must be seen to be done – in the Libran's eyes, at least. (Negative Librans will get their sense of justice a mite mixed up.) But even positive Librans will tamper with the balance they find in their lives, on their oh-so-sensitive scales, and wonder if they've got it right. ('On the other hand,' they'll sigh, 'I could be wrong.' This sort of soul-searching can go on for ever, and frequently does!)

Librans' love of harmony and balance extends to matters of the heart, as you might expect. They must have luscious lovers (they must be physically fantastic), and the Libran man must have the most beautiful bird in town in tow, even if he's as ugly as a vulture himself (though he'll have a smashing smile and delicious dimples.) Accuse Librans of this and they will say in a superior way that they're an intellectual Air sign, so plump for personality, first and foremost. But you try to get a Libran to go out with someone who's no oil painting, but has bags of bounce and *bonhomie*, and see what happens. That's right. *Nothing!*

Libra Man

Here's a real smoothie, but usually in the nicest possible way. Libran men are the knights in shining armour who gallop up on white chargers and rescue damsels in distress. They exude an aura of courtly love, even in the twentieth century. If a Libran man found a dragon in Dagenham menacing a maiden, he'd know just what to do. (No, dear, he wouldn't jump on a bus going in the opposite direction!)

Libran men often smell sensational, as well as look luscious. After all, it's no good looking as if you've just stepped out of the pages of a glossy magazine if you pong like a pig farm, is it? A lot of Libran men have large collections of colognes and aftershaves. They can spend hours lying in a sweet-smelling bubble bath, guzzling gin and tonics (possibly pink?), reading interesting books and having a whale of a time.

There can be something slightly androgynous about Libran men, though not necessarily in a sexual way. Think of a Libran man you know. Isn't he rather epicene and elegant? A perfect period in history for Libran men was Elizabethan England, when they would have been real fops, clad in flowing shirts, and rigged out in ruffles from ear to ear. Some of these men can seem too feminine, but what do you expect? Venus is a fantastically feminine planet, but she rules masculine Libra. Tricky, eh?

The tremendous trait of Libran men is their amazing ability to be sociable with either sex. There are many male signs of the zodiac who have to be seen with the lads, putting away pints in the pub. But the Libran man can be downing a drink at seven in the evening at the rugby club, sipping a sherry at the theatre with a girlfriend at nine and feeding on fish and chips out of a newspaper at midnight, tucked up in bed. (His girlfriend will be in the kitchen concocting the cocoa. He's not daft!)

These lovely lads are great diplomats who hate to upset

anyone. In fact, Libran men are walking, talking proof that the age of chivalry is not dead. These are the men who will stand up for you on buses and trains and open doors for you (yes, I thought you'd wondered where they were). They help you on with your coat, and don't even get the arms tangled up. They're wonderfully well-mannered, and don't care who knows it. What's so sensational is that they don't have to read books on etiquette first – these good manners are innate. That's why people find it easy to fall for them – they're such charming, chivalrous chaps. (How can you possibly resist?) But the problem comes later. (I know, there's always a catch.) If you marry one of these 'parfit gentil' knights, although he'll still be as charming as ever to you, he'll also continue to be captivatingly courteous to every other maiden he meets. He may not be unfaithful – it's just impossible for him to ignore a pretty phizog or a perfect pair of pins. But his partner may get hold of the wrong end of the stick. (And beat him with it.) After all, he does like to flirt; he and Leo are the two most flirtatious fellas in the firmament. And once he knows he can charm people potty, he'll trade on it. (After all, he *is* a Cardinal sign.)

Libran men love to look good, which is part and parcel of their persona, and if they could afford it they'd wear tailor-made suits and stunning silk shirts. This isn't because they're status symbols, but simply because Librans love the best. (Debonair and dashing Roger Moore is a Libran lad, and look how ladies lust after him, even when he's on the silver screen and they're in the stalls.)

One thing which people can find hard to swallow is the cold streak within every Libran. However, we mustn't forget that the emotions of a Libran man come mainly from his mind, and not from his heart, because he's an Air sign. Sometimes he'll find it hard to believe he can ever be cold. He thinks that, being a child of Venus, he's all love. But that's not always the case, and he can be remote and resolute, harsh and hard, and you'll wonder where your charming, cheerful, comfy companion went. (But don't worry, he's only popped out. He'll be back.)

Positive Libran chaps are charming, but the negative ones can be a very different cup of tea. (One without sugar.) They can be tipplers, tarts (yes, even the men!), messy, mucky, dirty and disgusting, and so unrefined that they're revolting. And they'll have no sense of justice at all. (Whereas the positive ones abound in it.) A negative Libran will think he's doing fine, when actually his scales of justice will be completely out of balance, with one way up in the air and the other down on the ground.

As a doting dad, the Libran lad will long for the day his child is old enough to talk to him. When his kid is a baby, niggling all night and with terrible table manners, putting pork and prune purée all over his Savile Row suit, he won't be very keen at all. (In fact, he'll hate it!) But once the child begins to chatter, and its personality protrudes through the purée patina, he'll start to enjoy himself. Mind you, some Libran dads never have much time for their kids. They prefer to go for a game of golf, or try a tournament of tennis, than play with the kids in the kitchen.

After reading this, you may think the Libran man sounds just what you've been looking for. You've always wanted a man who's seething with *savoir-faire* and sophistication? Right, dear. Here are two clues which should help you to track him down. Pay attention, and stop swooning. First is his great big grin, which looks like a lollipop laughing (you'll know it when you see it), and second are his dimples. (This is the bit you'll really enjoy.) He'll have them somewhere. And if they aren't on his face, then it's up to you to find out where else they might be!

Libra Woman

Libran women are peaches and cream sundaes on legs. (So if you ever see a woman wearing a *glacé* cherry, you'll know she's a Libran.) Some of them are breathtakingly beautiful, although you'll get the odd horrible old hag among them. (But she'll think she looks good!) Traditionally, they are the most gorgeous girls in the galaxy, and when I tell you that Brigitte Bardot is one of them, you'll see what I mean. A few Libran ladies bear more than a passing resemblance to a number 79 bus on a wet day in Worksop, or Dracula's mother when she's not feeling well, but they always have nice natures! (Well, I suppose they've got to have something, poor dears.)

Libran ladies usually have curvy figures. (They look like egg-timers. Bigger ones look like hour-glasses.) But whether they're a size 8 or a size 18, they are all fabulously feminine, and find it fun. Piscean and Taurean women are also no slouches in these stakes, but Libran women take the biscuit. (And preferably one covered in chocolate!)

The last word in Libran ladies will dress deliciously, with everything matching, and she'll look chic and *charmante*. Even if she's poured into a pair of old jeans, you can be sure they'll be clean, and blend beautifully with her sweater or shirt. The Libran lass is frequently fascinated by fashion, and may make her mark in it, especially as a designer. If not, she'll be content to create her own clobber, and crochet and knit like mad, churning out her own collections.

Like her male counterpart, she adores the company of others. It's rare for her to spend a lot of time by herself. And if she does live alone (unusual for Libran lasses, who always seem to share with someone), she'll have lots of pals around. She's also a dab hand at cocktail parties and coffee mornings. (Libran ladies are too lazy to cook five-course dinners.)

Librans are like Leos in lots of ways, but whereas the Lioness will use her best bone china to show her guests that she's actually got some which isn't cheap and cheerful, the Libran lass will use *her* special Spode because it's so sweet and she loves looking at it. She'll want to give her guests the best, and everything will be as good as she can possibly make it, but with the minimum of effort. (She'll serve up nice plates, nice cups – and Nice biscuits!)

If you're bowling along on the bus one day and a luscious-looking lady sits next to you, smelling like an English garden in the middle of the summer (but more of roses and sweet-scented stocks than rotting compost heaps), you can take a safe bet she's a Libran, or at least has a strong Libra in her natal chart. The Libran girl loves giving things that smell sweet, but finds it most important that she should top the list in the nasal ratings. One of the ways to her heart is with a bottle of perfume and a dozen roses. (But make sure the pastels of the perfume packet and the petals pair up. Otherwise, her hope for harmony at all times will instantly be upset.)

Should you want to have this Libran lady as your pal or your partner, you must make sure you pass the nose test too. If you offend her sensitive nostrils, she'll never forgive you. Libran ladies (yes, they *are* ladies) are without doubt the ones who walked through history with neat nosegays near their nostrils, rather than put up with the powerful pongs pervading the place.

Of course, you may see the other side of the Libran scales, and one day discover her decked out in her dirtiest, most disgusting dress. (Unless she always looks like this, she's coping with a crisis, and won't care how she looks.) You'll probably find that the root of the problem is a lovers' tiff. Like her male counterpart, she loves to be in love, and if she has no one in particular as the object of her affections, she may pick a popstar, a politician or the postman, to tide her over.

For all her loving and giving, the Libran lass doesn't make a natural mother. She hasn't got the maternal motivations of a Cancerian woman, or the protective personality of a Piscean, but she will try her best with her kids. However, it's often a case of 'Now you see me, now you don't', as she's always rushing off like the Good Samaritan to give a helping hand to lame ducks, and set them back on the lily pond of life. (A lot of Libran women should learn that charity begins at home.) If her scales have swung to the saintly side, she will be out nursing a needy neighbour while her own family flake out like flies from the flu. Not surprisingly, she'll come home to a right old row – if her nearest and dearest have got the strength to shout!

Nevertheless, on the rare occasions that she *is* at home, she'll be quite a loving mum. But like her Gemini sister, she'll be happier when her kids can communicate with her verbally, rather than causing horrendous havoc with the contents of the coalscuttle.

She'll understand the need to stimulate the minds of her kids, and will make sure they are introduced to books at an early age. (Just out of the womb.) Her sense of justice will make her treat her kiddies fairly – something they may even take advantage of.

One thing you can be sure of is that a Libran hen and her chicks will all be captivatingly clothed, and usually looking their best. (Colour co-ordination is a must.) But that's another reason for her not being overly enthusiastic about tiny tots. She may pick up her smashing son for a squeeze, only to find he's done a whoopsie all down her cherished cashmere cardi! In fact, bad baby bouquets can really bother a Libran mum, and she can be driven to putting air purifiers round the potty!

Libra Child

Even if a Libran child has been dragged up by the shoelaces, he or she will give every outward appearance of having gone to a finishing school! All Librans are born with a complete catalogue of the social graces firmly fixed in their heads. And while the right parents will encourage this instinctive sense of etiquette, even if the kid is brought up as a combination of the Artful Dodger and a guttersnipe those perfect manners will still be there, under the surface. Librans of all shapes and sizes hate coarse and callous folk, but are far too polite ever to say so.

Any early interest a Libran child shows in the arts should be actively encouraged. Whether a boy or a girl, this kid should be taken to the ballet, to see something sweet like *Sleeping Beauty*, to dancing classes, round museums and into art galleries. (No, not all at once!) He or she should join the children's section of your local library as soon as possible, and learn to love books.

Very often Libran lads find football futile, can't cope with cricket, and run from rugger like rabbits. Their parents shouldn't worry about this, and force them to join in games that are anathema to them. Instead they should let them do what they want, whether that's knitting or practising the violin. (They love to fiddle!)

Libran kids should be allowed to choose their own bedroom wallpaper. Even at the tender age of two, these children like to have everything matching – carpet, curtains and quilt. (Librans of all ages love duvets as they abolish boring old bed-making! And they're so snug.) Your Libran girl will probably be fantastically feminine, and will enjoy dressing up. There are the occasional tomboys, but they usually flower into frills and flounces in their teens.

When you want your little Libran to stop wearing out those beautiful blue eyes (although they're often grey too!) reading books all day, or dressing up in a tutu and pretending to be the

dying swan, buy your kid a tennis racket. Tennis is a very Libran game, because the ball is always going back and forth, back and forth, like a set of scales. You may find it's the only sporty activity a lot of Librans like. (They can be very lazy!)

Another good pastime for a Libran child is painting, so pop along to a place that purveys painting-by-numbers sets, or purchase pretty poster paints, pencils and paper. Then sit back and wait for a masterpiece or two. And don't forget music, which will appeal to the little Libran, whether tuning into the tranny, or serenading you with snatches of Schubert.

But don't let your diminutive Degas, Dickson (Barbara -- she's Libra too!), Dickens or Dior spend so much time on hobbies that any homework goes by the board, or is done by mum at midnight. Your lazy little Libran will procrastinate like anything and put off doing the maths until the last possible moment. But a Libran lovely can be luscious in other ways, so encourage him or her to help you with the cooking sometimes (they adore making radish roses or pastry posies), or the washing up, while you tackle the trigonometry, or fathom out the physics. These kids could make a car's gasket look perfectly pretty.

All in all, you must lavish a lot of love and laughter on your little Libran, and help him or her to master that innate indecision all Librans live with. Then you'll have a delightful daughter or a smashing son, who will grow up with all the best Libran qualities, blessed by the vibes of Venus. Now isn't that something to be proud of?

Libra in Love

Hold on to your heart-strings! Love for Librans is Abélard and Héloïse, Romeo and Juliet – and even Tom and Jerry! And when a Libran falls in love, it can be like a rerun of all the most romantic stories in the world, or like a Barbara Cartland creation come to Coventry. (Or Croydon, if you prefer.)

Librans love to love, and adore to amour. These Venusians join forces with Fiery Lions to be the two greatest signs of love in the celestial sky. As a result, some Librans can run away with the whole idea, and fall in love with love. Leos long for love-affairs and extramarital encounters, but Librans don't usually go in for amorous activities like these, unless they're already on the verge of divorce.

This is the old style of love, with heroes and heroines, knights in shining armour and damsels in distress. (No, dear, you're the damsel, he's the knight.) And just to add to the old-fashioned flavour, lots of Librans like love without lust. Some of them say sex is slightly squalid and a mite messy. If the Libran's scales swing out of balance, he or she can end up having terrible troubles, and may run away from any sexual shenanigans. (Don't worry, they're not all like that!) But to every Libran, sex will never be as romantic as wining and dining by candle-light. Most of this balanced bunch just need to know they're loved and adored, and to be given lots of kisses and cuddles. They aren't so keen on steamy scenes of unbridled passion.

Since this is the sign of marriage and partnerships of all ilks, nuptial bliss will be high on the Libran's agenda. And Librans can make perfectly pootchy partners, since they always consider their loved ones before themselves. (And that can't be bad, now can it?) Indeed, love will make a Libran's world go round, or make it grind to a halt. But this isn't to the same desperate degree of dependence as poor Pisceans. The Libran's

145

Airy, balanced view of life will always keep those (probably plump) tootsies on terra firma, while the Piscean will float off into a romantic reverie and pretend nothing has gone wrong. And because this is an Air sign, the Libran will feel love on an intellectual level; all the emotions will emanate from the mind, first and foremost.

One thing you can never say about these Venusians is 'Once bitten, twice shy'. (More like 'Once bitten, twice as keen'.) If a lover lambasts a Libran, he or she will go back for more time and time again, ambling in where angels (and every other sign except Pisces) fear to tread. If the light of love is put out, the Libran will languish until the next lover looms up. (When the Libran will make the same mistakes all over again!)

Another problem for Librans is that, once Cupid has shot them with his bow and arrow, they can shut off the rest of their lives to attend to their amours, and put them on pedestals. All their friends will get fed up, and if the Libran is stranded high and dry on the rocks of romance, there are no shoulders left to cry on.

Librans constantly analyse their love lives, like Cupidic chemists, trying to work out how to make them better, and how to smooth out the course of true love. They abhor arguments and will do anything to avoid them, preferring to sweep problems under the carpet, when they would do better getting them out and giving them an airing.

The profoundest pitfall in loving a Libran is that someone more elegant and eloquent than you may shimmer on to the scene, and push you off your perch. Librans are easily tempted to romantic reverie and aren't fantastically faithful (given half the chance!), but they don't always scram from their spouses. (It would start a scene.) So they try to have their cake (chocolate, of course) and eat it too.

Would you like to lure the love of a Libran? (Sounds like a good idea to me.) Right. First of all, you must have a bath, and then saturate yourself in some scent. If it's a Libran lady you long for, find out her favourite flowers and send her a garden of them. Then take her out for a whole month and don't mention sex once. And if you're looking for the likes of a Libran lad, pretend that you aren't. Be cool but courteous. Get matey with his friends, look your loveliest, be interesting and intelligent, and wait and see. It could be your lucky day!

Libra as a Friend

L ife is just a bowl of cherries if you have a Libran as a pal –
unless you find one who gives you the pip!

Librans make perfect pals – because they're so open,
outgoing and obliging. They're great fun to be with and usually
to know Librans is to love them. (There will be a few folk who
feel they're too sickly sweet to stomach, but Librans normally
have more fans than foes.)

If you plan to keep your pal pleased, make sure that you take
him or her off to oodles of outings. Trundle off to the theatre
together, coerce your chum into coming to the cinema, drag
him or her off to the disco (but not one that's too dazzling or
you'll both be devastated – Librans hate philistines), and
persuade your pal to a painting preview or a promenade in the
park (preferably by the bandstand). Be prepared to be the one
who has to tempt your mate out, because often Librans are
happy to hide away in their harmoniously-hued homes, eating
excessively and tittering at the telly.

Some of the lazier Librans will be even more enthusiastic
about going out if you can provide the pedal power – and I
don't mean a bicycle made for two! (That's too much like hard
work.) Sagittarians will willingly walk to Wales in wellingtons,
and Pisceans will paddle to Perth in a punt, but try asking a
Libran to join you on a jog to Jarrow, and your friend will have a
funny do!

Should you decide to take your pal off for a posh nosh,
instead of to a naff caff (Librans love luxury), he or she will
probably moan and groan about having to get ready. They have
such problems making up their minds that choosing what to
wear can take hours. (Tell 'em the table's booked for eight when
you know it's not till nine that you're going to dine.) But the
finished result always looks wonderful. (Capricorn chums
groan too, but step out of the bath and into the first thing they
see. It could be a little black dress, or a dark green dressing-

gown with a hole in the back where the dog took a bite out of it.)

When you're the friend of a Libran, you've got to make sure your brain cells are fighting fit. (Take them out for training sessions.) Librans are mentally motivated, and they like their cronies to converse concisely and cleverly about a cornucopia of contrasting conundrums. It's no good thinking you can get away with some wishy-washy words on the space race, for example. A Libran will expect much more than a mere murmur from a mate, and may even take the opposite opinion to yours just so you can have a dynamic discussion. (They love to hear both points of view. But before you get too hot under the collar, remember your pal may not believe a word of what he or she is spouting. It'll just be a game in mental mastery.)

Lots of Librans find it impossible to say no, because they hate to upset anyone. As a result, they'll be quite incapable of refusing their nearest and dearest, best and the rest, anything. And some Librans are so shocked at the thought of cancelling a date that they don't phone, don't write – and don't turn up! (But when you do meet, they're so charming that you forget it all in a trice!)

Next time you go out to a dreadful dinner, a dismal disco or a rowdy party, try to spot someone with a round face and normally bright eyes who looks like a moping Matilda. Seen 'em? Well, that's a Libran who's been unable to refuse an invitation and is having a horrible time (and can't find a mate!). Some Librans can be very put-upon as a result of their inability to say no, and can be unpaid nursemaids, chauffeurs, escorts and general dogsbodies.

So, if you have a Libran mate who always goes along with your suggestions, and spends hours when out with gritted gnashers, take pity on your pal. Let your Libran choose what to do. And then get out a good book. (Try *War and Peace* for size.) You might get half-way through it before your vacillating Venusian comes up with a suitable suggestion, by which time it will be too late to do anything but go to bed. Good-night!

Libra at Work

Team up with a Libran, and you've got it made. These folk adore working with other people, and help make dynamic duos and terrific trios. As long as they're working somewhere wonderful, that is.

Even the most creative creature born under this sign will feel completely claustrophobic and confused if the atmosphere at work is wrong. Any disharmony will send one scale shooting skywards and the other dropping downwards. Librans must also be able to cope with their colleagues. (Some of them don't care what they do as long as they can be with their pals.) They just can't bear to be with people they don't like. (And they don't enjoy being with people who don't like them, either! And often they'll try to win them over, which will make things even worse.)

Because this is a Cardinal sign, Librans are ambitious and know where they're going. (For a bar of choc, over the road!) Once Librans get over their innate indecision, they can make excellent executives, because they're full of the flair, fair features and finesse to do any deals, direct any discussions, manage any meetings and arrange any agreements. Their sense of justice and desire for fair play means that they can make balanced decisions and will always be able to see both sides of an argument. (Sometimes that's a bad thing, as the Libran will sit sucking a platinum pencil and weighing up the pros and cons of a deal till the cows come home.)

They can also be very cool in a crisis, and cope competently with any contretemps. Sometimes they may appear too cool, and give others the impression that they don't care, when actually they're just trying to be businesslike.

This is such an artistic and creative sign that Librans should make the most of any aesthetic expertise they may have. Being ruled by Venus means that music is often very important to them, and they can do anything in the musical line, from playing an instrument to working for a record company or just appreciating a melodious tune.

In fact, the Libran artistic talents are so great that nearly all of them play, paint or produce poems – or would like to! So, any profession that explores the artistic realms will be good for Librans. And once their interest is captured, they can become complete workaholics, leaving the adage of 'lazy Libra' far behind. (Mind you, when they're lying in their soft warm beds with the ones they love they'll want to turn off the alarm and turn over for another snooze.)

Lots of Librans make divine diplomats. They will always manage to pour oil on troubled waters, and can soothe ruffled feathers faster than you can say 'Who's a pretty boy, then?'. And to show you the other side of the scales, Librans also make smashing soldiers.

If you work with one of these human balancing acts, you may have noticed how your colleague reacts in different ways on different days. One Libran lad laboured in a large office with people he liked a lot. One day he would appear, wreathed in lovely Libran smiles, with bags of buns for everyone to scoff with their coffee. But the next day he'd walk in, as though suffering in silence. (This is the other side of the Libran's easygoing nature. When the scales are down, watch out.) And when everyone had agreed to let him get on with his mental indecision, he'd pop out of his office, fall over the fan-heater, and give a grin to melt the hardest-hearted Hannah.

Just remember that the keywords for Libra are partnership and harmony. Put them into practice professionally, and your Libran colleagues will love you for ever.

Libra at Home

Have you ever opened a glossy magazine and seen an arresting abode (no, not a police station!) and wondered who lived there? Well, you're about to find out. A Libran. These folk really know what they're doing when it comes to their homes. They lavish lots of TLC (Tender Loving Care) on getting them just right, and harmonising everything in sight.

Very often Librans choose the right decor rather than sumptuous comfort. Everything will echo everything else: the green of the house-plants will go with the green of the cushions, which will blend with the curtains, which will be made to match the lampshades, and so on, right down to the loo! Even the ashtrays will be the right colour!

On your first visit, you'll walk in, and gasp, because it will be so beautiful. You'll be invited to sit on the stunning sofa, only to fall off it instantly because it's so uncomfortable. (The Libran will have a soft seat, though.) As you chat about this and that, you'll wonder how soon you can scram and go home for a hot bath, to get rid of the backache brought on by the sofa. (It will feel as if it's made from solid steel.)

Of course there's a catch in having such a colour-conscious chum. When you next visit your Libran mate, you must try to make sure that *you* blend in with the background. Imagine sitting on the solid sofa, which is wearing a delicate Libran shade of almond-pink, when you're upholstered in your best fluorescent orange frock with matching magenta make-up. Your pal will be in paroxysms of pain, seeing you clashing with the cushions!

Generally speaking, Libra is not the tidiest of the Sun signs. (Leave that to vestal Virgo.) They may have one room (probably the one with the steel sofa) for visitors that is always tidy and another that is a glorious glory-hole. They feel uncomfortable living in a completely tidy house, but hate living

151

in a proper pigsty. So they'll strive for the happy medium, as in everything they do. Librans aren't usually too hot on hard work, and most only have a hankering for housework if they have a strong Virgo influence in their natal charts. But if they do have a craving for cleaning, the polishes and disinfectants will have to smell nice, and be the right colours. It's no good washing a blue basin with a green cleaner!

Talking of blue, this is the classic Libran colour, especially if it's a pastel shade. Librans should surround themselves with it as much as possible. It upsets them to live among colours that are too vivacious and vibrant, and should choose lavenders, lilacs, pinks and gentle greens, as well as all the blues in the spectrum.

Because this is the sign of togetherness, Librans should always try to live with someone. However, if they do live alone, they'll have tons of chums and a scintillating social life.

These Venusians aren't as animal-minded as some signs, because pets can be messy and need looking after. So, if they do plump for a pet, they're unlikely to choose a carefree cat or a doting dog. But the perfect pet for a Libran is a fluffy white kitten. (You know, the Kosset carpet type!) After all, white goes with everything! But the fur may go with everything too, so a practical Libran may decide that a ball of white mohair will look just as pretty and be a lot less trouble. It doesn't have to be fed or let out, and if the Libran puts a little black felt nose on one end of it and leaves it near a fire, no one will ever know the difference!

The bedroom is undoubtedly a Libran's most important room in the house, and it will be full of luxuries, matching sheets and quilts, and maybe even a four-poster bed. (All these fripperies can add a dash of rhapsodic romance to grubby gropings.) But by far the most important item in this harmonious household will be music, which all Librans adore. And as the Bard said, if music be the food of love, then fiddle away to your heart's content! (And don't Librans love a fiddle!)

Libra
Health and Relaxation

Librans usually glide along with their heads held high. But sometimes they shuffle like stand-ins for Quasimodo, because their backs will have given up yet again. You'll find that every Libran has lain supine because of their spine at some point in their lives. So, it's very important for all Librans to make sure that they have a comfy chair to sit on at home, so they don't put too much strain on their sensitive lumbar regions. They can easily get slipped disks, and the Venusian vertebrae can really play havoc. (If you go on honeymoon with your Libran husband, and he wants to carry you over the threshold, think twice before you say yes. It could be *him* who spends the week flat on his back!)

The kidneys can be another weak spot, and Librans should watch what they drink. (Though sometimes it slips down too swiftly to see!) In fact, lots of Librans have weak bladders. Give them a cup of tea and they'll toddle off to the bathroom ten minutes later! (If you wonder where your Libran's gone, look in the loo! My BBC producer Annie is often loo-bound while we're filming.)

In astrology, you should always look at the polar people when considering the health problems of a Sun sign. Aries is the opposite sign to Libra, thereby making these Venusians vulnerable to problems with their faces, eyes and ears. And they can be plagued with horrendous headaches.

However, unless the Libran is very ill indeed, he or she will want to get a divine doctor. Libran women, if they're having a home visit, will put on their nicest négligés and hope the doctor is handsome, while Libran men will asphyxiate themselves with aftershave, and pray for a pretty practitioner!

Librans who need to relax can do so in the company of the ones they love. Particularly vivacious Venusians should relax in an outside atmosphere, such as a nice (but not noisy) pub, or a bar, where the Libran can sip sweet cocktails. (Librans love sweet things, both animate and inanimate.)

Any Librans who are all het up and don't have hobbies should find themselves something, quick. This is an artistic sign, and Libran women could join an evening class in fashion or interior design, so they can look well turned out on the cheap. (Libran men enjoy it, too.) All Librans enjoy being practical in an artistic way, and they can love to crochet or knit.

To keep their minds working, Librans should take up some sort of study, such as the history of art or fashion. Music appreciation classes would be perfect for them, or they could learn a musical instrument if they don't already play one.

Some Librans, of course, will have had quite enough of work during the day, and won't want to do much at all in the evenings. So, they should be loafers on the sofa, and listen to something light and lyrical. Lots of Librans love Liszt and Lennon, Strauss or Sibelius, and they go barmy for anything baroque. (And that could be you, dear.)

A lot of Librans spend too much time just with their partners, and forget about their friends. It will do them a lot of good if, once a week, they trip off on their tod to the Tate, or meander off with a mate for a meal. (Librans love food and drink, so a marvellous way for them to relax is to go out with friends to a salubrious joint. And they're so generous, they'll even foot the bill. Capricorns dote on them!)

But all in all, whatever the Libran chooses to do will centre on looking and learning. This is such an intellectual sign that the Libran will love to keep his or her brain busy and buzzing, at all hours of the day and night, and will be charmed to chat to you.

Scorpio

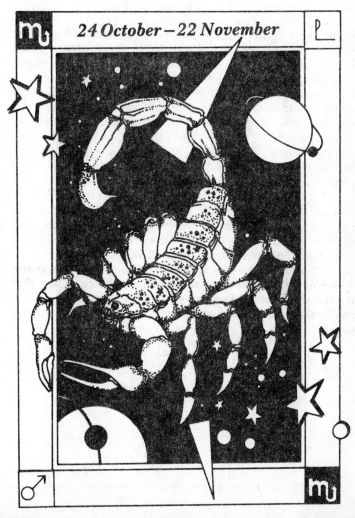

24 October – 22 November

What Makes Scorpio Tick

Listen. Do you want to know a secret? (Where have I heard that line before?) Do you promise not to tell? Scorpios are ace! Their coolness can be captivating, and their furtiveness fascinating. And they're so laidback it's luscious!

Scorpios have more undercurrents than a conger eel. You never know what makes them tick because they never give you a clue. (Is it clockwork or quartz?) They sit looking enigmatic, and you wonder what on earth they're thinking about!

In fact, enigmatic is the supreme Scorpio word. The normal give-away for this Plutonic sign is the eyes, which are like deep pools – you wonder what's going on below the surface. Scorpios are like icebergs; after all, if you combine their element, Water, with their Fixed quality, what do you get but ice?

Aries and Scorpio share the ancient rulership of mighty Mars, yet their temperaments are as different as chalk and cheese. Arians have flashes of Fiery fury, and act on impulse (they'll suddenly strangle you with a sock). Scorpios, though, simmer and smoulder on the back burner of life's cooker, plotting and planning how to get even with you. And they'll manage it in the end! Scorpios have psychological power, and use it to the full whenever they can. (They could manipulate Machiavelli!)

Never underestimate a Scorpio. This is a phantasmagorically profound placing for a person, and Scorpios are imbued with intensity. This is, after all, the sign of sex and death.

Death, for a Scorpio, isn't always something physical; instead these folk can kill off certain sections of their lives they no longer like in the twinkling of an eye. They can transform and transfigure their lives more than any other sign, making fresh starts with barely a backward glance. However, since this is the sign of obsessions, some Scorpios are fascinated by physical death, and can gad about graveyards, looking at the headstones and absorbing the atmosphere. They'll be engrossed and enthralled by the ritual of death, and almost have death wishes, because they

156

can't wait to know what it's like on the other side. Other Scorpios go to the opposite extreme, and are petrified of popping off!

Make no mistake, this is a sign of such compulsion, obsession and profundity that some people find Scorpios hard to handle. Just thinking about their intense inquisitions, interrogations and investigations makes some folk's hair stand on end! Scorpios can be like an oil rig, drilling deep into the heart of the matter. (I wonder how many of the men are called Derrick?) And if you want to know what makes a Scorpio tick you've got to do the same to them. Then you'll start to see what's submerged beneath that superficially serene surface. (A Scorpio may come across as cool, calm and collected, but underneath that elegant exterior is a sizzling selection of scorching sensations simply seething away!)

Power is very important to these Plutonians, but it's always gained in a secretive way. Scorpios operate behind the scenes; they love to manipulate others, but hate to be caught in the glare of the spotlight themselves.

But don't just think there's only one sort of Scorpio, who's like the Spanish Inquisition. There are three sides to this sign, from the angelic to the awful. Top of the list is the devout dove. This is the Scorpio who believes in peace and tranquillity, and strives for it at all costs. (Perhaps even becoming a nun or a monk in the process.) Next comes the exciting eagle – the daredevil hero who takes risks and laughs in the face of danger. Whether James or Jane Bond, this Scorpio works behind the scenes as a spy or a secret agent. (You can always spot 'em because they shin up drainpipes in the dark, clutching cartons of chocs between their teeth!) So far so good, I hear you say. But lastly comes the sly snake, that slithers through the undergrowth of life, then slinks out when you least expect it, and buries its fangs in your ankle. Ouch! These are the mass-murderers, the Charles Mansons of the world. (No wonder Scorpios can get a bad name!)

Luckily for the rest of us, that is the lowest level to which a Scorpio can sink. (It's the lowest level to which anyone can sink!) Higher-minded Scorpios choose to follow a positive path, seeking out the spiritual side of life. But a truly negative Scorpio will turn to black magic to fulfil that pulverising passion for power, taking a macabre interest in things most people shy away from. Once you've totally understood a complex Scorpio you'll have solved one of astrology's most ancient mysteries, and be shown sensational sights of life that no other sign can offer.

Scorpio Man

'**M**y name is Bond. James Bond'. And guess what sign he is. No, not Virgo. It's Scorpio! Good old 007, working behind the scenes, privy to state secrets, is sensationally Scorpionic. And he has enough magnetic charm to make the world stop spinning on its axis and start rotating in the opposite direction.

Scorpio men are all-powerful, and the ones most women would do almost anything for. (Yes, *anything*, Fanny of Falkirk!) Some girls can flip and flutter all over the place, just at the sight of one of these Scorpio men. (You too!)

A lot of the Scorpio men I know are very powerful indeed. They're the sort you don't see very often (too busy in the bedroom?), but they are busy running corporations, or are heads of firms, organisations and so on. (Oh! Too busy in the boardroom!) And even if they aren't in that sort of position professionally, they still exude a stunningly strong and acutely attractive ambience. And you know there are undercurrents surging away beneath the Savile Row shirt, or sophisticated suit.

These fellas are the darkest men imaginable. The Scorpio man usually has very black hair – although you'll find some who are as blond as anything (been at the bleach again) – and very black eyes, and even when he shaves he will look as if he hasn't seen a razor in days. Scorpio men have very penetrating peepers, which can pulverise – looking right into you. (And out the other side.) Very often both sexes accentuate their eyes in some way, by sporting strange specs or coloured contact lenses. (It's very disconcerting meeting a Scorpio in January when the snow is on the ground and the Scorp's in sun-glasses – and woolly mittens!)

There is a staggering strength about the Scorpio man, even if he's four foot nothing and has to wear built-up socks and a specially woven wig. He has such stature, magnetism and oomph that people turn to look at him when he walks into a room, and either sigh or shudder! (That's if he can *find* his way in, with his

158

blackened bins.) Because the Scorpio man indulges in drink, and probably food too, he can put on weight, although he tends to be quite sturdy in the first place. Richard Burton is a stunning Scorpio who springs to mind; he has hidden depths, and there's a mist of mystique all around him.

The Scorpio man can be very loyal in his relationships, because his is a Fixed sign. But it's very important that the woman in his life is extremely sexy, and has qualities he desires, to help his power games. Ideally, he needs a rather flimsy, fluttery female Fish, who will rely on him totally and believe he's right – even when he's so wrong it's ridiculous! He won't want his partner to be in competition with him in any way. (Cancel your application to the London Marathon and apply for the Mixed Doubles at Wimbledon.) He needs an emotional responsibility, but he also needs to know that his feelings are reciprocated. Because he is so sublimely sexy, he needs to express his emotions in that way (yes, *that* way!), and must pick a partner who has the same sexual sensations (and stamina) as him. (Remember that some folk *talk* about it, but don't actually do it!)

Usually, he will make a good dad, as long as he can curb his jealous, voyeuristic nature. (He's the one who reads his kids' diaries to see what they say about him.) Being a Water sign he'll find it easy to show affection for his kids – his feelings and emotions are very often more profound than those of Cancerian and Piscean men. But he'll happily let his wife look after the babies, only really becoming interested in his children when they begin to put forward particular personalities. He can also set tests for his children, to see how loyal they are – lying on the line in front of the 4.20 from Frinton-on-Sea, and waiting for them to rescue him! But he must guard against being so strict that his kids are frightened of him. Basically, he's a family man, and he likes the thought of his family being together as one unit. But in the long run (during the London Marathon, if you decide *not* to cancel), the Scorpio man will devote more time to his spouse than to his offspring, even though they'll still be special.

Some Scorpio men are very attracted by the seedy side of life, and many take great delight in indulging in illicit sex in the most seamy surroundings, dallying round dustbins and lurking in loos. Remember that Scorpio is the sign of obsessions, so a Scorpio can take any pleasure or pastime, and transform it into a total fixation. Sometimes this overriding obsession will become so strong that it'll destroy him, either physically or mentally.

Scorpios can bring their obsessions into their relationships. Their ferocious feelings can turn to jealousy, envy and possessiveness if they aren't reciprocated, and the loved one will feel swamped and suffocated by the Scorpio stranglehold.

This is by no means a light sign. Unsavoury Scorpios are far too intense and unsettling. But don't think you're dealing with someone dour and dull, because you're not. In every sign, you'll find folk who are melancholic and those who are merry and mischievous. And you can take it from me that a lot of Scorpios can be a real riot, although they will always keep their heads, when all around others are losing theirs. They will exude an aura of assurance, promoting themselves in such a way that you stand back in awe and wish you could be like that too. Yet, underneath it all, they are probably a welter of worries, full of phobias and phantasms. After all, this is a Water sign, and Water signs tend to worry a lot, whether they are strong Scorpios, captivating Cancerians or pretty Pisceans. But whichever way you look at it, Scorpios are simply sensational!

Scorpio Woman

N ow here's a cool customer. The superb serenity of some of these Scorpio sirens can bewitch, bother and bewilder you, making you long to know what they're really like. Surely they can't actually be that cool and controlled, can they? Well, it's up to you to find out!

Although Taurus is the astrological opposite to Scorpio, there's a similarity between these two signs, and both can be the strong silent sort. (Yes, even the women!) Taurean lasses are sensationally sensual, but there's more excess emotion in Scorpio girls. Meet one of these maidens for the first time and you'll know that still waters run very deep indeed. There's a fountain of fervent feelings under that flawless facade. (Got your snorkel?) But don't despair. Scorpio women are like complex stock-cubes, full of all kinds of amorous aromas and tantalising tastes. All you've got to do is get the recipe right!

As far as looks go, most Scorpioettes are exotic and enticing, sultry and seductive. Their eyes will speak volumes, even if they're totally tongue-tied! They can look like the back end of a bus but still folk will flock to them, because they're so marvellously, mesmerisingly magnetic. Once you're ensnared by their enigmatic, elusive and enthralling energy, you won't notice if they have perfect pins or a wooden leg.

There are two women who portray perfectly the stunning stillness of a Scorpio woman – cool Katharine Hepburn and glacial Grace Kelly. They have always appeared completely in command of themselves, yet beneath that icy exterior is enough heat to melt the hardest heart.

In fact, passion pervades every element of a Scorpio maiden's existence. She'll be intense about all sorts of issues, from the way you hang up your socks (you do *what?*) to the problems of the Third World. But what is so delightful about her is that she feels strongest of all about the ones she loves, and her partner in particular. She may be the sort of girl lots of men go gaga over, but if her heart belongs to you, then that's where it'll stay. These lasses are fantastically faithful, and lusciously loyal to those they love. Win over one of these maidens and you'll feel the gods are grinning on you.

But before you become complacent, remember that if you step out of line, you'll only regret it. That Bullish Bard was absolutely right when he wrote 'Hell hath no fury like a woman scorned'. If you cross a Scorpio siren she'll never, ever, forgive and forget (although she'll say she will), and she'll do anything to get even with you, no matter how long it takes. (Even at eighty, she'll still hold a grudge!) And don't think that you can two-time her, either. With her penetrating X-ray vision, she'll find out all about it, then unleash a fury on you that will get you running for cover. Scorpio lasses can be more jealous, envious, vengeful and vindictive than any other sign in the celestial sky. So if you incur the wrath of one of these women, don't say I didn't warn you!

Sex is important for all Scorpios, but that will mean that they either love or loathe it. (Not all of these folk belong in bed.) I used to know one Scorpio lass who was so panicked by passion that she ended up in a mental hospital. She just couldn't handle it. (She couldn't handle anything, actually, and that was her problem!) So don't be a chauvinist piglet, and think you can slide a Scorpioette between your satin sheets within six seconds of setting eyes on her. She'll be disillusioned and disgusted. Give her time to get to know you first.

Once she's a mother, the Scorpio woman will be a tigress, determined to protect her offspring at all times, and she'll fight tooth and nail to do it. She can also be ultra-possessive, and won't let her kids out of her sight. Very negative Plutonian mums won't let their kids develop their own individuality, and this can cause chaos if they aren't careful.

The Plutonian philosophy of life is that as one door closes, another one opens – and that's the way Scorpio lasses live their lives. One strongly Scorpio girl upped and left America, and bourréed over to Britain, so she could start again from scratch. At first, she hardly had two halfpennies to rub together, but now she's riding on the crest of a wave: an excellent example of how a Scorpio can call out 'All change!' on the bus of life.

Pick a positive Plutonian girl and you can have a tremendous time together. Whether she's a pal or a partner, she'll show that stunning Scorpionic solidity. Gosh, these girls are great!

Scorpio Child

Now this can be a weird one. There's a Scorpio kid I used to know who never so much as uttered a peep, and just sat silently in a corner all the time. These children can be enigmas, and leave one feeling in quite a quandary as to what to do with them.

Even though small, a Scorpio child will have the compulsive cravings for command, and the megalomaniac motivations of the senior Scorpio, and may try to get what he or she wants through manipulation of mothers and flattery of fathers. And, especially if there is a strong Pisces in the chart, he or she may become expert at playing one parent off against the other. The Scorpio child can also become very jealous of brothers and sisters. If you have a Scorpio kid, and a baby on the way, make sure that your child doesn't feel threatened or ousted by the new arrival. Reassure your child of the place he or she has in your affections, and try to bring out the positive characteristics of your Scorpio child.

Equally, some Scorpio children can become envious of their pals if they live in larger houses, or have more money or better toys. It is very important for you, as a parent, to nip these tendencies in the bud before they become deep-rooted. They will still be there, under the surface, but not as strongly as they will if they are left to grow unchecked. Otherwise, your Scorpio child may become spiteful and vindictive, and not very nice.

As you would imagine, Scorpio children can run up against sex at a very early age, so I strongly advise all parents to give them a good talking-to about the birds and the bees as soon as it seems necessary, but certainly by the time the particular kid has embarked on puberty. Otherwise, it could be too late, and you'll be locking the stable door after the horse has bolted!

But until puberty arrives, the Scorpio child will be strongly influenced by his or her parents, so make sure that this power is positive. Once the Scorpio discovers what life is about, and the consequences of physical attraction, he or she could be in for a lot of trouble. Scorpios can make whacky teenagers, and can need careful handling. As they are so emotionally motivated – and with their hormones in turmoil all through their teens, to make matters worse – young Scorpios can have problems coming to terms with their volcanic natures. They may even frighten themselves, let alone anyone else!

You might think that the minute a Scorpio reaches puberty, he or she will go wild, but some of them can have hang-ups about the whole business and find it difficult to cope. Remember that a Scorpionic obsession can mean love or hate, and some Scorpios will loathe sex.

If a Scorpio teenager suffers some sort of bitter experience physically, it can set him or her off on a very dire direction indeed. It can result in the Scorpio becoming paranoid, or it can poison every future relationship. For instance, a teenage party that turned into a drunken orgy might make some Scorpios believe that even a knees-up at the local pub could become a Bacchanalian bun-fight. (And of course, some Scorpios will dread the idea, while others will try to encourage it for all they're worth!)

Like Capricorns, some Scorpio children can be very attached to their grandparents, and will almost be brought up by them. They can be very close to the older members of their family, and if one of them dies when the Scorpio is young, he or she will be extremely upset; this can often set the pattern for future phobias about death.

If you have a Scorpio kid, tread very carefully. You will bring up a delightful dove, an entrancing eagle, or a shy snake. Which is it to be?

Scorpio in Love

If a Scorpio has fallen in love with you, rush out right away and invest in a fire extinguisher, then leave it within arm's reach at all times. (Especially in your boudoir). You'll need it. Scorpios perform on a pulsatingly passionate plateau when they're in love, and will smoulder and sizzle away until you'll swear you can see smoke emanating from their ears. (At least, I think it's their ears!) But don't make the mistake of thinking that all Scorpio stands for is sex, because these people need a lot of love, too. It's not exclusively a sign of rumpled sheets, but they will play a large part!

Scorpios can go at an affair hammer and tongs, but sometimes they push a relationship forward too fast and it becomes rather like a false growth in a plant. It will shoot up, bring forth the most beautiful bloom, and then keel over and collapse because it hasn't got enough roots to support it. And the same thing can happen to a Scorpio love-match, because it can be plunged into love's hothouse and not given time to develop naturally. So go easy on the Baby Bio, Scorpio!

The Scorpio emotions are torrid, and the feelings are sensationally steamy (well, what do you get when you mix heat with water but steam?), provocative and volcanic. (And that's putting it mildly.) They can be so sexual that many Scorpios think they're in love when actually they're in lust, which of course is something quite different. And that's the first problem for most Scorpios to work out – is it love they feel or is it purely a physical *frisson?* That may be why many Scorpios marry twice. Sex will have been the main attraction with the first partner, and then the couple will discover they have nothing in common, apart from that. But when wedding bells peal out the second time around, the marriage will be a mixture of sexual and mental attraction, and the couple will be able to have a good old chin-wag, when they're not wagging other areas of their anatomies.

165

Scorpios will ferret out all the shortcomings in their first relationships, and then put those lessons they've learned into practice in the next nuptial. But there's no getting away from the fact that this is an emotional sign, and a Scorpio in love has to have his or her passions, urges and surges assuaged. Love is so incredibly intense for Scorpios! Whereas most signs find they can love each other on a more day-to-day basis, the Scorpio will make a big thing about every minute. Some Scorpios can become overpoweringly jealous, imagining all sorts of ludicrous liaisons for their lovers, and putting their partners through real psychological wars at the same time. (If you spend too long in the bath, they can think you've been up to something.)

Very often the emotional rapport will depend on the intensity with which the Scorpio drinks. Catalysts always play a very important part in a Scorpio's life, and alcohol is often the trigger to spark off this very volatile sign. (A bottle of Beaujolais and the feelings flood out.)

If you are after a one-night stand with a Scorpio, you've got to flaunt yourself! (Better blatant than latent.) But if you want more than that, you must be subtle, in a very sexy, sensual and self-confident way! Because this is such an enigmatic sign, it's difficult to say how to get a long-term relationship with a Scorpio, but basically you have to be loyal, faithful, and where he or she wants you. (Flat on your back in bed.)

Scorpios like power, and won't be delirious if you challenge them a lot. And don't make the mistake of thinking that you must fall into bed with a Scorpio immediately, because if you do, you will only degrade yourself in his or her eyes. However, there is no point in pretending that once you do climb between the sheets together that the physical side of your relationship won't be important, because it will. In fact I would go so far as to say that if your physical needs don't match, that could be grounds for divorce later. Never underestimate a Scorpio, in bed or out of it!

Scorpio as a Friend

Have you ever been frightened of a friend? I've had lots of Scorpio pals whom I've adored, but I've always been a weensy bit wary of them. Even in a platonic palship, Scorpios hold an emotional half Nelson over you, one way or another. They can also make you feel guilty, and if you've done something which you know won't please them, you'll worry and wonder exactly how they're going to take it!

Nonetheless, if you have a Scorpio as a friend, you can be fairly sure that they will be a pal for ever and ever, as long as you play by the rules. (Their rules, that is.) As Scorpios belong to the quartet of Fixed signs, they need permanence within their relationships, and won't like to chop and change. However, you must realise that if you are a very strong person yourself, it can be like living on a knife edge to have a Scorpio as a pal. There are going to be times when you won't agree, and you can have a clash of wills as a result. And before you say 'I can win this round', go back into your blue corner and think again. It's *you* who has to concede, if you want the relationship to continue. It's no good coming out fighting with a Scorpio. (Not unless you are ready to throw in the towel half-way through the first round.) I know a Taurean and a Scorpio who used to be the best of buddies, until the day that the Scorpio decided that the Taurean had betrayed her. From that day to this the Scorpio has never forgiven her mate, and will stick the knife in at every opportunity.

This is a good example of the Scorpio destructiveness, and the ability to close one chapter of his or her life, no matter how important it used to be. Once a Scorpio has taken against you for whatever reasons, no matter what you do, how nice or nasty you are, you will never regain that friendship. What's more, you can be pretty sure that whenever your back is turned the Scorpio will be making subtly destructive comments about you, hinting about the possible skeletons in your closet. Scorpios can produce a powerful poison when they want to. Think of the sting in the

Scorpion's tail! (And witch-hazel won't help, so you can put that bottle away.) A relationship can mean everything to the Scorpio, but the minute he or she feels let down, that will be it. You may as well forget it, pack up and go home, because you will never make your mate change his or her mind, and you'll only make yourself unhappy if you try. Really wounded Scorpios can mail their ex-mates missives which can mangle, maim and mortify.

So the friendship factor will be important for a Scorpio, but it can be over as quickly as it began. And you won't get as stable a friendship with a Scorpio as you would with any of the other Fixed signs, of Aquarius, Leo or Taurus. The emotionalism of being a Water sign has too intense an influence.

If you want to keep a Scorpio pal sweet (and it sounds like you should), you could do worse than to take him or her down to a wine bar, pub or social club. A Scorpio with a strong Mars will be enormously energetic (remember a Mars a day helps you work, rest and play), and may enjoy doing things on water, such as sailing, swimming or skiing. But generally this is a sign that is quite self-indulgent, and Scorpios will love going to the ballet or the opera, and other ostentatious activities. They also like ghoulish, gruesome, grim and grisly get-togethers. I know two Scorpios who practically live in the Chamber of Horrors. The more their hair stands on end and their knees knock, the more they adore it!

In fact, a good night out for a Scorpio will be knocking back a bottle of booze, ambling off to the opera, and then going home via the graveyard, preferably at the stroke of midnight, which as any Scorpio will tell you, is the witching hour. And then they'll like to pull their partner down behind a towering tombstone!

If you go out for the day with a Scorpio, take a warm woolly, because he or she will probably want to walk around a couple of crumbling churches, and they can be cold. This fascination isn't usually for religious reasons, but simply so the Scorpio can soak up the age-old atmosphere, take in the tombs and discover who died when, and of what. Just remember to keep an eye out for a grey lady or two, or a knight from the days of gore. I mean, yore. (See how magnetic they can be – they've got me at it now!)

Scorpio at Work

S trong Scorpios have such sterling qualities that they can go far professionally, and their wills can propel them up the ladder of success. But then so can their jealousy. The Scorpio's envy of another person's success can be just the spur to get him or her moving. Of course, if the Scorpio uses this in a negative way he or she can decide to destroy that person's success, instead of emulating it. This is the Scorpio snake, who sneaks and sniffs about, storing up the smut and searching out the secrets, then sits in silence, sensing a suitable season to start the siege.

A Scorpio isn't always ambitious for status (unless there are strong Leo or Capricorn links in the natal chart), but he or she will want to wield a certain amount of power. In fact, Scorpios really *need* power and, if they can, they will manipulate behind the scenes, so even a Scorpio secretary will be much stronger than you might expect. Sometimes, this can be in a positive way, for the good of the company or her boss, but a negative Scorpio will be underhand.

This is a very capable sign, and most of the Scorpios I know who have made it to the top of their trees have done so through tons of talent and pounds of potential (and ounces of opportunism), and have worked resolutely against the odds. (What a weighty combination!) They have been able to promote their own positions and blow their own bugles in such a way that they've just bounded to the top. However, because most Scorpios don't particularly like the limelight, they will prefer to operate in the wings, working behind the scenes.

Professions that often attract Scorpios include police work, being private detectives, spies or even gangsters. (Scorpio ladies love being gangsters' molls.) There is often something a little shady about Scorpios – a sense of the underworld, of secret hideaways and ganglands – which I find fascinating! Some Scorpios are sensational at snooping which, of course, has to be done secretly, and there's nothing Scorpios like better than operating under cover. (Unless it's operating under covers.) For example, I know a Scorpio VAT inspector, and another of this sign who is a Social Security snooper – I mean, just how Scorpionic can you get? So, professions in which there is a certain amount of secrecy involved will fascinate them, especially if they can lead a double life as a result.

Not surprisingly, with their pulverising powers of penetration, Scorpios make perfect psychologists and psychiatrists. Some of them will even by hypnotists! Pluto is said to govern X-rays, so radiography can appeal too. (And guess what? Marie Curie, who discovered radium, was a Scorpio.) The Plutonic fascination with death can mean that some Scorpios will become undertakers or be associated with death in some other way, such as pathology work – or grave-digging! Scorpios with a strong Mars in their charts can choose a profession in the armed forces. And let's not forget that this sign rules big business and corporations, so you'll find a lot of Scorpios wheeling and dealing away at the tops of large organisations.

I know some Scorpios who, if they are open in their work, can be secretive in other ways professionally. For example, they can create some intrigue in their lives by canoodling with their colleagues. Sometimes this will be just another way for the Scorpio to achieve more power, and inject some excitement into his or her life. Sometimes it can be real love. I used to know one Scorpio man who managed to sleep with almost anything and anyone in a skirt. He adored the subterfuge and secrecy that was involved, and was always organising romantic rendezvous in restaurants, where he would keep one peeper on the paramour and the other on the door, in case someone he knew walked in. But he had such oodles of Scorpionic charm and charisma that he could always get away with it, and no one minded!

Scorpio at Home

Scorpios like their homes, and they'll be quite important to them. Because this is such an emotionally-motivated sign, the feelings will often evolve from the home.

They can be real homebirds, and during the week they are usually quite content to spend their evenings peacefully in their own places. They tend to make whoopee at weekends and have hysterics on holiday. And because they usually appear so laidback and inscrutable, when they let themselves go they can be wonderfully outrageous!

But Scorpios love their lairs, and I know many of them who nestle in very happily. Like Cancerians and Taureans, they like their grub, so the kitchen will be important to Scorpios. (They like their drop of drink, too.) Many Scorpios will enjoy the company of one or two close chums or a few members of their families, but they will also enjoy being with their partners very much. This is especially so for the Scorpio female, though her male counterpart may go out a wee bit more. In fact, he often needs his hour or so in the pub after work before he's ready to go home and settle down for the evening.

Nonetheless, there is a homely and cosy feel to the Scorpio abode, and the accent will often be on the lighting, as it is for all Water signs. Pisceans may go for fantasial fairy lights, but Scorpios will opt for soft lights (and sweet music), perhaps even with dimmer switches. Then they can plunge the room in gloom when they are feeling sexy and seductive and in the mood for amour. Lots of Scorpios have furry hearthrugs in front of their fires. Did you ever wonder why? Well, it's so they can push their partners on to the trimmed tiger, or lacerated leopard, and have a rampant romp without catching cold.

Normally the atmosphere in a Scorpio's home will be emotionally highly charged, either because there has been a terrible tantrum, or because the couple is very much in love. A sensitive Cancerian, always aware of atmospheres, strolling in for the first time for a cup of tea can come out reeling and have to push off to the pub to recover! You can get more of an electric tingling atmosphere in a Scorpio home than almost anywhere else. (Some of them have a higher voltage than the National Grid!)

Needless to say, the bedroom will be by far the most important room for the Scorpio, and it will be dramatically decorated, with the accent firmly on the bed. (What else? One Scorpio man was unemployed and flat broke, but he literally couldn't live without his four-poster, which looked rather incongruous in his one-roomed residence in Ruislip!)

A lot of Scorpios place a great deal of importance on their curtains. (Maybe so they can swing from them!) You'll notice time and time again that even in the smallest flat, Scorpios tend to have dynamic drapes which look as if they've been ripped off from the Royal Opera House. Scorpios can go to town, putting up plush pelmets, sweeping swags and dia-phanous drapes, even if the rest of the place looks a pigsty. I've met two Scorpios who both had beautiful burgundy-coloured curtains cascading in tatty old tips. So there is an aspect of the Scorpio home that will be quite grand – even if the Scorpio hasn't got two pennies to rub together. You will also find lots of rich, deep, dark reds, which are very Scorpionic shades. (Especially if they come out of a wine bottle.)

Negative Scorpios can be very jealous when other people have what they want, and they can bristle like brushes when they see their neighbours or next of kin with things they'd like themselves.

There is usually a lot of drink in evidence in the Scorpio home, and probably racks of robust red wines. Very grand Scorpios will have their own cellars, which they will turn into replicas of sets from Hammer Horror films. They'll be covered with cobwebs, and have slippery stone steps and creaking oak doors, so that when you go down for a bottle of booze you'll find yourself looking around nervously, in case the Phantom of the Opera or Dracula is about to leap out and grab you! (It'll probably only be the Scorpio, out for a quick cuddle!)

Scorpio
Health and Relaxation

Have you ever noticed that Scorpios eat lashings of garlic? They may say they like the taste, but actually they are warding off werewolves and avoiding vampires. Scorpios are sensationally superstitious. Some of them always put their left socks on first, or turn round three times and touch their toes if they put the sugar on their Shreddies before they pour on the milk. Does that sound obsessive? It is! And excessive, sometimes, when it can lead to trouble. Once a Scorpio gets a bee in his or her Easter bonnet, that can be it. The obsession will be overpowering, and the whole health can suffer. Those ever-present, ever-ready emotions can work to the good or the bad. But if they're channelled in negative directions, they can bring about the downfall of the Scorpio, who can hammer away at that one obsession until it begins to hammer away at *them*.

Most Scorpios seem to spend a lot of time at special clinics, being treated for some form of sexually transmitted disease or another. If they haven't got a dose of VD, they will have thrush, cystitis or something similarly problematic connected with the genital organs. And this is the area of the body ruled by sexy old Scorpio, as you might have guessed.

The health of Scorpios is also affected by their polarity with Taurus, so they can have problems with their throats too. They can also have troubles with piles and other ailments associated with their bowels, and these will be accentuated if the Scorpio has a strong natal link with Virgo, the sign of inner cleanliness.

But mostly, a Scorpio's physical health will revolve around the sexual organs, while the mental health will be at the mercy of any obsession that grips the Scorpio. Some members of this sign can become fixated about their health, and a few of them have actually developed anorexia nervosa, because they had such overpowering obsessions about their figures. Problems like these are all caused by the build-up of those strong, secret, subterranean powers in the Scorpio.

This is a sign that needs to relax, especially with all that intensity and passion smouldering away inside. Positive Scorpios can relax with a bit of a booze-up with their buddies, but negative Scorpios should watch they don't have too much of the hard stuff, because it can unleash torrents of destructive emotions. Alcohol helps to thaw the Plutonian ice on the surface of a Scorpio's character, releasing some things that might be better left in cold storage!

Ideally, a Scorpio should relax in quiet and meditative locations. For instance, a Scorpio, with a Capricorn for company, could parade along the peaks of Snowdonia, burrow through the Brecon Beacons, or ramble by a river. (No, walking, not talking.) This is a Water sign, after all, so watery places will be very attractive.

We mustn't forget the stupendously strong sexual urge – as if Scorpios would let us! They can often unwind by going to cinemas that show blue movies, or perhaps by seeing something just slightly sleazy. And of course, they can relax very well indeed by spending a whole weekend in bed, with a couple of crates of claret for company, either with the one they love or with someone they are paying to be there. Sex really is a very important outlet for most Scorpios.

Scorpios who are strongly Martian will enjoy a good rough and tumble on the rugby field, and all the exploits you would expect an Arian to indulge in. For example, pastimes like potholing will appeal to Scorpios, because they will like the element of risk involved. They also love delving deep into things, and may take classes in psychology, Ancient Egypt, or reincarnation, a subject many Scorpios find fascinating – perhaps because it serves as an awful warning that the worst sins and excesses they commit in this life may backfire on them in the next.

Sagittarius

23 November – 21 December

What Makes Sagittarius Tick

alk about clumsy! If Sagittarians aren't putting both feet in it verbally, they're doing it physically, and landing up to their necks in trouble. If you ask an Archer round for afternoon tea, don't get out the best china. It'll only get broken. (Use some plastic plates instead.) Your Sagittarian pal will rush into the room and trip over the tea table, sending the cups and saucers flying in all directions. Then, to add insult to injury, as your mate dashes off for a dishcloth to mop up the mess, he or she will step on a cream cake and crunch it into the carpet. Still, having your residence wrecked is often better than hearing the truth about yourself, Sagittarian style. Your friend can say 'I saw someone who looked just like you yesterday.' However, before you feel pleased, and start to preen, wait for the punchline. 'Then I realised it was someone else, because you've got more spots.' See what I mean?

But let's look on the bright side – something that's second nature to our jovial pals. Sagittarians are incurable optimists (their beer bottles are always half full, never half empty), and they will inject others with their infectious enthusiasm, given half a chance. If you're feeling really down in the dumps, your Sagittarian pal will bounce up, tell you a joke or two and try to get you giggling again. Go on, give 'em a grin! Jupiter, the planet that rules these Archers, makes them magnificently merry, and they'll try to jolly everyone else along too. The terrific thing about them is that they usually succeed. You can't mooch about moping for long when there's an Archer about.

Because this is the polar sign of garrulous Gemini, Sagittarians are also blessed with the gift of the gab, and can talk the hind leg off a donkey. But there is a mighty difference between these two signs. Astrologically, Gemini is the lower-minded sign, dealing with subjects superficially and knowing a little about a lot, while Sagittarius is the opposite, full of philosophy and worldly wisdoms. (In ancient mythology, the Centaur – the

Sagittarius symbol – was the master of teaching and healing.) During a deep discussion with an Archer, you'll find that they're searching for the meaning of life, and will ponder on the problem all through their existence. ('What's it all about, Alfie?' is definitely the Sagittarian's song!) Faiths and beliefs are all-important to Archers.

Now, it's not for nothing that Sagittarius is the sign of the Archer. There's the hunter, poised with his bow and arrow, all a-quiver, taking aim at a target. Archers do this throughout their lives (always aiming for the bull's-eye), but the trouble is they often aim too high, and miss the target by miles. They set their sights too high (literally!). Sometimes, of course, an Archer will get it right first time, but usually life to these folk is like a rerun of the Battle of Hastings, with arrows flying in all directions. (If you're called Harold, you should head for the hills!)

It's all gigantic Jupiter's doing. Because he's the largest planet in the heavens, he gives some of these Sagittarians ideas above their stations. This can be a terrific trait, because it means that the Sagittarian is always striving for better things. But some Centaurs can go to the opposite extreme and exaggerate everything they come into contact with. As a result, they get everything out of proportion; they bounce about, blowing their own bugles, believing the world can't turn without them. You see, Jupiter knows no bounds – and neither do Sagittarians. (The world doesn't just end at Ambridge for these Archers!)

This is the universal sign, and all Archers are tantalised by travel and the thought of far-flung corners of the globe. Think of the Sagittarians you know. You'll find that lots of them went round the world as soon as they could, or lived in a foreign country at some point in their lives. (Their passports contain more stamps than a Stanley Gibbons catalogue!) This desire to get out and see the world for themselves can be the making of positive Sagittarians. Negative Archers, though, can wax lyrical about their exotic adventures, name-dropping like mad, so it sounds as though they spent a weekend at the White House, when actually they only whizzed past it on a bus.

Jupiter is the planet of luck and opportunity, and some Archers are just like cats, with nine lives. (Some of them are so accident-prone, they need all the help they can get!) You may

think they're gauche and rude, but they call it being honest! They make the most of every opportunity that arises, and can often spot a chance when others don't think it's there. Sometimes that'll be their brilliant perception and vision, and other times it'll be blind faith and living in Cloud-cuckoo-land. It's up to the Archer to decipher the mystical morse code.

Meet a positive Sagittarian and you will be fulfilled in many ways, and imbued with a zest and a zeal for living. But a negative Archer can be crafty, or will let you down in some way or other, whether emotionally or materially. These folk can waste everyone's time, and will bite off more than they can chew. All Sagittarians need challenges; they need to know where to aim their celestial bows and arrows so they can hit the target fair and square. After all, it's much better to climb the ladder of life, rung by rung, than to take a flying leap at it and miss by miles!

Sagittarius Man

Would you like to know a debonair, fancy-free playboy who wins at roulette and is often more at home in Monte Carlo than Monmouthshire? (Unless he comes from Monte Carlo, of course!) Well, then, find yourself a Sagittarian man!

These chaps don't like to be tied down. They're the free-ranging fellows of the zodiac, who can scorn and shun ties and commitments – at least, until they're ready for them. The Sagittarian man needs space to breathe.

When he's young, wherever he hangs his hat is home. He can hanker to hang up his homburg in Hamburg, or his bowler in Bolivia, until he's got the worst of the wanderlust out of his system. I know a Sagittarian man who hiked around the world the minute he left school, got married, divorced, went to live in America and then capered off to Canada. He didn't come back for ten years! These men aren't content to be told that the world is round or that the Antarctic is ice-bound: they've got to find out for themselves. The archetypal Archer was Sir Francis Drake, who couldn't sit still but had to set sail to see the world.

Many Sagittarian men are bachelors, born and bred, and will still feel free even when they've marched down the aisle. Let's not kid ourselves – these chaps like to have the cream of the crop, and they're not ready to make up their minds until they've sorted out the ewes from the nanny goats, and know what's what in the world. Up till then, they need as much variety in their lives as possible. If you're at all possessive, you won't suit the Sagittarian chap, unless he's got a few home-loving planets in his personal make-up. At some point in your partnership your Archer will want to get up and go. He may just meander off for a month, but he might be gone for good if your first reaction is to chain him to his chair and bolt all the doors and windows so he can't escape. You mustn't make this man feel threatened or tied down – even if he is, the trick is to make him think he isn't!

It's the same old story with every Fiery fellow, and the Centaur is no exception. If you want him to notice you, you've got to pretend to ignore him. Remember that this is the hunter of the zodiac, so the Sagittarian man will be a past master at pulling the girls. Show that you're intelligent and interesting to know, and play love's Ludo till you're sure of your ground. Many Sagittarian relationships don't get past the starting-post for ages, because initially the couple don't hit it off. But as they discover facets of each other that they didn't know existed, so their friendship usually grows. Indeed, life with a Sagittarian man can be like your very own voyage of discovery, even if the nearest you get to setting sail for the New World is when you both go boating in Brighton!

When it comes to being a dad, the Sagittarian man doesn't do very well. Very often, he won't be keen on babies, although once he's heard the patter of tiny feet, he'll change his mind. (Unless he feels too hemmed in for words.) Even so, he won't be all that understanding or sympathetic, and his partner might literally be left holding the baby, while he does his own thing without her.

But once his children begin to grow up, he'll change his tune, and enjoy them more. They'll be able to participate in proper conversations, and he'll get them thinking about the meaning of life and similar serious subjects. Jupiter will have shone his jovial rays on him, so he'll be full of fun, and will make his children chortle with mirth and merriment when the mood takes him.

As far as looks go, he's usually tall and fair. Keep your beady eyes peeled and you'll see that stacks of Sagittarians have very high foreheads. It's not a polite way of saying they're going bald, but that they have so much brain, they've got to make way for it! Christopher Cazenove looks very Sagittarian. Another archetypal Archer is Ian Botham, who's not only an international cricketer but also, so they say, a playboy. And you can't get more Sagittarian than that! As for Winston Churchill – no one sounded more Saggy!

Sagittarius Woman

What a friendly female! With her lively mind and frank face, she can't lose. (Till she puts both feet in it.)

This is a liberated lass, and she'll want to be liked for herself, not because she's got long blonde locks or big blue eyes. She's not usually quite as footloose and fancy-free as the fellows of this sign, but she'll still want to skip off to the wide blue yonder every now and then – even if the nearest she can get to it is a holiday programme on the telly.

It's very important that the Archerette shouldn't get spliced at sixteen. She's got to get out and see the world before she can settle down for good. Otherwise, she'll kick over the traces later, which could cause havoc.

One thing she'll never stop doing is learning. Sagittarians of both sexes have a never-ending need for knowledge and self-discovery; they're always discovering new subjects and learning about them, running the whole gamut from Abyssinian to Zen Buddhism. So, a Sagittarian girl who got married too early, and now feels stifled, should join an evening class or the Open University.

The Archerette isn't the most maternally-motivated of maidens, but she'll do her best to bring up her kids to be bright bundles of joy. She'll also respect her children, and put them on an equal footing with herself. She'll really excel as her kid's *confidante*. She won't be an old fogey or stick-in-the-mud; instead she'll encourage her children to be themselves. She's so honest that she has to tell them the truth as she sees it. After all, she's always followed her own star, so why shouldn't they? The most important part of her children's development, though, will be their brains, and she'll see they're as clever as they can be and use every ounce of grey matter.

Any man who expects his Archerette to play the part of the little woman, and be treated like a sexy servant, is going to get a nasty shock. She's a feminist through and through and will show flashes of her Fiery temper if her man only mutters mundane things to her. She believes that she's a woman in her own right. Jane Fonda is a typical Sagittarian; she's not afraid to speak up for what she believes in, and she combines a career and a family by working hard at both of them.

An intellectual focus is important to the Archerette, who needs something to stimulate her mind. Otherwise she'll become furious and fed up. Restriction is anathema to all Archers, whether they're living in miniature maisonettes, or married to people with minute minds. So, if a Sagittarian girl is spliced to someone who can't keep her in the manner to which she's mentally accustomed, she may float off with the first fellow who comes along blessed with brainpower.

Don't forget that all Sagittarians are rovers. (No, dear, I said 'rovers', although they are ravers too.) They like nothing better than roaming about the world, meeting people and having captivating conversations. So, ideally, the Sagittarian girl needs to find a fella who loves travelling too, and then they can rove off into the sunset together.

Because they are ruled by Jupiter – the planet of expansion – some Sagittarian women promise far more than they can ever deliver. Many moons ago I was really down on my uppers, and an Archerette offered to lend me some loot any time I needed it. When I was down to my last crust of bread, I went to borrow some boodle. 'Oh!' she said. 'If only you'd asked me yesterday. I've just paid the gas bill and now I'm broke, too.' Sometimes they mean their promise when they make it, at other times they have no intention of coming up with the goods, even when they're saying otherwise – it just sounded good at the time!

Archerettes can also drop names in all directions, and lead you up the garden path till you truly believe what they're telling you. A Sagittarian woman I once met kept mentioning someone called Charles, who'd been at a gala theatre do the night before. Pretty soon the penny dropped that it was Prince Charles. It sounded as though she'd shared not only the royal box, but the royal choc ice with him too! Imagine my surprise when the next day someone said the Archerette had just been selling programmes, and hadn't even got within curtseying distance of our next, royal ruler!

So take it from me. Don't believe everything you hear a Sagittarian say, and you won't go too far wrong. Then you'll see the right and bright side of these sensational Sagittarians.

Sagittarius Child

Baby Centaurs are like miniature whirlwinds, whizzing about and making your hair stand on end. (Either because they're so fast or you're so frightened. What are they going to do next?) You've got to keep them occupied, otherwise who knows what will happen. And if you've got any Archer kids, for goodness' sake don't leave them to their own devices, or you could return from the shops to find you have no house left! They'll have gone through it like a dose of salts!

One thing you need if you have a Sagittarian child is plenty of patience. You've also got to devote a lot of time to your kid, and be prepared to do something together every day. You may be lucky enough to have a babe who buries their bonce in a book for an hour, but just when you've made a cuppa and put your feet up, your kid will toss the book on the fire and start rushing around again.

Make sure that, even at an early age, your Archerette has lots of little pals to play with, and pack 'em off to kindergarten as soon as you can. Even if you're a Cancerian, and can't bear to see your fledglings leave the nest, you must let your Sagittarian kid get a taste of the big wide world at an early age. After all, he or she will still scamper home from school ready to play.

Once your child's a little older, he or she will love going to school. But there has to be at least one free-ranging teacher who can let that already open and enquiring mind expand even more, and soak up knowledge left, right and centre. These children will give classes like carpentry a miss, but go bananas over subjects such as geography, English, religious studies and foreign languages. Then, as for their Gemini opposites, school will be something they really enjoy.

You may as well know now that if the school is organising a trip to foreign parts, whether to Ostend or Omsk, your Sagittarian kid will want to go. In fact, it'll do him or her a world of good, so try to scrape together the loot. Remember that Archers have an innate ambition to see as much of the world as they can and it's only fair to give them the chance at an early age to peak at parts of it.

If you do mollycoddle your Archerette, or restrict him or her, you may have a wayward child on your hands. After all, this is a Fire sign, so you must get your kid's mind working on a positive level. Like Geminis, a very negative Sagittarian child will turn to petty theft, such as shop-lifting, in order to relieve the boredom, and rebel against the world. Don't let your Archerette go to waste in this way, because this is a sign that has oodles of intelligence to offer, if it's channelled in the right directions.

Watch out for religion, if you have a Sagittarian kiddie. A lot of adult Archers adopt a different devotion to that of their parents, simply because they weren't allowed to think for themselves when they were young. Sagittarians question the creeds on which they were brought up, and you must let them do this. Don't rant and rave about religion – let them work it out for themselves. This is such an interesting and intelligent sign that your Sagittarian kid is bound to come up with an answer. It might even set *you* thinking!

Sagittarius in Love

Don't expect life to be one long lullaby if you tumble for a
Centaur. It's more likely to be a swift Sagittarian serenade,
followed by a Jupiterian jive, and then an Archer
arabesque. In fact, it can be all sorts of things, rolled into one.

Sagittarians aren't naturally amorous or romantic, and could
take a few leaves out of a Libran's book in this delicious
demonstrative department. Because they're the hunters of the
celestial sky, these folk go all out for the chase. They can woo you
till it's swoonsville season, and you wonder if what you've heard
about them is true. But once Archers have you lined up in their
sights, and have fired that bow and arrow, it'll be a different story.

The Sagittarian won't race off in pursuit of the next quarry,
unless you were a passing fancy, or your amour is too superficial
for words. But you can kiss goodbye to those rhapsodic romantic
renditions you used to hear. It'll be different now, dear! Your
Archer will still adore you, but may forget to say so. Try dropping
a few hints; and if they fail, come straight out with it! It's no good
beating about the bush with these Fiery folk – they just won't get
your drift. On your birthday, for example, you might wake up and
expect to see a pressie waiting for you at the breakfast table. But
you'll get nowt. Now, it's no good sulking all day, because your
Archer amour won't know what you're on about. Be positive
instead of petulant, and say 'You've forgotten my birthday!'
(If still nothing happens, then it's time to have a tantrum!)

Love may mean never having to say you're sorry to some folk,
but to an Archer it means 'You go your way and I'll go mine'. (To
selfish Sagittarians it's 'I'll go my way and you stay at home
waiting for me to come back'.) Sagittarians hate to be tied down,
either by people or places; they need to feel they're free – even if
they never do anything about it. And because they're such
intellectual individuals, they'll let you know of their love by
lending you their library books, or taking you off on a trip to
Turkey. They often prefer to sit chatting into the wee small hours

about reincarnation rather than romance. Don't be too disappointed if that happens to you – because it's the Sagittarian way of showing they care.

One word of warning. Because all Sagittarians are superficial to some extent, they can get love and lust all muddled up. They don't realise that there's a sublime and divine difference between the two, and can leap in and out of bed like a Yo-Yo, naively thinking it's love, when really it's something quite different!

If you've set your cap at an Archer man, forget what your mother told you about being coy and coquettish. You've got to play hard to get, but not in a flimsy, whimsical way. Flirt outrageously, tease and tantalise him, but don't give in too soon. Keep him on his toes, but don't mess about so much that he gets bored, or he'll career off after the next conquest, leaving you high and dry.

And if you want to grab a Sagittarian girl you must be some sort of social success. (Even if it's just the caller at the local bingo parlour.) Alternatively, you must own something scintillating. Take your pick between a smashing sense of humour or a wallet bulging with credit cards. It all depends on the Sagittarian. She might be after your flashy white sports car, or she might be after your heart. Try her and see!

Sagittarius as a Friend

A re you feeling a mite moody and morose? Has your dog developed distemper, or is your bank manager getting obstreperous about your overdraft? Yes? Then seek out a Sagittarian. If anyone can cheer you up, it's an Archer.

There is a slight snag, though. You can't be low-spirited for long. If you're still wandering about like a wet weekend after a fortnight of the Archer's attempts to animate you, you could find yourself friendless. Their Mutability means that these folk get bored easily and some of them will ditch a friend who's spouting the same sad story for months on end. It's sad to say that Sagittarians aren't very loyal. (Unless a Fixed sign colours their natal chart.)

Like their opposite numbers, Geminis, Archers have very few real mates, but an army of acquaintances. To become the friend of a Taurean, you've got to have known 'em for yonks before you're accepted and allowed into their select circle. But with a Sagittarian, it's quite a different story. A pal can be a drinking partner, a business acquaintance, or even someone the Sagittarian has spoken to at the bus stop! And if you're the faintest bit famous, you may be surrounded by shoals of Sagittarians, because they're the groupies of the zodiac. Of course, not all Archers are hangers-on, but many of them can't resist the chance of a soirée with a starlet.

So, sometimes, to be the buddy of an Archer, you don't have to do much and, if you've got a claim to fame, your success is secured. (Say you've just finished your latest film – and don't let on that it's one that's sitting in your Kodak Brownie!) But if you want the palship of a positive Archer, you must be bright and brainy, and a bundle of laughs. It also helps to have a hotch-potch of hobbies, because Sagittarians love doing lots of different things. They get bored very quickly if you always go to bingo together and then buy fish and chips on the way home. If you want some Jupiterian jollification you must be more adventurous than

that. Ring the changes every now and then (are you a campanologist?), or beat these Sagittarians at their own game and take up archery together. (But for goodness sake make sure you're never within fifteen feet of the target when the Archer's taking aim. These creatures are so cack-handed they may miss, and get your bum as the bull's-eye!)

Because Sagittarians have such a fund of friends, they're always out and about, and have different mates to do different things with. They won't have just one best friend. So you might see your Mutable mate for an hour, as you glide round a gallery together, before the Archer ambles off to see someone else. It's all go for these jocular Jupiterians.

With their love of travel, you're bound to be asked to go on holiday with your Sagittarian pal. If your plans actually come to fruition (some Sagittarians always let you down at the last minute, come what may), don't expect to lie on a beach for two weeks, sizzling in the sun: you'll be bounding about in all directions, marching up mountains, tiptoeing through the tulips, canooing down a canal, reading the Dead Sea Scrolls or free-fall parachuting. (Rather you than me, dear!) Then, just as you've fallen into a soothing slumber at the end of a dynamic day, your buddy will burst in, clutching a guidebook. 'Guess what!' they'll yell. 'Our hotel is built on an ancient burial ground. Get a spade and let's go digging at dawn!' There's one thing you can say about this sign – life is never staid with a Sagittarian!

Sagittarius at Work

Fancy a holiday? Well, trip off to a travel agent and check what's behind the counter. If the person you're prattling away to knocks all the brochures on to the floor by accident while expounding on the exotic excitement of Egypt, you've found an agent who's an Archer. Make the most of it, because you'll see a Sagittarian at their most stupendous, but be careful you're not carried away by this enthusiasm and talked into a trip to Tibet instead of a weekend in Wigan, which was what you wanted! (Some Sagittarians have powerful powers of persuasion!)

In fact, anything associated with travel is the perfect profession for most of these Jupiterian girls and boys. They all crave to get out and about to see the seven wonders of the world. (Though they'll turn them into seventeen sights, with their effortless exaggeration!) And if they're not blessed with the boodle to do it under their own steam, they'll get a job that pays them to fly off into the wide blue yonder, or at the very least be in contact with other countries. So, you'll find lots of Sagittarians who are pilots, and others who rush about on runways, encased in enormous ear-muffs, clutching two table-tennis bats! Other Archers hear the call of the sea, and sail off round the world. (After all, any port in a storm!)

But not every Sagittarian wants to travel as a profession. Other jolly Jupiterians embark on jobs that are journeys of the mind. Make no mistake, this is an intellectual sign, and Sagittarians can be real clever clogs, blessed with bags of brainpower. Because they're Mutable beings, they can see both sides to a story, and make superb solicitors and brilliant barristers.

All Archers are born with a thirst for knowledge that will never be quenched, though some will spend their whole lives trying to do so. So Sagittarians make stunning students, especially if they nurture the mental discipline to see something through from start to finish and not give up half-way through because they're bored.

(What they shouldn't do, though, is dive in at the deep end and enroll for a course on politics, when they think that Karl Marx is one part of the pair that makes the nation's knickers!) Archers who've drunk deeply at the well of wisdom and paddled in the fountain of knowledge will want to impart that knowledge to others, and will become teachers and lecturers, even if only in their spare time.

Being batty about books, many Archers pick publishing as their profession. (No prizes for guessing that they'll want to work on tomes on travel and philosophy!) You'll get a few Jupiterian jockeys, too, because Archers adore horses. Actually, they enjoy all of our four-legged friends, and can make great vets. (Sagittarians with a love of the large will fly off to Africa to become elephant doctors!) Higher-minded Archers can have vocations, and will become anything from a Dean to a Druid. (Did you know that plenty of Popes have been born under this sign?)

But whatever job the Jupiterian goes for – whether it's working in a fast-food franchise, handing out the hamburgers, or being a guru in Guildford – the one thing it can't be is full of routine. Archers abhor nine-to-five jobs, and are at their happiest when they don't know what the next hour will bring. They hate to be stuck in offices and factories day in, day out, doing the same old things with the same old people. They'll always find some excuse to escape; so if you work with an Archer who's unaccountably absent, you'll know why. They'll either have peeked in at the pub for a pint, or will have hared off to Heathrow and popped on a plane to Peru! (Don't say I didn't warn you!)

Sagittarius at Home

Amble into an Archer's abode, and you'll think you've landed in the local library by mistake. There'll be books on shelves, books on floors, books on tables – even books in the bath! (Well, they've got to keep them somewhere!) And it doesn't matter whether the Archer likes reading Agatha Christie or Anton Chekov – there'll still be tons of tomes.

You'll find a mixture of moods in the Sagittarian residence, ranging from culture to kitsch. Because Archers have a hundred different interests, these will be reflected in the decor. As a result, the Sag's pad will be like a colourful cocktail, and it'll either make you feel as high as a kite or as sick as a parrot!

Since Sagittarians are so spasmodic – fired with enthusiasm one minute and overcome by *laissez-faire* the next – it's always a toss-up whether their homes will be spick and span with not a smudge in sight, or knee-deep in dust and dross. You've just got to take pot luck! (If you're a clean Virgo, you'll take a portable air-freshener, too!)

You know that geezer who yelled 'A horse, a horse, my kingdom for a horse'? Well, he must have been an Archer, because Sagittarians love anything equine. (After all, they're half horses themselves!) So there'll be some equine evidence about, even if it's just a glass galloper sitting on a shelf. There's bound to be a pet or two about. Archers aren't crazy about cats, preferring to have a pooch on the mooch. (Better than having a mouse about the house!)

Nearly all Sagittarians suffer from itchy feet (no, it's not something they do to their socks!), and are always dreaming of their next foray into foreign parts. So, during the dreary winter months, the home will be littered with travel brochures and holiday guides, as the Centaur plans a pleasure trip or two. (Ask if you can go along for the ride.) There will also be some subtle signs of the Jovian junkets to Java or Jutland – a pile of plates brought back from the place, or a pretty picture. (Sagittarians don't go

overboard, the way some signs do, hanging Spanish sombreros on the walls or dotting terribly tatty trinkets about the place – although there are always the exceptions who like to prove they *have* been there!)

What you might find, though, are reminders of religions, ranging from ancient to modern, Eastern to orthodox. It's not unusual to see a Buddha nestling next to a rosary. (Rummage through the bookshelves and you'll see books on philosophy and the world's religions, too.)

The foreign flavour will flood over to the furnishings, too, and there'll be Turkish carpets galore. All the colours will be rich with imperial reds, blues and purples, making you feel as if you've come to the kasbah. Keep a protective eye on the possessions, though. Sagittarians can own the most valuable vases, giving them pride of place. But the next time you turn up, they'll have vanished without trace. You'll have to hold on to more than your hat when you're told where they've gone. 'Oh, I threw them in the dustbin,' the Archer will announce. 'I got bored with them!' (If you're a careful Capricorn, you'll cry!)

Saggittarius

Sagittarius
Health and Relaxation

The heavens have just opened, and you're standing at the bus stop with your brolly. Suddenly, you see someone striding into sight, smiling through the shower. 'Lovely day for a stroll' says this wet and wacky walker, whizzing past. Don't label them as a loony – that was a Sagittarian.

Archers have to be active; they can't bear to be cooped up. Many Sags are sporty, and find that sprinting themselves silly works a treat when they want to unwind and relax. (*Relax!* I should think they collapse and keel over, then start snoring on the spot!) If an Archer doesn't fancy bowling a maiden over on the cricket pitch, or winning game, set and match, he or she will still be sporty somehow – even if it's just dispensing drinks behind the bar at the cricket club. (Or consuming them!) A Sagittarian stuck in front of the telly on a dull day will watch all things sporty, from *Grandstand* to racing at Newmarket.

If an Archer can't be active physically, then he or she will go on a journey of the mind, and relax that way. That can mean reading about far-flung places, or becoming immersed in something philosophical or literary. Astrology is one subject which can really get them going, and they love to delve deeply into it, looking for the real reason people are the way they seem. Sagittarians are truly the philosophers of the zodiac, and can shrug off situations that would stun other signs. It means they don't get quite so het-up when things go wrong, although you can still expect a tirade or two. (After all, this is a Fire sign!)

As far as their health is concerned, Sagittarians don't do too badly. When you think of a sign's health and well-being, you have to consider their opposite numbers in the zodiac, because they can suffer from the same complaints. Geminis have troubles with their chests, so Sagittarians should avoid that by cutting down on cigarettes and wrapping up warmly in the winter. They may also find it all too easy to hurt their arms. (And they're already so clumsy that anything could happen!)

Because these folk are ruled by jocund Jupiter, the largest planet in the solar system, they in turn rule the liver, the largest organ in the body. (And if an Archer guzzles too much, it'll get even larger!) So, all the ailments associated with the liver will afflict the Archers – from cirrhosis to hepatitis – if they don't control the amount of rich grub and booze they put back. Another Sagittarian danger point is the thighs, and they're often where the flab falls when an Archer expands.

Sluggish Sagittarians will probably be feeling under the weather because they've had one over the eight. It's a very Jupiterian thing to go over the top, and be indulgent, but it can only lead to problems for these people. So they should take extra care, and make sure they don't bite off more than they can chew – literally!

Capricorn

22 December – 20 January

What Makes Capricorn Tick

Right, repeat after me, 'Capricorns are captivating'. Say it again. Got it? Good. Now remember it, and forget what you might have heard about these folk being morose and melancholic. You will find some Goats with a grouse, because there are positive and negative folks in every sign, but a together Goat can be gorgeous.

Let's get the worst over first with this sign. Some Capricorns can be the original wet blankets, moaning and misanthropic, complaining and carping, and generally being gloomy old things. You'll look at them and think 'I don't want to know you'. But if you bother to get to know them, you can have the time of your life. Talk about giggle!

One of the tremendous traits of this bunch is their superb sense of humour and wit that's as dry as a bone, but much more fun. They can take the mickey out of everything – including themselves, which makes them very endearing indeed. And they really do act the goat, making you laugh until your sides split. Once you've glimpsed the sensational side of this sign, you can turn a blind eye to its more *triste* traits, because you'll have found the silver lining to the Capricorn cloud. (And the crock of gold at the end of the rainbow, if the Goat has Taurus rising.)

Some negative Capricorns can pick holes in everything – even if they hit the jackpot at bingo, they'll moan about having to spend all that money. The poor things can't express their emotions, either, and will bottle up all their feelings and frustrations.

When you meet a Capricorn, expect them to act older than their years. Goats age in the opposite way to the rest of us, behaving as if they were fifty when they're only five, and seven when they're seventy. This means that Capricorns make elderly-seeming babies and young-at-heart pensioners. When the rest of us are being put out to grass, Goats are just coming into their own!

This is a sign that believes in experience, with a capital 'E'. They never have an easy life until they've blown out all the candles

196

on their thirtieth birthday cakes. Until then, life will have been one long struggle; the only way for them to survive is to learn by experience. (Capricorns hate wasting *anything!*) Many of them will have had cramped childhoods, awful adolescences and terrible twenties. But they'll have terrific thirties, fantastic forties – even naughty nineties!

There are two types of Goat – the ones who cavort and curvet up the crags to the summit of their own mountainsides, and the ones who are domestic, and like to potter about their own pieces of pasture, never straying far from the fireside. Capricorns are Cardinal, making them astoundingly ambitious, and even the domestic ones will be determined to do well. Success for them, though, isn't totally based on boodle (although they'd never refuse owt for nowt!); honour, public position and status all smell sweet to them.

Capricorns need security, which they get from the tried, true and tested. They love history, and anything with a past (this could mean you), because then they feel safe. Capricorns are conservative, canny and cautious, and are suspicious of new-fangled things, until they get used to them. They hate to fly in the face of convention.

They're very wary of wearing out their wallets, too. They believe that if they take care of the farthings, the pennies will look after themselves. More positive Goats would call them-selves careful, and will be generous with their loot when they've got it, and laugh about it when they haven't. (Always with a note of caution in their grin!)

Guilt is a very Goaty thing, and some Capricorns thrive on it, putting everyone through the mill, including themselves. They can set themselves impossibly high ideals, and almost galactic goals, and then hate themselves when they fail to reach them. Because just as they hate waste, they also can't abide failure. (It's a good job they're imbued with endurance and endeavour!) They are deeply determined and disciplined, so can drive themselves to hit heights others only dream of.

But not all Goats are quite so positive. Some delight in the doldrums, like grumpy old Eeyore in *Winnie the Pooh* – a donkey who's always down in the dumps. But still everyone adored him. In fact, with a little understanding, you are sure to have fun with even the most morose Goat: laugh with them, but never at them, and you'll never feel down!

Capricorn Man

Gosh! Now here's a man who knows where he's going (No, not round to the pub for a pint!) Straight to the top! Want to see how he does it? Come on, then.

Capricorn chaps have got it all worked out in advance. Just as their stern ruler, Saturn, is surrounded by circles, so Capricorns are limited by their very own rings. They know exactly what they can do, and will do it well. No more and no less. Whereas some signs can go mad, and try to take over the world (or Penge at the very least!), these men know their limitations, and abide by them. Sometimes this will ensure stupendous success; but at other times it can mean the Goat is hidebound by his own hangups, and won't step out of line or take a risk, strangled by his own rules and regulations.

Money and these men seem to go together, like cheese and chutney, or curry and chips. Just to show you how accurate astrology can be, the multi-millionaire Howard Hughes was a Capricorn.

Because this is a conservative, careful sign, Capricorn men have an aura of respectability, and many of them will become pillars of society. (No, dear, I said pillars, not pillows. We're talking about *suc*cess not sex. Better read Scorpio if that's what you're after!) They will worry about the opinions of other people, and try to toe the line in everything they do. But don't think that they're one long yawn, because nothing could be further from the truth. When these fellows let their hair down, it'll take you a week to recover!

Now, fathers are very important for all Capricorns, and the Goaty lad will feel he has the shadow of his dad hovering over him all the time – like a ghost that won't go away. (Look what happened to Hamlet!) Even if he didn't get on with him, he'll be beset by guilt (a very Capricorn complaint) and wracked with worries that he hasn't done his duty to his dad, whether by following in his footsteps, or carrying out his laws to the letter. If the guilt gets too ingrained he'll be pulverised by a lack of self-confidence. But if he re-routes this sense of responsibility into the correct channels, he'll go from strength to strength, and the sky will be the limit. (He could become a pilot, although most Goats prefer to keep their hooves on terra firma.)

As a result of these feelings about his father, he won't be the most dynamic of dads, and there may be a hint of harshness about him. He'll find it difficult to figure out what makes his tiny terrors tick, because he was never really a kid himself – even when he was knee-high to a grasshopper he was a tiny adult. When he's feeling witty, he'll have his offspring doubled up with mirth, and at other times he can be wonderfully wise. But the minute his kiddie's satchel swings over the step, he'll become like Rumpelstiltskin – always putting his foot down. In fact, he can be a real old wotsit when it comes to his kids' homework, standing over them until they've done it. (There's no maths while watching *Minder* in this house!) But when the patter of tiny feet is heard second time around, and the Goat is a grandfather, he'll be a riot. By now, he may say he's sixty, but he'll behave like a sixteen-year-old, given half the chance! (Ever seen an old age punk, with his pension book chained to his cheek? That's a Goaty grandad!)

The Capricorn man, if he's a Goat that's going places, can become a workaholic, sacrificing the needs of family and friends to his files, facts and figures. 'Not now, Norah, I'm working' can become the constant Capricorn cry, as he clicks away at his computer or calculator into the small hours. He's got to learn to let go, and show his family that he does care about them, before he's left with just his briefcase to go to bed with!

Both the men and the women of this sign can be appealing or austere, *soigné* and sophisticated, or scruffy and smelly. Some of them look like walking dustbins – I knew a Capricorn fella who wore the same sweater for two solid years! (The sweater was solid, too, because he didn't wash it once!) These men sometimes baulk at baths too, and think that if they get caught in a cloudburst, that's their wash for another week! But before you give the elbow to your Capricorn chap, or grab a clothes peg for your nose, not all Goats are like this! Some are quite clean and tidy, and exude the sweet smell of success, not an awful aroma at all.

Whether clean or not, Capricorn men are usually wiry; their ruler, Saturn, makes most of them dark. They tend to be short, but what they lack in inches they they more than make up for in

personality. When he's young, this fella often looks older than he really is, and a fifteen-year-old will look twice his age. But once he reaches thirty, that's the way he'll stay. (By the time he's sixty, he'll almost be able to pay half fares on the buses!) Goats can grow old very gracefully. Capricorns in the public eye include Cary Grant, who's got the lot – looks and laughter – and Michael Aspel, who's incredibly boyish. And last but not least is my friend Frank Bough, who sits beside me on the *Breakfast Time* sofa. What more can I say?

Capricorn Woman

S trong is not the word! Some Capricornettes (Italian Goats are Capricornettos!) can make Henry Cooper look as camp as a row of tents! Don't think they're butch, because they're not. It's just they they're imbued with an astounding authority, which can make you think twice (or even three times!).

Now, it's a funny thing, but the Goaty girl often ties the nuptial knot with a man as wishy-washy as a cup of BBC tea. This is so she can be the boss and the breadwinner, and feel like the father-figure of the family. Of course, not all Goatettes marry men who are mice, but a surprising number of them do. (At least it makes supper simple – goats' cheese on toast!) When they feel that things are getting out of hand, they'll be coy and coquettish for a day or two, and then revert to ruling the roost! If you spy someone striding round the supermarket on a Saturday while her husband hurries along behind, clutching a carrier bag and trying to keep the trolley on the straight and narrow, you've just glimpsed one of these Goaty girls. Other Capricorn women marry men who are sitting in the biggest branches at the top of the tree, and they feel profoundly proud of them. Then it's the men who wear the trousers. But it's all or nothing – there are no half-way houses for Capricorns.

For another astrological exercise, next time you pop along to the Post Office, keep your peepers peeled. See that old man with a pension book, and his glamorous granddaughter next to him? Well, if she's a Goat she won't be his granddaughter – she'll be his wife! Capricorn women often adore older men, and sometimes think nothing of an age gap of anything up to thirty years. Most of them like a father figure.

Once a mum, this girl will be emotionally wrapped up in her kids, and will want to guide them through life, pointing out pitfalls and helping them over them. Sometimes she can be interfering, offering too much of a helping hoof, wanting her kids to meet ambitions she was unable to fulfil herself. But she can also be supremely supportive, and a great help to her kids (giving them a nudge with her horns if they need it!).

Capricorns are the salt of the earth (you can ignore the health warnings), and these girls make great mums. But what you must remember is that they will never be over-emotional, claustrophobic and cloying. Instead, they'll be determined, disciplined, law-abiding and loving. (A sort of Mighty Mum!) Sometimes they can be too firm, causing clashes and confrontations, especially when their tots turn into teenagers. ('You're not going out looking that that,' they'll yell. 'What would the neighbours think?')

You'll never catch a Goatette gushing like a geyser, unless she has lashings of Leo, Libra or Watery placings in her chart. But even so, she'll be more emotionally effusive than her male counterpart, simply because she *is* a woman.

At an early age, this nanny goat will have had to decide whether she's going to be a domestic damsel, content to caper among the cabbages in her garden or the go-getting girl, bounding up the mountainside of life, bopping over the boulders and being tipped for the top. But work is so central to a Capricorn that she's bound to do something to bring in the boodle, whether it's a few bob or a couple of hundred quid. Most girl Goats need a special goal in life to aspire to.

Nothing in life ever falls into this lady's lap (unless it's a spider or two – money ones, of course!). Instead, she'll have to scrimp and save, or drive herself like a dervish, to get what she wants. But the gorgeous thing about these Goats, if they're positive, is that they put down trials and tribulations to experience, and try to profit from misfortunes and mistakes. And when they turn their sensational sense of humour on themselves, you know you're looking at a winner.

These women can work themselves up from nowt, and tip the very top. Take Gracie Fields, for example – an excellent example of a Goat who got everything through sheer hard graft.

When you meet a Capricorn woman for the first time, take a peek at her pins. Lovely, aren't they? This is a sign full of sense and style, and a classy Capricornette is a sight to behold! Some girl Goats can glow with grace and glamour, and stun in their smart sophistication. (Others can look like something the cat brought in.) All that and a sense of humour, too – who could ask for anything more?

Capricorn Child

Now, let's get one thing straight before we go any further: there's no such thing as a Capricorn child! But hang on a minute before you have a butchers at the birth certificate. Your Capricorn kid may look five to you, but he or she is much older inside. Actually, if you have a gander at some kids, you'll find that they can look like pint-sized pensioners. But don't worry, they get younger as they become older. Your little Goat will be much more canny, clever and clear-thinking than you!

It's an odd thing, but Capricorn kids often have one parent who's stronger than the other in some way. I don't necessarily mean that their mum is the strongest woman in the world, while their dad is a seven-stone weakling. Instead, one of their parents may have died, they may be divorced, or the mum's a missionary in darkest Africa. Grandparents often play a large part in a Goat's early years, and may be the ones who bring the kid up. But whatever the reason, it'll make the kid grow up much earlier than his or her pals, and be mature at an early age. (Like a precocious Cheddar cheese! And in some cases a stringent Stilton.)

As a result, Goatlettes learn to live with the slings and arrows (must be an Archer about!) of outrageous fortune at an early age, and are imbued with responsibility and resourcefulness. Sometimes it means they stick out like sore thumbs at school, and find it hard to fit in with kids of their own age. In fact, it's more than likely for a Goatlette's best mate to be a couple of years older.

If your kid hasn't got any grandparents, see if you can adopt some, fast! Capricorn kids get on great with these folk, because they understand each other, and will have cosy chats together.

You must remember that a Capricorn child has an old head on young shoulders. (No, you can't see the join!) Your kid won't want to play all the time, and may prefer to mooch round a maths book, or go for a walk. (But that doesn't mean these children are boring, because they're not, especially if you encourage their straight-faced sense of humour.) So next time you bake a cake, get your kid

to lend a hand, rather than pack him or her off to play. Capricorns are constantly learning, and need to experience life at first hand.

With all this miniature maturity, you'd think your child would be sensational at school, but that's not always the case. This is an Earth sign, after all, so your kid will be phlegmatic, and not as alert and active as an Air or Fire child. But unless you dropped your Goatlette on the head when a baby, this kid won't be stupid. Sometimes, school reports will leave a lot to be desired, because your child will be bored, having already read all the textbooks! (These kids love reading school-books while their buddies are buried in the Beano.)

If you understand your Goatlette, are kind and bestow a lot of love, you'll bring out the pure gold that lurks within this sign, and bring up a real kid to be proud of. Your kiddiwink will be happy scouring statistics, and gazing at gazeteers. Now, who wouldn't want a babe like that? Saves you constantly washing out football shorts or party frocks!

Capricorn in Love

L ove isn't a many-splendoured thing to Capricorns. It's not an easy emotion for them to feel. Some of them are more at home with ambition than amour. (It's safer.)

Capricorns don't give themselves a chance when it comes to love. Very often, they erect obstacles between themselves and the objects of their affections, which give them a good excuse not to act upon their feelings. The trouble is that they're terrified by the thought of rejection, and will do anything to avoid it. As a result, gaggles of Goats (OK, I know you only get gaggles of geese!) opt for unrequited love. It's easier that way. They'll go through the agonies and the ecstasies of amour, but from afar. The thought of inviting their inamorata to come dancing or go bowling will send them into paroxysms of panic. And if they do pluck up the courage and are then turned down, they may curl up and die on the spot. Instead of saying 'What about next week?', they'll slink off, scarred for life and feeling very, very sorry for themselves.

You see, all Capricorns are convinced that folk find them funny, and laugh about them behind their backs. Even if they're having a happy relationship, they can find it hard to believe that their amour doesn't really think they're one big belly laugh. This is often a figment of their imaginations, but they can torture themselves terribly. They underestimate themselves, often to a dramatic degree.

Capricorns who've been caught by Cupid can be quite melancholic and masochistic, so their loved ones should try to jolly them up, and make them feel cherished. Give your Goat a hundred hugs a day and see what happens. (Probably, your amour will scowl at you suspiciously and say 'What are you trying to hide?'. They're a suspicious lot.)

Because love can be confusing to Capricorns, married Goats may more often be seized by a sense of family duty than by fervent desire. This can make them seem slightly chilly, and in fact most Goats find it hard to show their feelings. They don't lavish you with love, although it'll be there under the surface. Capricorns aren't adept at announcing amour, because they think they sound a mite trite. If one day you throw a wobbly and say 'You don't love me', your old Goat will gaze at you and say 'Yes I do. I've lived with you for twenty years, haven't I?'.

Being an Earth sign, Capricorns are no slouches when it comes to sex. (Some of them are really randy ruminants and bounce in and out of beds like a jack-in-the-box.) But sometimes even sex will be seen as a duty.

Now, suppose you've set your cap (or your hair-net) at a Goat, but don't know what to do. Well, there are three golden rules, and if you follow them, you can't go wrong. Firstly, punctuality is a must. Goats hate to waste even a minute. Secondly, take your loot with you, and offer to pay for something, whether it's the port and lemons or the plaice and chips. And lastly, make 'em laugh! Be warm, witty and wonderful, and as bright as a button. Do all this and you'll be well on the way to success. (What a Capricorn word that is!) Good luck!

Capricorn as a Friend

Friendship, friendship, that's the perfect friendship! Whoever warbled that must have been going on about the Goats. They make perfect pals, and are loyal, level-headed, and a lot of laughs. What more could you want?

Like their fellow Earth signs, Taurus and Virgo, you can always count on a Capricorn when you're in a spot of bother. They're supportive and sensible, and real pillars of strength. Goats have a stupendously strong sense of duty and responsibility to the ones they love. They will always rally round and hold your hand in a crisis (you lucky thing!), drawing on their wealth of worldly wisdom to find a scheme to save your skin. And well-hoofed ones may even lend you some of their loot to tide you over if your bank manager is seeing red. (Your overdraft.) However, they'll expect to be repaid when you're back in the black!

A Capricorn chum will stand by you through thick and thin. (In fact, he or she won't care how many diets you indulge in!) But when the boot is on the other foot, and it's your mate who's in misery, you may not be allowed to return the compliment. These Goats are stunningly self-sufficient and self-contained, and like to cope alone. When you offer advice, the Goat will grin and say 'Not today, thank you'. (You're not a milkman, are you?) Negative nanny goats, of course, will take your offer of help as their cue to totter at your tootsies, saying they can't go on.

Though Goats make fine friends, you may have hassles getting them interested in the first place. They're not the most sociable of signs, preferring an evening by the fire to a night on the tiles, and only gad and gallivant about like giddy Goats if a lively sign is part of their natal make-up.

When you first encounter a Capricorn (usually through work), pay attention. When the Goat thinks the coast is clear, he or she will clock you carefully to size you up and see that you're suitable. (As you might imagine, Capricorns like to sort out the sheep from the goats. They don't want woolly one-hit wonders when they could have hairy humdingers.) Capricorns don't like socialising for the sake of it, because they've got better things to do with their time. So you've got to be worth getting to know, or you'll never climb on to their social lists.

And talking of climbing, that's just what these Goats do. Capricorns may not be aware of it themselves, but they are socially ambitious. As a result, you must be able to offer your Capricorn chum something apart from friendship at some point in your relationship. If you're a failure, you may be on dangerous ground; your Capricorn pal will begin by helping you, but if all is in vain, slowly but surely you'll be eased off their social register. This might sound cold and calculating (sometimes it is!), but Goats can't abide waste of any sort. And time *is* money, where Capricorns are concerned.

But don't get all het-up and have the heebie-jeebies because you're not about to become Prime Minister, or can't afford your own airline, and are worried that your mate is going to give you the elbow. Just show an atom of ambition, a molecule of magnificence, and all will be well.

If you want to take your mate out for a treat, have a day trip to a place pulsating with pageantry and heaving with history. (Any old castles, abbeys and Roman relics will do!) But whatever you do (and it's bound to be fun), you'll soon see that one thing Capricorns aren't keen on is eating out. It's much too expensive! (Cheaper at home, at half the price!) But Goats will have a good go at the grub when someone else is footing the bill. After all, they're not daft!

Capricorn at Work

'If you want something done, do it yourself.' That's the Goat's motto, and it works every time. And then the conscientious Capricorn will add: 'And if a thing's worth doing, it's worth doing well!' You've got to admit they're absolutely right!

Capricorns may be momentarily captivated by soft lights and sweet music, but what really gets their hearts beating extra-fast is work. They love it! Because this is a conservative, careful sign, you won't find many Capricorns working for fly-by-night firms, doing daredevil jobs, or something outrageously out of the ordinary. They don't even dare be self-employed in case the business goes bust and they find themselves bankrupt. (They need to know where the next 597 meals are coming from!) Instead, they'll choose a company that has a pronounced path of promotion, which the Goat can scamper up as though it were the Yellow Brick Road. (Hopefully with an Aquarian Wizard of Oz at the end of it!)

Some Capricorns with get-up-and-go are astoundingly ambitious and deliciously diligent. They may commence their careers as Goat Fridays, but you can bet your bottom dollar that they'll end up being in charge every day of the week! You might have a pal who seems to be dawdling about on the slopes, but just wait, my dears. Some signs make a song and dance about their aspirations, but Capricorns keep quiet and plod along determinedly. Remember that slowly but surely wins the race. Most ambitious Goats get what they want in the end, long after acrobatic Arians and jumping Geminis have fallen flat on their faces.

Because this is the sign of status and public recognition, Capricorns love jobs in which they can rise to great heights. (No, not as window-cleaners, dear! Haven't you heard of the giddy Goat?) Some Capricorns will be custodians of social mores, and become politicians and Members of Parliament. Others may become local councillors and end up being mayor or mayoress. It could mean the Goat is just the greatest grocer for miles around, or wins the Queen's Award to Industry. (Gosh!) But Capricorns aren't constantly looking for pats on the back, like Leos – though they do like their hard work to be appreciated. Then, they're happy.

Because of the Saturnine link with teeth and bones, Capricorns make delightful dentists and outstanding osteopaths. And as you might have gathered by now, they make fantastic financial directors, telling other people how to spend their money! They also make marvellous mathematicians and stunning scientists. Creative Capricorns will plump for practical professions, such as pottery. (They like to know they're working twenty-four hours a day for a good reason.)

Capricorns will burn the candle at both ends, then try to have a go at the bit in the middle, too! This is a stupendous sign to have around, work-wise, but you may find your dear old Goat starting to look a teensy-weensy bit haggard. You see, they have dreadful difficulties in delegating, and prefer to do everything themselves. Take a Capricorn chef I know. He got a great new job, in charge of a kitchen, with six chefs to boss about. But because he didn't like the way they minced meat and pounded potatoes, he sacked the lot of them. And did he employ six more? Of course not! Instead, he got up even earlier every morning, and did all their jobs as well as his own! Now you know why every workplace should be graced with at least one responsible, dutiful Capricorn!

Capricorn at Home

The Saturnine setting is as traditional as can be. Capricorns get the collywobbles in flats that are futuristic, and like to abide in buildings that are Victorian at the very least. They need to have a sense of history in the homestead (no, that doesn't include last week's washing-up) if they're to be really happy.

A dream dwelling for this sign is a country cottage, creaking with age, and bursting with beams. But it'll probably have a septic tank in the garden, and wandering woodworm. (Capricorns don't mind a bit of hardship, and can exist on bread and cheese, with a sprout on Sundays, if they have to.)

But whether it's a country cottage or an Edwardian edifice, it'll be comfy and cosy, tasteful and traditional. Like Taurus, Goats won't lavish their lovely loot on furniture that will fall apart in two ticks. Instead, whatever they own will have been made to last – and last, and last. (Some of them will have beds that Catherine the Great could have kipped in!) If they've got the dough they'll have lots of antiques, which are investments, but can be used in the meantime.

If you visit a Capricorn chum, and then pop off to your pal's parents, you may see a certain similarity in the styles. Most Goats don't stray far from the tried and tested, which could be what they grew up with. They may have the same kinds of carpets and curtains, or even knick-knacks taken from the parental pad. These reminders of home and halcyon days will make Capricorns feel safe and secure. They hate to break from any tradition.

Very often, the parents of a Capricorn end their days living with their child. Goats feel a real responsibility to their folks, and if one parent passes on, they'll ask the other one to move in. (Sometimes, that's too terrible a thought, and the parent will find somewhere nearby, where the Goat can keep an eye on mum or dad, but not have them at home all the time.)

Capricorns like slightly sombre, sober shades, such as black, grey and white, although they'll throw in the odd pretty hue to brighten things up a bit. Without doubt, the Goat will love the study best of all, or wherever he or she can work. (Capricorns like to keep their noses to the grindstone even at home.) He or she will relax by reading, sipping some sherry, listening to the stereo or even by just sitting still in silence.

Capricorns often potter about in their kitchens, but like to keep things simple. They're not mad on gimmicks, and often prefer a spot of elbow grease to an electrical gadget. (There's nothing like the old days!) They enjoy cooking, and will probably invite you round on a Sunday, for a traditional lunch or tea. But don't bowl up in your best bib and tucker expecting edibles that are *outré* or avant-garde. Instead, your tastebuds will be tantalised with a traditional juicy joint and succulent spuds, or a terrific tea, with scones, shortbread and a superb sponge cake. Goats go for grub that they're used to. They'll consume cod and chips if that's what they were brought up on and steer clear of anything slightly strange. (It's no good taking a Capricorn out to a foreign restaurant unless you know it's a firm favourite. Otherwise the Goat will go green and bolt for the bog!)

But Capricorns usually prefer to entertain their pals in the comfort of their own homes. It may mean they're bombarded with the washing-up afterwards, but at least they won't be bankrupted by the cost!

Capricorn
Health and Relaxation

Ask a Capricorn how he is and he'll tell you. 'Not too good,' the Goat will gasp. 'It was touch and go last night.' Now, before your eyebrows shoot off your skull, that doesn't mean what it would if a Ram was replying. Instead, it's a Capricorn being outrageous. (If you ask what the ailment is, you'll be told it's an ingrowing toenail.)

Capricorns love a dash of drama every now and then, and one of the best ways of livening things up is to be ill. Some Goats are stoical and suffer in silence, but others can make a melodrama out of two sneezes and a suspicion of a splutter. Trundle round for tea and you'll find the Goat bedridden, behind a battery of balsams and bandages. (Better safe than sorry. He or she could take a turn for the worse!) There'll be grapes galore, and enough orange juice to drown the town of Jaffa!

One great girl Goat I know says she has a dicky ticker, yet she's as strong as an ox. She strides up to the seafront in great leaps and bounds, and promenades her pooch until it's exhausted. But when you ask her how she is, she says she's not well! But she's got such a grand Goaty sense of humour, that after she's told you it's lucky she lasted the night, she'll have a good giggle.

Goats can cry wolf so many times that even Johnny Morris would get confused. Sometimes they really believe their supposed symptoms, other times they exaggerate them a wee bit, just to get your sympathy, and to have you on. (Goats adore good jokes, even when the laugh is on them.) You can watch a Capricorn sipping a stout ('It'll build me up') and shovelling down a steak so swiftly you can scarcely see it, only to hear your chum say 'I could go at any minute'. (Maybe they've seen the waiter bringing the bill?) And half the time your pal is much stronger and fitter than you are!

All this means some folk see Capricorns as hypochondriacs, always moaning and groaning. If you have a pal or partner like this, try to see the funny side. (You can bet your Goat will.)

The bits of the body ruled by Saturn are the bones and teeth. Some Goats can have awful arthritis and rampant rheumatism, and will have to spend days at the dentist. Capricorn also controls the knees and kneecaps, and when a Goat bends down, he or she may sound like an old banger backfiring as their knee joints crack away.

Many Capricorns find it very hard to relax. They're such workaholics that they feel guilty if they spend ten minutes in front of the telly. Ideally, they should allow themselves a few moments every day just to sit still and do nothing. If the thought of that drives them demented, they should pick a pastoral pastime, such as gardening or fishing. (They'll enjoy both because they'll save money by fending for their own food, and growing their grub!) They're not very sporty, though, and won't get further than the bar at the local rugby club!

Goats also enjoy creating things, especially if they have a touch of tradition to them. So they'll love tapestry (making their own Bayeux bedspread) and embroidery (they can create their own coat of arms − just right for an old-fashioned octopus!). One Capricorn lass makes candles, so is especially useful when the lights go out during a power cut! And I don't need to tell you she sells them at a profit!

Aquarius

21 January – 19 February

What Makes Aquarius Tick

Y ou learn a whole new vocabulary when you meet an Aquarian. Forget about the usual words, and ponder on ones like 'contrary', 'bizarre', 'radical' and 'outrageous'. In fact, you'd do well to remember them, because you're going to need them.

Before I go any further, let's get one thing straight. Well, two, if you're going to be pedantic. (And if you are, make sure it's not in front of an Aquarian. They aren't particularly pleased by pedantic people.) There are two types of Aquarians: those ruled by Saturn and those ruled by Uranus. It's strange, I know, but then a lot of people think Aquarians are strange. . . (Watch it, because I'm one of them.)

Saturn is the ancient ruler of Aquarius; when rebellious, revolutionary Aquarius was revealed he was given to the Sun sign most fitting that description – Airy Aquarius. (Some people think Aquarius is a Water sign, but it isn't. Its symbol may be the Water Carrier, but it is actually the third of the Air signs. Confusing, isn't it?)

Saturn Aquarians tend to be conservative, reliable, and positive pillars of proper society. You won't catch them wearing lampshades for hats, unless you've spiked their sherry. If that sounds a bit like Capricorn, you're right. Saturn Aquarians do have a lot of Capricorn's characteristics, so if you think you know one, turn back to the previous chapter and have a gander at the Goats.

I'm going to deal mostly with Uranus-ruled Aquarians here. (Usually, you will discover which planet is strongest by studying the birth chart. Sometimes it will be easier – you may meet an Aquarian who is so Saturnine it's not true, or so unusual that they have to be Uranian. Unless they're just plain mad.)

An ancient astrological adage says you can't tell Aquarians anything because they know it already, and very often will tell you so. One of the negative qualities of Aquarians is their one-

216

upmanship. You can meet an Aquarian mate for a meal, and arrive in a wheelchair with your bonce in a big bandage. As the waiter whizzes you to the table, you will smile through your layers of lint, expecting a sudden show of sympathy. The Aquarian will look up, and ask you what happened. So far so good. After you've mumbled in a muffled manner that you were weeding your window-box and fell off, fracturing your femur and splitting your skull, the Aquarian will sigh, say 'Oh is that all?' and go on to recount how they once broke both arms *and* both legs, wrecked their ribs and biffed their back, while morris dancing at Kew Gardens. It can make you mad, but don't kick them with your cast, because it'll hurt you more than them. The negative Saturn Aquarian can be like the negative Capricorn, and be plagued with pessimism, downcast by depression and doubt, and worn out with worry.

The two halves of Aquarius are so very different. If the Saturn type is black and white, then the Uranian Aquarian has all the colours in the spectrum. They can be completely confusing, contrary, unpredictable and incomprehensible – qualities that set them completely apart from their Saturn brothers and sisters. Uranus Aquarians are all of a jitter, rushing here and there, and constantly changing their moods. They remind me of Merlin (or me on Breakfast Time), popping up when you least expect it. In astrology, Uranus is known as the great awakener, as if a magic wand had been waved, the word 'abracadabra' said. He will create change in something that was static. So, the Uranus-ruled Aquarian is ceaselessly craving change.

On a positive level, this means that the Aquarian is eternally excited and exhilarated by what may lie round the corner, and there may be sudden changes of career, luck or partners, when Uranus decides to stage a shake-up. Negatively, an Aquarian will want to change things just for the sake of it, because he or she longs to rock the boat. Routine can be anathema to an Aquarian; the Saturn Aquarian, on the other hand, may find it rather reassuring. This is the quintessence of the Aquarian quandary – complete contradiction, with one half of the sign panting for pastures new, and the other following the furrow.

You never know what's going to happen next with an Aquarian. Life can be a lot of fun, or you can find it very tiring. Aquarians are unconventional, but they are also original, and along with Geminis, are said to be the geniuses of the zodiac. They can be inventive and brilliantly clever, although sometimes they are spectacular in such a strange way, so abstract and off at such a tremendous tangent, that no one knows what they're talking about! Aquarians are really born way ahead of their time. (After all, they all laughed at Christopher Columbus when he said the world was round!) Other people, who are rather less free-thinking and original, will conclude that they are completely cranky.

Another Aquarian contradiction is that although Water Carriers are said to be humanitarians, they can be emotional ice cubes in the cocktail of life, and don't easily express their emotions. They can be humanitarian – helping others, sending cash to charities, or being affectionate on a large scale – yet find their own close relationships difficult to cope with. Aquarius is a Fixed sign, so it can be intolerably inflexible and intransigent. For all their brainpower and brilliance, Aquarians can be staggeringly stupid and stubborn, standing their ground over a long-lost cause and unable to admit they are in the wrong.

Since Aquarius is an Air Sign, the Aquarian will be much more mesmerised by a marriage of the minds than a partnership of passion and physical fulfilment. Very often, they pick the most unlikely-looking person for a partner, because they will have chosen them for their mind rather than for anything else. Aquarians can have some very avant-garde relationships! (Ever heard of Beauty and the beast? And guess who's playing Beauty!)

Aquarians think of the future a great deal; often when they have just crossed one hurdle, they will think 'Where will this lead?' and 'I wonder what's going to happen next?' And this brings me to another Aquarian attribute. They are the only sign to answer a question with a question. Ask an Aquarian if it's raining, and he or she will ask you why you want to know. (A Piscean would say yes, and offer to lend you their green gamp.) The first word Aquarian children learn is 'Why?', and they will continue to ask that question all through their lives.

You can never get really close to an Aquarian. Unless they have plenty of Pisces and Taurus in their charts to warm them up, they can be aloof and cold and difficult to cuddle. But for all that, life with an Aquarian, either as a pal or a partner, will never be dull, and that's something to think about!

Aquarius Man

Apollo, Adonis, Aquarius. . .It's all the same really, because the male Water Carrier is traditionally the most attractive man in the zodiac. To give you an idea of just how attractive an Aquarian man can be, here's a list of just a few famous ones – James Dean, Paul Newman, Alan Bates, Clark Gable, Mikhail Barynishkov and Martin Shaw. See what I mean?

Aquarians of both sexes can become corpulent from the age of forty onwards, but, in spite of that, Aquarian men do have very godlike features and physiques, and can set many a heart fluttering. Aquarian men, even if they don't look like Paul Newman (who, incidentally, is the archetypal Aquarian as far as looks go) can be even more appealing because to all outward appearances they are cool, calm and collected, even if the real story is somewhat different. An Aquarian man doesn't chase people, and because he is oblivious to the effect he has on women, he may appear even more attractive! All men born under this sign have cratefuls of charisma and masses of magnetism – legacies from their ruler Uranus – and both sexes can attract people to them like magnets.

Very often, the more aware a male Aquarian is that you are chasing him for all you're worth, the more he will run in the opposite direction. Get to know him first at a local club or society (places in which you'll find lots of Aquarians, both single and married) and become his friend. Aquarian men love to be part of a group. The weaker ones will just be members: the Uranus Aquarian should never be given any responsibility, because he won't know what to do with it. The Saturn-ruled Aquarian, on the other hand, will rise rapidly through the ranks to become president emeritus, or secretary at the very least.

In fact, Aquarian men will do well in any club or society they join; they will always make lots of friends, and bring a breath of fresh air into a stuffy environment. Some Aquarian men, however, can capitalise on their charisma, and use it for nefarious purposes, chasing whatever takes their fancy – power or people. (A lot of Aquarians are bisexual by nature, even if not by action. They are an Air sign, so they will try anything once, sexually or any other way you care to mention!)

In general, Aquarian men are marvellous to have on a committee, because they are one of the few signs of the zodiac who can have a complicated conversation and listen to what's happening at the other end of the room at the same time. So they can always tell you what's going on!

They are also incredibly observant – until it comes to amorous intentions, when they will be as blind as a bat. But if you're talking about intellectual wizardry, they're the tops, whether they take a leaf out of Gemini's book and know a lot about nothing, or make an Aquarian effort and become an expert on something. They will often pick a subject that other signs shun or simply see as silly. They love flying in the face of tradition and respectability.

If you have an Aquarian son, you may have felt a mite miffed that you don't see much of him. Most Aquarian boys leave home at an early age, wanting to spread their wings. Aquarians, you see, are on a continual quest to learn new things, and will take Open University courses long after a hundredth birthday telegram from the Queen has plopped through the letterbox, along with a syllabus for a course on fibre optics at home.

If an Aquarian man finds he's failed to fly to the top of the club he's joined, he may set up a rival society, and make himself president! He will love doing sports that are different, and will enjoy activities like chess, bridge or even stamp collecting, because he has to use his mind. What he hates though, is being told what to do, and he will make this very obvious if someone steps out of line (as he sees it) and asks him to do something demeaning.

Aquarian men are not the social butterflies of the zodiac, flitting off to a ceaseless round of cocktail parties or propping up the pub bar just for the sake of it. They have to have a reason for their social gadding about. They love to widen their horizons, and have no time for idle chit chat about the balding budgie next door or the shocking state of the supermarket.

Even if your Aquarian man isn't called Frank, you'll discover that that's what he's like. Frighteningly frank! He can be cuttingly candid too, and you may have to develop the sort of skin normally only seen on old rhinos to cope with some of his comments when he's feeling tetchy. Alternatively, he can be cool and contrary, and upset you that way.

You either love or hate an Aquarian man. There are no half measures either with his feelings towards you. He is extreme to a degree, and will revel in his ability to shock, no matter what chaos he causes those around him who are caught in the crossfire. There can even be an element of spite with some Aquarian men, who will see that a friend is upset about something, and then put the verbal boot in, going straight for their Achilles heel. It's all part of Uranus being disruptive and outrageous, and when ultra-unusual Uranus is being bolshie, you just have to run for cover, if you don't feel able to cope.

Aquarian men, by the way, always want the last word, and if they can't have the satisfaction of that, they will go instead for the last sound – they'll slam a door or smash a window!

Lots of people have been involved emotionally with Aquarian men, and come out of the experience sadder and wiser, convinced that they have failed. They haven't, but they just haven't understood the contrariness and outrageousness that governs the actions of the average Aquarian. (Except, of course, there is no such thing as the average Aquarian anything!)

Aquarius Woman

I t's very hard to describe what Aquarian women look like, because they don't really conform in that way at all. (They often don't conform in any other way, either.) In fact, whatever the current fashion is, you can bet your last Pools coupon that an Aquarian woman won't be wearing it. If long hair and miniskirts are all the rage, she'll be wearing a skirt that sweeps her ankles, with her hair cut to half an inch all over. Aquarian women were the first to wear peach, pink and puce eye shadows and purple lipsticks, because they are outrageous trendsetters. But by the time their trend has caught on they'll be wearing something else, equally shocking.

A good example of the two halves of the Aquarian woman would be to picture a Greenham Common woman (Uranus Aquarius), sitting in her tent, glaring over a fence at Margot Leadbetter (Saturn Aquarius), clutching her pearls and cosy cardie, from *The Good Life*. Both are extremes of the same sign, with strong principles neither of them will surrender.

We all want to be loved, but in different ways, and the Aquarian's need for love is quite different from a Cancerian's or an Arian's. You have to give an Aquarian as much freedom and independence as you possibly can. If you marry one, don't expect her to settle down, putting your slippers in front of the fire, tucking the kiddies up in bed, and making the cocoa every night. Otherwise one night you'll come home and discover she's rebelled, put the kids in front of the fire, tucked the cocoa up in bed, put your slippers on and walked out.

She's far more likely to want to reverse sexual roles, and go out to work herself while her husband stays at home holding the baby. She wants to retain her brilliance, not see it tarnished by a pile of nappies. All Aquarian women want the world to know how clever they are, and to get the praise they feel they deserve.

If married, she will certainly want her own bank account, but that is just the tip of the iceberg as far as this lass is concerned. The most obvious example of a liberated Aquarian lady is Vanessa Redgrave, who typifies the Uranian need for putting out not so much the dove of peace as the eagle of extremes. She has raised more eyebrows than most, but has always done so with consummate class.

A negative Saturn Aquarian woman can be pompous while positively, she can use her Capricorn qualities to become a JP, head lots of committees and be a pillar of local society. A Uranus Aquarian woman who is prey to the negative side of the sign will be the one who breaks the law; or she might use that extreme outlook to protest against the Catholic Church's attitude to abortion, and adopt all the causes she feels affect her as a woman.

The Aquarian woman can be prey to fits of egotistical mania, behaving like a combination of the Queen of Sheba and Boadicea on a bad night. She will swan about, being arrogant, pompous and rude, and thinking she is absolutely wonderful. Of course, she'll appear really silly, but you won't know if she's behaving badly because she is so pleased with herself, or because she's about to shock you.

The Aquarian motto is very much 'Live and let live' (by the way, a lot of them are into health fads or are vegans), yet the female Water Carrier may fly off the handle at something other signs will shrug off, or be acquiescently Aquarian over an issue everyone else is up in arms about. It's just one more example of the Aquarian contrariness – the Mary who had a garden full of cockleshells in the nursery rhyme was definitely born when the Sun was in Aquarius!

She can almost be a hypocrite sometimes because it may suit her to change her mind about something. It's not that she's vacillating vaguely like her Venusian sister, Libra, but that she's purposely trying to confuse you and drive you mad! Very often she will succeed. You will hear people saying time and time again of an Aquarian woman 'I just don't understand her', whether she's decided to ban fish fingers from her fridge for evermore, or save the whale personally in a rowing boat. The day before she will have had completely contrary claims, and she will have only announced the change in convictions to confuse you, and to liven up life a little.

In fact, the best way to treat an Aquarian woman who chops and changes, setting you in a spin normally only seen at a launderette, is not to say a word. Don't utter a peep. Never suggest she should do something, or not do something, because she will instantly set out to do the complete opposite of what you want. You are constantly playing a game with Aquarians, and the sooner you realise it the better!

Aquarian mothers treat their offspring as equals, sometimes to the consternation of other relatives, who have rather different views on bringing up children. Saturn Aquarian women will be just like Capricorn, so flick back a few pages and find out about them there. But those ruled by Uranus can be really radical, and will have no qualms about breast-feeding their baby on the bus. They will want to bring up their children for the new age, sending them to strange schools where they will be taught by a Swiss acupuncturist and fed on a diet of pulverised prunes, porridge and peanuts.

Aquarian women ruled by Uranus love revolution and disorder, havoc and chaos, although they would prefer to describe it as 'a change is as good as a rest' (as they watch you being wheeled off to the funny farm sporting a strait-jacket and foaming at the mouth). There is nothing worse for Aquarians than to see things ticking along nicely. They positively itch to liven things up a bit. But, like her male counterpart, the Aquarian woman can be perfect in a crisis, so if you feel one coming on, make sure she knows about it!

Aquarius is the thunder and lightning of the zodiac, the gales and the hurricanes, whereas Libra is balmy breezes, and Gemini is gentle zephyrs. It's up to you to decide, when encountering an Aquarian woman for the first time, whether you want to put on your waterproof and wellies, or stick with your sunshade.

Aquarius Child

Aquarian children are way ahead of their brothers, sisters and classmates, and can be terribly precocious. They love to make friends with children many years older than themselves.

These kids can be unbearable: they are so far advanced that you may want to help their advancement along a bit further by booting them into the next room with your foot. Their level of obnoxiousness will depend on their parents. If they are rebellious and contrary, it may well be because their parents are Water signs, and are trying to make them into ordinary children, when in reality that is the last thing they are, or ever will be! Whatever else an Aquarian child may be, the one thing it is impossible for him or her to be is ordinary. You will either have a silent genius or a loud, obnoxious, rude brat. Nearly all Aquarian children should be seen and not heard! (I was one once!)

But it is hardly their fault. If they have parents who are as liberated as they are, they may be able to bring out some of the more positive traits of their Aquarian children, the main one being an incredible intelligence.

Some Aquarian children have amassed so much information at such a young age that by the time school starts, they can tell the teachers when they've made mistakes. These kids can be real know-it-alls, and their little Aquarian voices will constantly be heard piping up from the back of the class. The hand waving in the air when a question is asked will inevitably belong to an Aquarian kid, giving his or her brain cells and vocal cords an airing. What's more, these little brainboxes won't be afraid of showing off their knowledge, which can make them disliked by both their teachers and their fellow schoolmates.

All Water Carriers, except those who are very Saturnine in character, hate authority, and teachers will be the first taste of it that Aquarian kids encounter. And don't they hate it!

A perfect solution will be if the Aquarian child can find a guru or

225

mentor in his or her life, and ideally that person will be at the child's school. If an Aquarian kid can find one teacher who understands their need for knowledge – and their antipathy to authority – and can help the child on his or her journey of exploration into the uncharted seas of knowledge, they won't become precocious, because their negative traits will be channelled into positive directions.

Parents of Aquarian children should take note of this. If they try to rule them with rods of iron, they will have a revolution on their hands. They will instantly provoke that wilful, rebellious side of this sign, leading to tantrums, slammed doors and possibly even an attempt at running away from home.

If you think you have a wayward Aquarian child, because he or she won't go to the Scouts or Brownies, think again. Aquarians loathe and detest being like everyone else because, even as children, they know they are different. They will refuse to wear a uniform because it makes them look like every other kid. You must understand that your Aquarian child, who may be only seven, is an adult, and quite possibly more adult than you. He or she is very much an individual, and knows it. Aquarian kids feel so unique that they don't want to be put into a classroom full of other children who they know are idiots by comparison.

The Aquarian child needs to be understood and handled with care. If you become a friend of an Aquarian kid, especially if it's your own, and get him or her to trust you, then you will have won the battle. But don't send your child to join the choir in the local church if they show signs of being a true individual. Because no matter how cherubic your kid looks to you, they will probably wreak untold damage on the church, the choir stalls and the other choir boys and girls!

Aquarius in Love

How do you know when Aquarians are in love? Very often you don't, but before you reach for the Kleenex, I should tell you that neither do they. It takes a long time for their heart-strings to ping, and when they do they are far more likely to twang for a person's brain, or a hobby or a group of people, than someone who's six foot two with eyes of blue.

Love has to grow for an Aquarian. Friendship comes much faster. Aquarians are much more likely to be in love with an idea, and fall in love with someone during a conversation because they adore the way a person's mind works, then fall out of it again afterwards. If you are looking for love at its tenderest, the sort when you hear music and can't see two feet in front of you because of all the dry ice swirling around you and your amour, don't try to find it with an Aquarian. So, if you are planning to pronounce your passion to an Aquarian, and when you do, he or she says 'Oh dear!' instead of 'Oh, *darling!*' either grin and bear it, or move on to fresher, more fantasial fields.

Aquarians spend their whole lives avoiding routines, running away from ruts, and because they are so obsessed with the idea of their lives being monotonously mapped for them, they *can* get into a routine. They can be like this emotionally too.

Love for an Aquarian is much more a state of mind than one of the heart. They will say that they love people, but it is in an abstract Aquarian way, rather too mental – loving people in general rather than one particular person. When they are with one person, their relationship can become a matter of habit. They are likely to stick around and wait for love to grow; sometimes it will blossom long after the Aquarian is established in a relationship. Often they will love someone when they realise they can rely on them, as a mate, a mentor, a guru, a helper. But even then they won't spell out their sentiments with orchids and roses, but with books and words.

Love is a hard lesson for some Aquarians to learn, especially if

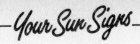

Venus hadn't shimmered into Pisces when they were born. If the Fish were floating about in the waters of the planet of romance and rhapsody, they will be much warmer, and their partner will probably be a lot happier. But if Venus was in Aquarius when they were born, they must learn how to give love, and how to express it. They belong to the Air element, and so are driven by their desire to communicate, although, of the three Air signs, Aquarians can spend the most time by themselves. On the whole, though, they are much happier with humanitarian, altruistic love.

A lot of Aquarians have long spells of being celibate; it doesn't worry them a bit. They can also go for long stretches without sex within a relationship, and be perfectly happy about it. (An Aquarian will be much more sexy if he or she has Aries, Taurus or Scorpio strongly placed, or a dominant, virile Mars – then you can expect a few fireworks.) They also don't actually *think* much about sex, unlike a lot of other signs. Imagine a Taurean not thinking about sex and you must have a Bull with amnesia!

If you have an Aquarian you crave and live for, try to understand them, and give them a little help from time to time. If you can cope with a lack of Moons and Junes from your Aquarian amour (unless Leo, Libra or Pisces is rising), and accept instead their unique blend of love and affection, you will be blessed with a friend who is a lover too, and one who knows you've bothered to work them out. They might even forget a little of that Aquarian coolness and thank you!

Aquarius as a Friend

Aquarians are really far better at friendship than anything else, if you discount disruption! If they are very clever (and they usually are), they will make their friend their lover too.

Aquarius is a Fixed sign so, like Taureans, Leos and Scorpios, Water Carriers are endowed with more than average amounts of faithfulness and loyalty, and will stand by you through thick and thin.

They enjoy their friends and can use their incredible intuition to check out a chum's character. They are great levellers, so can be a princess with a plumber for a pal, and neither of them will notice any social differences at all.

Like their fellow Air signs, Gemini and Libra, Aquarians like their friends to be intellectual and intelligent, and they want them to enjoy doing the things they do. However, they don't like their chums to be too clever and compete with them, because they want to be in the driving seat in their relationships, telling their friends what to do. They can be a bit bossy, which is a trait you can trace from their polarity with Leo. (Leos always want to be top cat.)

Be careful with your Aquarian acquaintances. Uranus, with its desire for disruption and revolution, can make its Aquarian subject suddenly sever a seventeen-year social solidarity with a sidekick overnight. They can rhumba away from a friend, as well as a lover, with hardly a backward glance, if they feel strongly enough about it.

Aquarians can be very adventurous and will often do things you wouldn't normally expect people of their age group to do, such as going to a musical instead of a rock concert at the age of fourteen, and taking up hang-gliding when they're eighty.

Water Carriers can be driven by desires and cravings, and sometimes these take an unlikely turn. You can be sitting with an Aquarian pal, who says he or she wants to spend the day quietly at home, reading. You say OK, and scuttle off to make a sandwich. Ten minutes later, your Aquarian chum will be standing in the doorway, wearing their hat and coat, and a scarf knitted from cat fur, with matching mittens (no, mittens, not kittens, though I wouldn't put it past some of them), and asking you if you're ready yet. They've decided to take a day trip to Doncaster. A quiet day with an Aquarian can often turn out to be quite nerve-racking! But whatever else they are, you have to admit, with a forced smile if necessary, that they are never boring. Tiring at times, but not tedious.

Their Fixed quality can come to the fore and they will stick to a viewpoint like chewing gum to your best frock. If you let them go on in their own sweet way, their current obsession will die a natural death, but if you try to chivvy them along and utter inanities such as 'Snap out of it', they will become more firmly entrenched in their views than ever. They will be determined to be proved right even if they drop down dead in the process.

Aquarians like mates of both sexes: they really don't mind whether their best pal is a woman, a man, or a bit of both. They just need their mates to be tolerant of them and allow them to do what they want. A friendship between two Uranian Aquarians would be a disaster, but a pairing between a Saturn Aquarian and a Uranus Water Carrier would be brill, as their relationship would be well balanced.

Like everything else about them, the zany Aquarian sense of humour can be directed at the weirdest things. Unlike Taureans, who love knock-about slapstick comedy, Aquarians appreciate subtlety or sarcasm with their sniggers, and will love comics like Woody Allen and John Cleese. They adore dry humour, and send-ups of authority and red tape (a pet Aquarian hate) will have them rolling in the aisles.

So, if you want to jolly along your Aquarian mate, take them to a funny film, buy them some popcorn, and help them laugh their troubles away.

Aquarius at Work

Watch out for the red tape if you work for an Aquarian. The minute they come into contact with it, they will try to fight it for all they're worth. Just because something has been done in a particular way for year after year, century after century, doesn't mean that the Aquarian will want to toe the line and do it that way too. Age-old rules and regulations often go by the board when an Aquarian encounters them.

The Aquarian at work is a reformer, adding new dimensions to the most mundane of meetings with brilliantly inventive ideas. He or she will be best in a profession that allows scope for unusual, inventive or technological talents. Media professions – especially jobs relating to television – are perfect for an Aquarian. What could be better than for a Water Carrier to work with a product of the Aquarian age?

Unusual professions will attract Aquarians, and they will go for jobs that don't have a regular routine. They hate working in a standard nine-to-five job, and you will find they devise their own flexitime, swanning in at sunrise and leaving at lunchtime, even if that isn't the practice of the rest of the company! They may be an astrologer or a PE teacher on an oil rig – just as long as it isn't run of the mill. Trouble will start the minute a Water Carrier feels hampered, hemmed in and hidebound.

If an Aquarian works with someone who provokes problems, he or she will oppose them all the way. There is nothing passive about an Aquarian at work, and although he or she may ultimately be defeated, it won't be without a brave fight. (Though the Aquarian's boss may well call it obstreperousness!)

The modern age is tailor-made for an Aquarian, with jobs in computers, television, videos, and electronics of all kinds. They are very adventurous in their work, trying out things that haven't been done before. A job at NASA would suit an Aquarian down to the ground, or rather, up to the stars! (Incidentally, show an Aquarian snaps of the Moonshot and he or she will yawn and say

'Haven't they reached Mars yet?') One of the biggest hurdles an Aquarian has to face at work is convincing others that his or her futuristic ideas are worth taking a chance on, and aren't just pie in the sky.

Many of those signs who like routine, or say 'That's not the way we do things here', will probably bore an Aquarian, who will ignore them all and carry on. So watch Aquarians at work, because they can be brilliant. But allow them the odd fault because, like most geniuses, they sometimes get things completely wrong! (They won't admit it openly, but they'll have a sneaking suspicion that they've blundered.)

You may find it rather hard to be chummy with an Aquarian acquaintance at work, which may seem odd as they are the sign of friendship. But for an Aquarian, work is work, and friendship is friendship, and don't expect them to mix the two in the office. They can be loyal to friends, finding them jobs, but they will make it plain who's the boss once the pal arrives, albeit in a nice way. They may go off to the squash club together in the evenings, when they will be mates, but at work they will have a business relationship and nothing more.

Self-employment was invented for Aquarians (they'll tell you they're all invention), because it means they are free to do what they like when they like. Within reason, of course. (They know that if they spend every day perfecting paper darts they will soon be bereft of the boodle.) Aquarians are also more self-sufficient than some of the other signs, and don't mind being alone all day. Given the right surroundings, their true genius will gush out.

What you must remember with an Aquarian – write it on a piece of paper and stick it on your wall if you work with one – is 'There's method in their madness'. Remember that and you won't go far wrong. Well, not too far, anyway!

Aquarius at Home

I f an Aquarian is settled, either emotionally or geographically, the home will be very important. It can be the centrepiece of work or the family.

A Saturn Aquarian will fill the home with tradition, choosing lots of wood, and even log fires, as any Capricorn would. But the Uranus Aquarian, of course, is quite different, and likes everything to be as up-to-the-minute, even futuristic, as possible. The first time you visit them, you may think you've strayed on to the set of *Star Trek*. (Maybe you'd better check your chum's ears for points.) There will be every electrical gadget you can think of, with videos, telephones in every room, typewriters, word processors, computers, the best microwave oven you can buy, and televisions that make the tea.

To make anything work at all, you will have to press this, plug in that, and pull something else. If they have the boodle, they will have rooms that go up and down, lifts – the lot! When you call on them you'll find yourself firmly flung into the twenty-first century. Aquarian abodes can be so sparse, so space-age, that they don't feel like homes at all, because they are so lacking in warmth. The atmosphere will be cold and functional, with the positioning of everything worked out on their solar-powered calculators. You can walk into a Uranus Aquarian's home and sit in mortal terror of being savaged by the standard lamp, or falling through a grating in the floor if you've been on a diet. It can be too cold for comfort.

But before you shudder and turn up the fire just thinking about it, remember that the more mellow Aquarians become emotionally, the more they will return to their Saturn roots, decorating their homes in a more comfortable, cosy manner, with traces of space-age technology in the kitchen.

An Aquarian home can be completely haphazard, and a perfect paradox, with all the paraphernalia of the modern age nestling (never seen a computer nestle? – if not, you've never been to an

Aquarian's home) alongside comfy sofas, squashy cushions, roaring log fires, rows and rows of books, and oil-paintings. It can be a complete contrast of the most modern with the totally traditional, illustrating perfectly the two sides of the Aquarian nature.

Aquarians wanting a harmonious home should surround themselves with electric blues, silvers – in fact, all the colours of the rainbow. They may have a different dominating colour in every room of their house, and sometimes will give a different character to each room too. One can be quite fantasial, another very cosy and comforting, and another decorated like a Chinese pagoda, where you might expect to see Madame Butterfly or Suzie Wong appear at any moment. Saturn Aquarians will prefer rather more sober surroundings; they should turn to Capricorn to discover what is best for them.

Like fellow Air signs Gemini and Libra, Aquarians won't mind having a pet, but will want it to be independent. Bringing up a budgie would drive them round the bend, because they'd be forever feeding it and checking its cuttlefish for cracks. Although they like animals in the abstract, they are not so keen on individual beasties. The most likely animals for Aquarians to keep are cats. They don't demand much attention, and don't need cuddling. (Mind you, don't expect these cats to be like your normal moggie. A cat kept by an Aquarian will be as cranky as its owner!)

If they choose other pets, they may opt for a dog, but it won't be a mongrel. The really *outré* Aquarian will keep an alligator in the outhouse, a leopard in the loo and a boa constrictor in the bathroom cabinet.

But whatever pets they plump for and however they decorate their dwellings, you can be sure that Aquarians' unorthodox approach to life will shine through in every respect. And would you really have it any other way?

Aquarius
Health and Relaxation

Aquarians live so much on their nerves that their nervous systems can become quite weak. They pack so much into a few seconds, minutes or hours. Because of their polarity with Leo, they can suffer from high blood pressure, and it is very important for them to make sure they have regular check-ups for their hearts and circulatory systems. If you get into bed with an Aquarian, be prepared to be chilled to the marrow by a pair of frozen feet. A lot of Aquarians have poor circulation, and they may have ice cold tootsies!

Saturn Aquarians have to watch out for rheumatics and general problems with their bones. I know one Aquarian girl who is forever falling over. It's not because she's drunk, but because she has weak ankles, as have many Water Carriers.

Aquarians and Capricorns both face a danger of being workaholics, because they are two signs who like to be kept busy. They are easily bored, and need to be constantly occupied. Aquarians especially need to do lots of different things. For example, they can find it terribly tedious to talk to one person for too long. They want to wander off for a walk, or rush off to the roller-skating rink (when they should be watching those weak ankles!).

Aquarians like to do things with their hands, whether it is knitting, crocheting, sewing, tatting, carpentry – anything, just as long as they can keep their mitts and their minds occupied. They love to mix with people who have the same interests, or they will start up a society and run it from their own homes.

Very often, in case the dreaded boredom strikes – and boredom is one of their illnesses – they will go visiting and say they can only stay for a short while. Geminis may act the same, but this is because they have another party to go to; Aquarians are playing safe, and giving themselves an escape route. If Aquarians find someone to their liking at a do, they will try to drag that person away from the party. Aquarians aren't big party lovers, and will not spend the week wondering where the weekend wing-ding will be. They are much happier mooching about a museum and then taking off to the theatre.

It may sound a contradiction (although Aquarians are full of them), but the best way to keep Aquarians relaxed is to make sure they have something to do. If they aren't totally occupied, they will begin to fidget; unfortunately, they sometimes find it difficult to concentrate on one thing, unless it is right up their street.

Like Capricorns, Aquarians have the marvellous ability of knowing when to stop drinking, so a lot of them are saved from the hazards of a hangover, or the denigration of dead drunkenness. Uranian Aquarians are so high anyway, they don't need stimulants in the shape of drink or drugs! Being creatures of extremes, of course, they may have a week of being permanently plastered, and then six months of drinking nothing stronger than orange juice. (Or mango juice if your Aquarian is really way out. And rich!) They have such tremendous will-power that they can do whatever they put their minds to, so if you know an Aquarian who sometimes reels about clutching a bottle of booze and trying to dance the hornpipe, don't worry too much. They probably have months of abstention to make up for it. You should only begin to take serious notice if your pal spends a year sloshing about in neat Scotch and one week on orange juice.

If Aquarians decide to do something, whatever it is, ten teams of wild horses won't stop them. If the excesses become habits, then that is the time to beware. But generally speaking, they are so naturally inquisitive, and scared of getting into a rut, that they will even see polishing off a bottle of vodka a day as being a boring habit, and give it up. (They'll give tequila a try instead. After all, it *is* made from cacti.)

Pisces

20 February – 20 March

What Makes Pisces Tick

Saintly Pisces! Some of these Fish should be canonised, they are so far advanced along the road to spiritual enlightenment. (Others still seem to be waiting at the heavenly bus stop!)

Now, there are two sorts of Pisceans; this last sign of the zodiac is ruled by two planets – jocular, jaunty Jupiter, and nebulous, nectarine Neptune. The Jupiter-ruled Pisceans are very akin to Sagittarians, because they share the same ruler. But Jupiterian Pisceans aren't so prone to the flights of fancy shown by Sagittarians. Their ruler represents wealth and good fortune, and the Jupiterian Fish will always have an eye on these things. In fact, Pisces brings out these Jupiterian qualities beautifully, making the Fish full of fun and clever at bringing in the boodle. Negatively, there will be a tendency towards over-expansion, whether in girth, mirth, or wheeling and dealing. But these Jupiterian Fish do burst with bounteous *bonhomie*, and can be gloriously generous and marvellously magnanimous.

Because of the saintly side of this sign, Pisceans can be very devout and pious. (It depends on the Fish whether that will make you awed or bored.) If they are ruled by Jupiter, they will accept the faith or religion they have been brought up in. A Neptunian Piscean, however, will be more unusual, even mystical, and may find Eastern religions especially attractive.

This is a profoundly psychic sign, and the Piscean should use this ability positively to live a better life. Many Fish become fascinated by black magic and the occult, like Scorpios, because they are seduced by secrecy. But, generally, Pisceans have an inspiration that can draw them wholeheartedly into the realms of the positive supernatural and mystical. They are also intensely interested in spiritualism, because it helps them to get in touch with that unseen lot they feel so much a part of.

Neptunian Pisceans waft along on clouds, day-dreaming away to their heart's content. They really aren't part of this world at all!

238

(This isn't the same as Aquarians, who are futuristic, and one step ahead of everyone else. Pisceans are unworldly in a filigree, fantasial way.) These Fish will appear magical and mystical, and they can be profoundly artistic and unworldly sometimes to the point of being gullible or geniuses. Lord Byron had powerful Piscean placings, and Mozart and Chopin both had the Sun in this sign, as does Rudolph Nureyev, who brought a whole new concept to ballet. (And to tights. Pisceans love to leave something to the imagination.)

What you must remember about Neptune is that this planet gives an illusory image to everything it encounters. Neptune represents something that can never be captured or held on to. Think of an intangible will-o'-the-wisp, or a piece of thistledown floating through the air that always eludes you, and you have the perfect picture of Pisceans.

They can bring this quality into their everyday lives, imbuing them with illusion, and smothering them in strange sea mists. You will think you're looking at one thing, then the shadows shift and you discover you're seeing something quite different.

Everything that Neptune does is intensified in an ethereal way, so Neptunian Pisceans will be hypersensitive, and as fragile as a butterfly's wing. They can feel neurotically nauseated by anything ugly, whether it's society, sights, sounds or situations. Some Fishy folk can't stand the slightest facial flaw, let alone anything else. (Better talk to them with your head hidden!) Yet such is their spiritual self-awareness, that often they will devote their lives to the very vocations which you'd think they couldn't bear. For example, they might join the prison service (but not behind bars!), look after the old and infirm, and the mentally and physically handicapped. These positive Pisceans force themselves to face up to their phobias, and bring some good out of them. (Other Pisceans will only want the erotic, exotic, seductive and sumptuous side of life, and none of the unpleasant parts.)

I can hear you saying 'That sounds like Libra!', and you'd be right. Neptune is said to be the higher octave of Venus, a sort of top C of the zodiac. It's like a dog whistle, which has a note that's too high for humans to hear. And this is what Neptunian natives are like – they're listening to a high-pitched tone that the rest of us can't catch. Equally, Jupiter is said to be the higher octave of Mercury, and Jupiterian folk can understand all the deeper things of life that a Mercury-ruled person skims over. Between them,

Mercury and Jupiter rule the four Mutable signs – Gemini, Virgo, Sagittarius and Pisces. (Interesting, isn't it?)

Neptune is a fantastically fantasial figure. On a positive level, its influence means that Neptunians can be wonderful writers, divine dancers and profound poets. (And incurable romantics.) But negatively, they can be monstrously Machiavellian, playing one person off against another. Some of them make Lucretia Borgia look like Little Bo Peep; they can be malicious and malevolent, vicious and venomous, treacherous and two-faced. (They have a wonderful way of believing their own fibs and fables.) And this is how we get the symbol of Pisces, which is a fish swimming in different directions. Pisceans are either way up at the top of the tree or at rock bottom; either the nurse helping the drug addict or the addict himself.

Fish are vulnerable, and can be victims of the unknown, murky depths of their imaginations and subconscious minds. They are either inspired, or they're the dregs of the earth, who rely on society to look after them.

There's no getting away from it. This sign is a mystery, but not in a Scorpionic way. Rather, it's unworldly, in a delicious, delectable, gossamer-like way. There is a floaty, flimsy veil hiding what is really going on in the Piscean's life. The Fish can inhabit a very weird world, and the worst thing Pisceans can do is to drift along on an aimless sea, when their phobias, fetishes and fixations may well get the better of them. They are very impressionable indeed, and negative Pisceans will be plagued by psychosomatic problems that they have brought on themselves. Positive Pisceans can direct that abundant artistry, that magnificent mysticism, into a brilliant conclusion. Or they can live such serene and spiritual lives that nothing else matters, because their tremendous inner peace brings them total fulfilment.

Think of your Fishy friends, and you'll realise that something strange sets them apart from everyone else. You can't put your finger on it, but you know it's there. Remember those sea mists. One minute the view is as clear as a bell, the next you're sinking into a ferocious fog! It's a magical, mystical mystery.

Pisces Man

Have you noticed how you get a collection of one sign in a particular area of your life, such as all the doctors you've ever met being Virgos? Well, a lot of the men who have steered my career along have been Pisceans. You can find these men in artistic professions, such as directors in television or editors of magazines. They tend to congregate in, and be captivated by, all the professions and careers that are glam and arty. And they're so sensitive that these sorts of professions are perfect for them.

Most Piscean men send out an aura that attracts people to them like bees around a honeypot, or a wasp to a jam sandwich. Neptune makes some Piscean men strong, silent types, but in an ethereal, aesthetic way, so they don't seem to quite belong to this life at all. Folk (especially female) are attracted to them because they seem slightly strange, or wonderfully weird, and everyone will wonder what they're really like. (And that can be a hard problem to solve.)

In spite of the flimsy, fantasial feeling to the Fish, Piscean men may further their careers by being clever, and behaving in a Machiavellian manner in meetings. Neptune can give these men a degree of camaraderie, conviviality and cordiality that makes them appear charming and captivating to other people, who will be slightly stupefied by it all. There is more than a touch of the Svengali about this sign, and a Piscean man can wave a magic, mesmeric wand over people. They may not understand, or even like him, but he'll have exerted a strange sort of hold over them.

If you have a male Fish floating about on a cumulus cloud near you, grab him, because in many ways Piscean men make wonderful lovers. (Mind you, have you ever *tried* clutching a cloud?) While you're busy working out the celestial side of the Fish, don't forget to look for the romantic one. (As if you would!) The Piscean man can make a woman really *feel* like a woman. He can lavish love and affection on her, sympathise with her moods, and be utterly understanding. She'll know she's wanted, and he'll treat her properly.

Some male members of this sign like ladies who are stronger than they are and will go all out to get them. Then they can drift along in their dream world, content in the knowledge that their partners are working hard to keep the wolf from the door. These men may even complain to their chums that their hard and unfeeling wives don't understand them. (In fact, they probably understand them all too well!) This is a similar Piscean to the Fishy drug addict who finds the real world too brutal to bear.

As a result, some Fishy fellows – strong and weak – can lead a double life, with no trouble at all, thank you very much. They'll skip to Soho, or the nearest knocking shop, at the first opportunity, or leap off to Luton with a lover. Netfuls of Piscean men love blue movies and pornography, because neither will get them into trouble. They won't run the risk of catching VD, which they would hate, and their wives and families won't be any the wiser. Like Scorpios, Piscean men love secrets – anything in fact, that goes on behind the scenes, and keeps their fantasies working overtime. No matter how upstanding a citizen the Piscean man may appear, there is a lascivious side to him which will always enjoy a bit of saucy smut.

Some male Fish want to be all things to all men, and have a deep desire to be everyone's friend. But they find it impossible to face up to the responsibilities and duties involved (7,341 Christmas cards). Then the mask can slip, and they can be double-dealing and deceptive behind their buddies' backs. That's when the Fishy fellows become confused by it all, which is a very Piscean problem indeed.

This is one of the most psychic signs of all, and Piscean men can often sense instinctively how their loved ones are feeling. As a result, male Fish – unlike most men in the zodiac – are emotionally and physically fitted to fatherhood. (Although you'll have to see the natal chart to be sure.)

Because this is a Water sign, and therefore full of emotion, Piscean men aren't frightened to show a lot of love to their kids, and by doing so can draw very close to their children indeed. The Piscean man can be very devoted, and radiate a lot of warmth. He doesn't always feel he has to be as macho as some of the men from other signs. And that can't be bad!

Pisces Woman

Goodness, these women can dream! Try accusing a female Fish of floating along in a fantasy, and she'll regard you reproachfully (in her disarming way) and say that you're quite wrong, she's a realist. Then she'll go back to reading her spy story or romantic romp, or she'll turn on the telly and sob over a sad film. See what I mean?

These women swoon and walk around in a haze of love. They tend to be at the beck and call of their partners, forgiving them their transgressions, and never causing rows. (They hate unpleasant atmospheres, and would rather be walked all over, with footprints on their faces, than start a scene.) After all, this *is* the sign of the saint (no, not the Leslie Charteris chap), and saints have never had an easy time of it. They've always been burned at stakes or stoned to death, poor dears. And so Piscean women can be perfect martyrs. Being incurable romantics, they may be roasted on the spit of love, suffering in silence for the ones they love. (Sometimes it's inspiring. Other times it's irritating.)

But don't forget that there are two types of Pisceans, and therefore two sorts of Fishy females. The first is the glamorous Hollywood woman, who is sophisticated and chic, yet a chimeric chameleon. Hollywood reached its heyday when Neptune was nestling in luscious Leo, the most creative sign, and gave birth to a charming confection. (That's entertainment!) These women can lead a double life with no trouble at all. They have such a strong power of pretence that they can actually believe the webs of fantasy they weave about themselves.

Some female Fish can be attracted to male strip joints, saucy soirées, and the like, while living a tremendously tedious life in Littlehampton. Piscean women can get dolled up to the nineteens the minute their husbands leave the house in the morning. Then they totter into town for the day, on high heels (why do you think Fish have funny feet?), have a really good time, and get home before their spouses so they can say they've been in the abode all day, dusting. Some of them can even keep a lover quite happily, while their other life jogs along nicely.

But don't think they're all like this. Some Piscean women are so devoted to their partners that they couldn't possibly live with the guilt they'd feel if they were unfaithful in any way. But they may still have fantasies, and need to dream about them, even if they never put them into practice.

Fishy females really are romantic, and they do adore their families and fellas. But because of their intense idealism, which is even stronger than a Libran's longings, they can find it very difficult to call a halt to a relationship when it's over and done with. They hate to hurt people and, like Librans, will often sweep things under the carpet, rather than face them.

To look at a different kettle of Fish, the other sort of Piscean woman will devote her life liberally to good works, helping in Oxfam shops, running Meals on Wheels from her shopping trolley, or looking after her invalid parents or her spastic child. She can be quite happy living with other people's problems, and trying to solve them.

Because of her Piscean ability to empathise with other people, she makes a very good mother, and doesn't flinch from the task. But sometimes she can smother her children in love, and will try to protect them to such a degree that they can lose their sense of individuality. Then when they face the real world all is lost – it's very different to the picture Mum painted. She can also find it very difficult to discipline her kids; telling them off can sometimes upset her more than them. (One Piscean mum got so exasperated with her two terrors that one day she announced she was leaving them. She made a great production out of slamming the front door – and then hid in the broom cupboard! No matter how cross she was, she couldn't walk out for even five minutes.)

All Water signs can have troubles with drink, and lots of Piscean women turn to the bottle, following a trauma of one sort or another. Then they can drink sherry from dawn to dusk as though it's going out of style, or pour whisky on their Weetabix.

Another dangerous period for a Piscean mother is when her children fly the nest, as they inevitably will. With her little fledgelings gone she can slide into fantasy, and pretend that her children are babies again. There is an ever-present danger of the female Fish slipping back into the silent, still waters of her own dream world. Buy a fishing-rod and hook her out.

Pisces Child

You know those children who seem to be too good to be true, and smile and simper until you want to smack them? Well, they're Fish. While positive Pisceans can be absolutely angelic, others can be noticeably nauseating. Some of them can be so delicate and dreamy that you want to shake them, and give them something to be delicate about!

As with the other Water signs, much will depend on the parents of the Pisces child. Little Fish (fish fingers!) who have been spoiled to death will be done for. The problem is that Pisceans find it hard enough to face reality at the best of times. And if they aren't taught as children to see the world as it really is, they can be ruined for life by the time they reach adulthood. Some of these small fry will dream through their childhoods, reading books and living in a fairy-tale of their own making. In fact, they'll be just like Alice in Wonderland, the epitome of a fantasial Piscean child. (One Piscean parent still buys pop-up books at the age of forty-seven!)

If you simply protect your small Fish too much, and not let him or her develop a good backbone, your kid can grow up to be a quivering jellyfish, rather than a friendly, intelligent dolphin. (I know – it's a mammal!) Over the years I've encountered a lot of negative Piscean kids, who have all been spoilt, spineless wonders! The minute the parental peepers are off them, they look for ways of regaining attention, staging screaming fits and having hysterics. Some of these children can be too sugary for words, so that in the end you want to clip them around the ear or throw them to the sharks so they'll see what life is really all about!

Piscean children can be extremely clever artistically, and will be involved from an early age in music, drama and all things arty. And this is the best direction in which to channel a sensitive Piscean child. A lot of the children born under this sign have been child prodigies. An excellent example is Mozart, who was tickling the ivories like a frantic Fish at the tender age of four.

But academically they may lag behind some of the brighter sparks in the zodiac. They'll need a good push every now and then, because they can slide into indolence very easily. At school, they adore literature, drama, art and music, but they'll avoid PE and all things academic, coming up with clever excuses. (Don't forget they're great at twisting the facts, even at *that* age!)

So, when your Piscean child says, fixing you with a wide-eyed look, that he or she has been given the day off school, I should ring to check. You might find that your innocent little Fish hasn't got a day off at all, but is just playing trout. (Sorry, *truant!)*

Pisces in Love

C ue violins, and bring on the hearts and flowers! A Fish in love can be really daft and soppy, quite batty, casting caution to the winds and throwing him or herself totally at the feet of the loved one.

There was one Fishy fellow who, though very happy with his other half, met someone else and thought this was love. It got so bad that one day he dashed off to spend ten hours outside his loved one's front door, in a lonely vigil, all through a nasty November night.

Fantasy can take over from reality when Pisceans are in love, and it's only when other forces come into play that the Fish will see the folly of it all. Another Piscean pal lived a wonderful game of love for three years, and regaled her mates with all sorts of intimate details about her love-affair. It was only later that she admitted that not a word of it had been true.

If Fish can find someone who reciprocates the limitless love they can dole out, then they'll be on cloud nine, and bluebirds of happiness will be forever tweeting in the background. But the Piscean problem is that because they give so much, they have got to know early on whether that love is going to be returned. (And that's where the difficulty lies.)

This is why more Pisceans are victims of unrequited love than any other sign. The Fish can love from afar, sometimes secretly. He or she may not need the other person to know, because the reality will never be as divine as the dream. (Disillusionment is a bitter pill to swallow.) The Piscean sensitivity is so profound that very often Fish can build barriers around themselves, shutting off the rest of the harsh, cruel world. Pisceans can pretend that their partners love them a lot, when actually they couldn't care less. But when a Piscean's paramour says that love is dead, the Fish will be flummoxed, flattened and filleted, and in such a turmoil it can take years for him or her to get over the experience.

I once wrote an article on Pisces called 'The Fish That's

Hooked on Love', and that's Pisces to a P. Unless someone can get the Fish off that hook and throw him or her back into safer waters, the Piscean will drift along, believing everything is dandy when really it's disastrous. ('Gone fishing' gets a whole new meaning when you're in love with a Piscean.)

Fishy love can be very clever stuff, but it can also be nail-bitingly neurotic. Fish can literally fall in love at the drop of a hat (or a fin). But sometimes they confuse love with infatuation: their Neptunian natures mean that they can be beguiled by beauty and deceived by desire, yearning for an unattainable amour!

Negative Pisceans can drown their sorrows by getting sozzled or stoned, because they have reached the ends of their emotional tethers and nothing else can help. Piscean emotions run devastatingly deep, which is why some of them are adept at emotional blackmail, and why their subconscious has such a hold over them. Some Fish can play games all the time. Others can imprison themselves for love and become complete and utter martyrs. This can be like Libra, but at least *they* have rational natures. All Pisceans have are bottomless oceans of love.

If you're thinking this sounds just like your cup of tea, you may want to know how to procure a Piscean. First of all, look in the mirror. Have you got what it takes facially? If not, never mind! Be kind, charming and cherishing and the Piscean will fall for that side of your nature.

Although some Piscean women fantasise over big butch men, you won't catch your Fish by being aggressive and belligerent. In many ways you should kill Pisceans with tenderness (no, not literally, dear!) and woo them with it too. You must be as romantic as they are, but not to the point of being weak and wet. Pisceans need strong partners who can look after them. (Virgos are perfect, because they're such rational, logical folk.) Cuddle and caress your Fish, nestle your amour in your arms, and say the world's wonderful. Your Piscean will believe you. After all, these Fish will believe anything!

Pisces as a Friend

If you want to make a Piscean pal's day, be ill. Honestly! Ring up and croak like a flu-ridden frog down the phone. Your Fishy friend will be happy to play Florence Nightingale to your Lady (or Lad) of the Camellias. That's if your pal is positive. Negative Pisceans can be real fairweather friends, first in the queue for the champagne when you're celebrating, but nowhere to be seen when the cork has hit you in the eye!

This is a Mutable sign, so Pisceans will flow in a very fluid way in whatever directions their fancies take them. And unless there is a lot of Fixity in a Fish's chart, he or she will tend to have a colossal collection of chums, and circulate freely among them, like one of a million plankton. In fact, because of their love of fantasy, it is important for Pisceans constantly to meet new people. The type of friendship you get will depend on the Fish, of course.

Like Librans, Pisceans will often do anything to avoid an argy-bargy, and some Fish won't say a word to friends who are being rude and repellent. (Though they'll despise themselves later for having no backbone.)

A Piscean pal will be a smashing social success, and you'll have a whale (I know it's not a fish!) of a time together, especially if you like dancing and getting into the swing of things. But sometimes the Fishy friend can lean too heavily on a very capable chum, and irritate them.

Friends can also get very fed up with Piscean pals who tell whoppers and become completely caught up in the webs of fantasy they weave. (It's not so much gilding the lily as over-decorating the orchid!) If you discover this trait early on, you can accept it as part of the Fish's character, and chuckle about it when you're on your own. However, if you have such high morals and principles that you can't stand the lying that may go on, a Fishy friend is not for you. You'll find it a trial to put up with the Piscean's embroidery of life's rich tapestry, making Spanish tangles out of French knots.

Don't make the mistake of mixing up duplicity with Mutability. Some Fish seem to be lying when actually they're telling you the truth. They just change their minds a lot! One day they'll say they adore something and the next announce that they loathe it. When you accuse them of lying, they will look hurt and then confused.

All in all, a Piscean pal might be a bit of a luxury, unless he or she is a highly-developed Fish – more of a salmon than a sardine. Otherwise, you may find that unless your friend can prove him or herself to be a pal, and not drown you in double-dealing, it can all be a lot of hard work for you. You'd do better just to meet once a month for a good giggle, and let someone else sort out the truth from the tall tales.

So, it will all depend on the sort of Fish the Piscean is. Angel Fish will swim about, little halos shining like mad, radiating beauty and cherishing everyone and everything in sight. But swordfish will mooch about, be nice to your face and then poke you in the ribs. (Ouch! You've heard of back-stabbers, haven't you!)

Pisces at Work

Well, it's got to be glamorous. As you will have gathered by now, Pisceans need some escapism in their lives, especially at work. If a Fish can't have the sort of profession that is slightly divorced from reality, they may pretend that their job is more than it's cracked up to be.

Pisces is a refined sign and a lot of Fish work in the beauty business. Many Piscean men are very happy working as sales reps for perfume companies, because they are selling feminine fragrances and sensational smells. The very nature of their business is beauty. Even though they'd make equally excellent salesmen for car firms, they'd hate it, because the product wouldn't be pretty. (Unless it's a Rolls-Royce, of course!) More mundanely, Pisceans make good bartenders, as long as they don't swig the stock! In fact, Pisces is Paris, London, Rome and New York – the four cities you see listed on the world's most expensive perfumes. This is the sign of sophistication and top class stuff, and Pisceans like to live and work in a world far removed from any area that's slightly slummy!

So, the Piscean will need to work in an enchanting, entrancing environment. Many Fish are found in ballet or opera companies, and film sets are full of them. Fish who don't work in nice places will fall apart. But not only does the workplace have to be elegant, the Piscean's colleagues have to be charming, and the atmosphere serene and tranquil. A row and a rumpus will set a Fish all a-flutter.

Other Fish swim in different directions, taking up the professions other Pisceans pass by, such as nursing the ill and the infirm, helping the aged and the ailing, and being social workers in some very *louche* locations.

Jupiterian Pisceans will want to travel the world through their careers, as do Sagittarians, although the Fish will have more finesse. Other Fish may join the Navy or the Wrens. (Arians choose the Army, Aquarians and Geminis the Air Force.) But

many Pisceans like to bob about the briny in one capacity or another.

Ambitious Pisceans are very few and far between indeed. They much prefer to be big fish in small ponds and, once they've achieved that, they don't want anything more. But usually, Fish are happy to swim along in safe, serene waters. Sometimes when Pisceans are pushed to go along for an interview, they will deliberately set out to fail, because they don't want the extra responsibility and duty that promotion entails.

Whatever work they do, Pisceans need to be happy. Aquarians like hectic jobs, and other signs thrive on hassle. But Pisceans need soothing surroundings and aesthetic atmospheres, otherwise their finely-tuned sensitive systems get jangled and jarred, and they become very flustered Fish indeed!

Pisces at Home

Strangely enough, Fish who are footloose and fancy-free don't care much about their homes. They're not in them enough, because they're often out on the prowl, looking for a full-time lover, husband or wife. But once nuptial bliss strikes and they settle down contentedly, the home will become the be-all and end-all of everything.

The perfect Piscean place is a pretty little cottage by some water, such as the sea or a river. But wherever or whatever it is, whether a council flat in County Cork or a mansion in Manchester, the Fish's home will be very cosy. It can also be rather mysterious and mystical; some Pisceans will smother everything in sight in Turkish carpets and Indian cottons. There will be an oriental influence somewhere about the place, even if it's just an empty carton of take-away chow mein!

It goes without saying that fish, and the sea, play an important part in a Piscean's home. There may be paintings of fish, seascapes or fishing boats about, the design on the curtains may be of seashells, or there'll be tanks of the finny things themselves. One Piscean man I know has tanks of tropical fish lining all four walls of his sitting-room. Pisceans also love cats, and there are bound to be a couple running around, even if they've just come visiting from next door.

With the Piscean predilection for pick-me-ups, there will be a drinks cabinet abounding with booze. If the Fish is teetotal, there'll be a bathroom cabinet full of pills and potions to attack any ailment. (Don't forget that Pisces is polar to Virgo – a sign which is obsessed with health. So, like Virgos, Pisceans may have to buy bathroom cabinets that are especially reinforced to take the mighty weight of all their wonderful medicines.)

A general feeling of sumptuousness will pervade the Piscean home and, like Librans, Fish will have satin or velvet curtains and silk-soft furnishings, if they can afford them. The armchairs will be comfy, with lots of cushions to sink back into, and delicate,

drapey and diaphanous fabrics will be floating about, in a host of harmonious hues.

The main colours of the Neptunian Piscean's home will be those that make you think of the sea – turquoises, blues, emerald greens, aquamarines, peacock blues and sea greens. (Phew!) Jupiterian Piscean's places will be pulsating with purples, and other shades of that imperial ilk.

It's difficult to say which will be the Fish's favourite room. He or she will love the bathroom, which will have a profusion of pampery products; the Fish will want to wallow in the water for hours, dreaming. And as this is the sign of dreams, the Piscean will also adore the bedroom, where he or she can sleep and have delicious dreams about their dreamboats – even if they haven't met them yet! Whichever room has the best atmosphere will be the one that appeals most to the Piscean's taste (usually the one with the home-made bar!).

Now, the garden will also be important, but it must be full of prettily-petalled perennials for the Piscean to pick. Water – the Piscean's element – may well be in evidence, and Pisceans often have fish ponds or waterfalls in their gardens.

All in all, the Piscean abode will be a bit of an odd mixture, especially if the Piscean is strongly Jupiterian. (A sort of seafood cocktail.) It won't be very large – just big enough to cater for the Piscean's needs. Of course, Jupiterian Pisceans may have large homes, because of their love of expansion, but Neptunian Pisceans will go very much more for atmosphere, and the lighting will be soft, as it is in underwater grottoes.

Just to show you how fantasial a Fish can be about the abode, listen to this. I have three planets in Pisces, and I once kept a string of fairy lights up all year round, because they looked so pretty! Twinkle, twinkle!

Pisces
Health and Relaxation

Pisceans drink like the fish they are, and this can land them in a netful of trouble. Jupiterian Pisceans also love their grub, but lots of Neptunian Fish don't give a fig for food, preferring to get their nourishment out of various alcoholic nectars! An odd thing about Pisceans, though, is that they tend to be either ridiculously reliant on drink or truly teetotal. And if drink doesn't get the Piscean who needs a prop, drugs will.

The Fish who do enjoy eating will be partial to elegant, escapist French and Italian food. Then, as they sit stuffing a scallopine, they can sigh soppily about the sexy signor or signorina they spent a sensational Sunday siesta with in Siena! (If they get tears in their eyes, it may not be because the grub's gone down the wrong way!)

Sometimes, the Piscean's ultra-high sensitivity to situations can lead to a lot of suffering, as anything unpleasant can jar a Fish's nervous system. Many Pisceans can be plagued by psychosomatic problems. Obviously, this won't be the case if your pal turns up encased in plaster from head to toe, and can only eat soup through a straw. If that does happen, negative Fish will moan and groan twenty-four hours a day, while positive Pisceans will suffer in silence. (Though the cast may creak a bit.) Very often, the root of an illness will be a nagging neurosis or pervading phobia, which will have preyed on the Piscean's susceptible and suggestive subconscious. Elizabeth Barrett was a Piscean, and she used to languish on a *chaise-longue* all day, writing poetry, until she discovered love. And it took a Bull, Robert Browning, to get her moving! (It's not often you can say that about a Taurean!)

Alcohol can play havoc with the liver of a Jupiterian Piscean, causing complaints such as cirrhosis and hepatitis. The feet will be the weak spots of a Fish ruled by Neptune, and a Piscean can have anything from corns and callouses to truly terrible times with the tootsies. (Ever noticed how Pisceans hate standing for long, and will complain about their shoes hurting?)

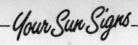

When it comes to relaxing, a Piscean can really only unwind in a soft, soothing environment, with a Romeo or Juliet in tow! If this isn't possible, Fish can feel better if they go dancing, take up painting, or throw themselves unreservedly into a spiritual subject. Otherwise they will be like Fish out of water. Pisces is the sign of the recluse or hermit, and some Fish recharge their batteries constantly and only show parts of themselves, hiding the rest away from the world. (There are a lot of Piscean priests.)

As well as artistic endeavours, which are pootchy for Pisceans, they can have a good time at a pub or club. (A very famous Fishy friend of mine has just one ambition – to work in a pub!) Very Piscean pursuits include window-shopping (and dreaming about what they could buy if only they had the boodle), going to the cinema to watch an old weepie, joining a video club, reading romantic novels and, of course, being with the ones they love!

Don't forget the link with water. A Fish who fancies a break should pack a bucket and spade, and shuffle off to the seaside. Then, after paddling along the seashore, and waving at the whelks, the Piscean can go off to guzzle some grub, whether fish and chips on the front, prawns on the prom or jellied eels on the jetty.

And, as you might expect, a lot of Pisceans enjoy fishing, though they can feel so sorry for the fish that they have to stop and go home!